Allison's Suncatchers & Chains

A Journey with Autism

Kris Jones

Kris Jones
2002.

Detselig Enterprises Ltd.

Calgary, Alberta, Canada

Allison's Suncatchers and Chains

© 2002 Kris Jones

National Library of Canada Cataloguing in Publication Data

Jones, Kris

Allison's suncatchers and chains: a journey with autism/Kris Jones.

ISBN 1-55059-234-3

1. Autism--Patients--Canada--Biography. 2. Parents of autistic children--Canada--Biography. 3. Autism--Patients--Family relationships. I. Title.

RC553.A88J65   2002   616.89'82'0092   C2002-902318-1

Detselig Enterprises Ltd.
210-1220 Kensington Rd. N.W., Calgary, AB T2N 3P5
Phone: (403) 283-0900/Fax: (403) 283-6947
E-mail: temeron@telusplanet.net
www.temerondetselig.com

We acknowledge the financial support of the Government of Canada through the Book Publishing Industry Development Program (BPIDP) for our publishing activities.

Special thanks to Barry Weaver, President, and Skyreach Equipment Ltd., for their financial support of this book.

ISBN 1-55059-234-3

SAN 115-0324

Printed in Canada

Dedication

This book is dedicated to all those special people living with disabilities, their courageous family members and those people who are committed to working with the disabled, appreciating their uniqueness and helping to enhance the quality of their lives.

Acknowledgements

Throughout the writing of this book I have had considerable support from my family, neighbors and friends and it was through their faith in me that I have been able to actualize the dream I had of telling my story about my experiences with my daughter Allison.

First and foremost I thank my husband Gord, who believed in me from the start and stood by me throughout the writing process. Not only did he read, edit and critique each chapter as I wrote, but he offered suggestions and guidance as well as cooked many meals and generally took care of me. Throughout the process we shared many memories, shed a few tears and grew to appreciate even more all the joy and lessons Allison has provided us with. I thank Gord for his unending love, support and encouragement and I am very grateful for his incredible patience.

I thank my sister, Shelley Younge, for giving me the final push to get started after I shared my dream of writing my story with her one weekend. Her encouragement and enthusiasm were my impetus to launch this project and I have appreciated her enduring support.

Gord and I were teaching and hosts on an Elderhostel tour in the fall of 2001 and met a lovely couple from Toms River, New Jersey, Walter and Edith Gabriel. After I shared some of my poetry and told them I was going to write my book, Walter volunteered to help. Walter and Edith knew nothing about autism, did not know us well and had not met Allison, but wanted to help by editing for clarity. Walter promised to be "brutally honest." I e-mailed each chapter as I wrote and they responded with suggestions and comments. There was nothing brutal about their comments and responses. However, they helped me to ensure that the content was understandable to readers with no direct knowledge of or experience with the disability of autism, pointed out some problems with chronology and generally kept me on track. It was nice having someone to discuss my ideas, thoughts and plans with, someone unbiased and willing to be direct and honest. I thank them for their input, their wonderful support and encouraging comments. I also thank them for their kindness and the friendship that we have developed via electronic mail.

Foothills Advocacy in Motion Society in High River, Alberta, man-

ages Allison's day and residential programs. I want to thank Vince Kimura, Executive Director, for his support and encouragement. After reading my draft he invited me to a Board Meeting where I outlined my book and my reasons for writing it. As a result of this the Board offered their support and have provided endorsement for my book.

Many friends have also provided me with encouragement. I thank Rob and Lorraine Irvine for reading my draft and their comments and support. I offer a special thanks to Cheryl and Bill Holmes and their daughters Jade and Keara, not only for caring for Allison with such love and devotion, but for helping me with the writing of the details of Allison's residential program and her life with their family. Throughout the process I have received encouragement from my neighbors, friends and former colleagues and have appreciated their backing. Edith Larsen, Allison's first babysitter, has been a tremendous advocate for my book, as has been her family. Thanks too to my friends from Mount Royal College including Dawn, Lynne, Jean, Maria and Kit who have listened to me talk about my book over lunch and have offered their support. To my colleagues in the Healing Touch Calgary group, I thank them for listening to my stories and poems and a special thanks to Ann Welsh-Baskett for her ongoing caring in my healing journey.

I want to extend a special thanks to my friend, Ann Mortifee, for reading my draft and writing the preface. Ann has been an inspiration to me in many ways and I am truly grateful for our friendship and her sincere willingness to do whatever she could to support my project. I thank her for giving me permission to include words of some of the songs she has written. Her music resonates with my soul and I am honored to have such a gifted friend.

The love and support I have received from my family and relatives have been remarkable. I thank Richard and Patricia Jones, Gord's brother and his wife, for helping me find a publisher and their faith in my writing abilities. My brothers Brian and Derek Younge and Gord's sister and brothers have all been very encouraging. I thank my son Derek and his wife Angie for their enthusiasm and ongoing trust and support. Derek has been such a blessing in our lives as our son and Allison's brother and he too is very special to us. His love for his sister is unconditional and he has looked out for Allison and cared for her in an exceptional way.

Barry Weaver, President of Skyreach, has graciously offered to spon-

sor my book and I thank Barry and his company for the generous support. It is Barry's belief that this book will be helpful to other parents who are faced with raising children with disabilities and he appreciates the challenges they must deal with and therefore he was most willing to help out.

I must thank my publisher, Ted Giles, President of Detselig Enterprises, for his patience and belief that this book warranted publishing. As well, I must thank Linda Berry, editor, for all her work in reviewing and editing my writings. When I saw the cover designed by Alvin Choong, graphic artist for Detselig Enterprises, it took my breath away. This artist was able to capture the essence of Allison and incorporate her suncatchers and chains in such a beautiful way and I am grateful for his talent and am moved by his design of the cover of my book. As well, I am grateful to the photographers who have shown patience and understanding when given the challenge of photographing Allison, not an easy task. Thanks to both Ted Dawson and Steve Hofland of High River for their work.

Above all I want to thank my daughter Allison. Her courage, strength and ability to live with her disability of autism with such tenacity and grace have been an inspiration to me. She has been the one that has made this all possible. Our journey with autism and the many experiences we have shared have enriched my life and provided the substance to my writing. I thank her for being who she is and for awakening me to the important things in life. She has been an amazing gift to me and to all who know and love her.

Table of Contents

"At times one turns to fiction for interesting reading but this isn't needed if you read Kris Jones' story of her love and experiences in raising Allison, her daughter. Although Alli is autistic and unable to speak she gives love to so many besides her own family. In writing her book Kris touches on both the joys and tribulations of raising her daughter … From reading Kris' book one feels that they know and love Allison and can imagine all those experiences she has shared with her family and multitude of supporters."
Walter Gabriel, BS, MS Geophysics, Toms River, New Jersey

"First and foremost, I would like to express my sincere gratitude and appreciation to both Allison and Kris for allowing me to participate in their unique journey through life. Reading this book has truly been an enriching and moving experience! I believe it has been Kris' destiny to write this book, to deliver this message. I was deeply touched by the complexity and yet the simplicity of Kris' message. Life can be many things and can be filled with innumerable challenges but the key is to be true to your intuition. Now knowing the path that Allison and Kris have traveled, since we have been involved in 1992, I have gained a deeper appreciation and profound insight into Allison's history and roots. This unique journey with autism has forever etched a new respect and reverence for *Allison's Suncatchers and Chains.*
Vince Kimura, Executive Director, Foothills Advocacy in Motion (AIM) Society, Endorsement for the book received for Foothills AIM Society, Board of Directors February 2002

"A touching, revealing, comprehensive chronicle of a family dealing with Autism, *Allison's Suncatchers and Chains* helped us to understand both the brightness and the ties of this human puzzle. Mostly, it shows how a child can reach out and exert the bonds of unconditional love that last a lifetime and the courage of her family to recognize her gifts."
Rob Irvine, Retired Principal. Okotoks Junior High School
Lorraine Irvine, Retired Teacher

"In her authorship Kris has reached well into her very soul, and in so doing has found the way to intellectualize a lot of feelings, and yet put into clinical perspective a deeper knowledge of her child and her

illness than any clinician could ever know. That she has laid bare the anguish, the hopes, and despair, and then had the courage to actually create something so positive from this is a real tribute to her character. I am profoundly touched by her writings. The substance of her writing is superb. Her role as a teacher is not by any means, done!"
Dr. Brian Younge, MD, Mayo Clinic, Rochester, Minnesota

"I must commend Kris on her courage, persistence, and of course her undying love for her daughter. As I read the book I could visualize both Kris and Allison and developed my own personal bond to both of them. I strongly feel no matter who reads her words they too will be able to enjoy the same closeness to the author and the subject. The content is easy enough to read yet contains enough textual information in order to give the reader an understanding of the magnitude of Allison's disability. By far however, the best part of the book was the way it was written. Despite the author's obvious intelligence and grasp of the medical theory behind her story, the words are hers and in my opinion come from her heart not her head. She is able to illustrate the challenges faced by a mother dealing with a disabled child from a purely common point of view all the while opening her heart to the reader. Personally I feel the book would be a wonderful addition to any parent or person's repertoire of human-interest readings. Kris expresses a deep and unconditional love for her daughter and a need to tell the world....
Lori Larsen, Masters of Criminology, Author

I come from a family of five children. I remember a card that was taped to the door of one of our kitchen cupboards when I was a girl. Presumably someone had given it to my mother in playful recognition of her amazing devotion and service to us all. It read...

"God could not be everywhere, so She created mothers."

I love that saying. Humor so often carries an underlying acknowledgment of a truth that is made more real through the laughter it evokes.

There are many strange and extraordinary forces in Nature, and the love of a mother for her child is certainly one of the most mysterious. There is a deep resolve in the feminine heart that is willing is swim over vast distances, through heavy seas in order to carry a loved one to safety. This is a gift of the universe to make our journey through the realms of planet earth less treacherous. This fierce love makes sorrow more bearable, survival more possible, and adversity an obstacle rather than an immovable obstruction.

The account you have before you is a heroic tale of love and dedication. The fact that there are families everywhere being asked to take this same journey and face these same challenges every day, makes it no less heroic.

Perhaps you have watched a parent with their disabled child from a distance in a shopping mall, and you have held the hand of your own child more closely. Perhaps you know someone personally who has had to face the challenges of living with disability. But I am clear that there is no way to know the gifts and grief's of another, until you have "walked a mile in their moccasins." We are bystanders all, watching from the sidelines the lives of those around us. We cannot know, we can merely seek to intuit a corner of their experience.

This book affords a glimpse into the heart of a mother and the world of her ongoing longing to find safety and fulfillment for her autistic child. It is an extraordinary account of the daily demands and frustrations, the joys and gifts of learning to surrender to a fact of life that you did not choose and would do anything to change.

I first met Kris at a workshop in 1998; I knew that she had been

under great strain and had committed herself to a path of self-healing. But until reading the book you now hold in your hands, it was not possible for me to fully understand the depth of pressure – emotionally, spiritually, physically and mentally – that has been her daily fare for years. She speaks of all that a family must bear as they seek to find their way through the myriad medical hoops, the numerous healing modalities, the possible care supports, the ups and downs of swelling hopes and devastating disappointments.

But within these same pages, you will see that peculiar gift that has been given to us as human being. By some miraculous inner resource, some of us are able to create value out of what we do not desire, beauty out of heartbreak, and wisdom out of the sorrow and the setbacks of this incredible journey that is our life. I have felt somehow ennobled to have had a glimpse into the daily unfoldings of this amazing family. Gordon, Allison's father, Derek, her brother, and my dear friend, Kris.

The Buddhists say that at the gateway to the Inner Temple of the Self there stands two guard dogs – paradox and confusion. And if we can accept these two and cease our resistance to them, we may pass into the inner sanctum of acceptance and peace that exists beyond duality. Here hope and hopelessness, disillusionment and expectancy, joy and sorrow walk hand in hand. Both knowing that life is not life without the companionship of the other.

Introduction

Over the years I have come to believe that there are reasons for our lives on this Earth and there is much to be learned and experienced while we are here. Things don't just happen; there is a reason for everything. We may not truly know and understand the reasons why things occur as they do, but the challenge is to give meaning to our lives and to grow through our experiences. I also believe we create our own reality, although this may sound contradictory. As humans we have the ability to make decisions and choices, which influences the direction we take. The script belongs to us and we have a hand in how it is written. Of course there are times when we stumble and even fall, but it is in the getting up that we grow and learn. I see life as a journey and through the writing of this book I am sharing my personal story, the journey I have been on with my daughter, Allison, who has autism.

I believe and understand that my purpose in life is to teach. Throughout my life I have been a teacher in many different ways, both formally and informally. For many years I was a nursing instructor, teaching mainly medical-surgical courses in different nursing programs. Teaching, in part, defines who I am. I retired from teaching nursing in the year 2000 and at first I felt like I had abandoned my path. Transitions are like that, rather unsettling, but I knew the time was right for me to leave my professional career. Although it has not been easy, I have had to let go of some aspects of my life, freeing me to move into a different phase with new challenges. My journey continues and although the direction has changed, I have found another way in which I can teach. For some time I had had a dream of writing a book about my daughter Allison and our journey together. Although the content and methods have changed, it is through my writing that my role as a teacher expands. My students are the readers – other parents, professionals, caregivers, students, friends and anyone else that happens to read this book. Others may be able to learn from my stories. One cannot really walk in the shoes of another, but one can at least wear them for a moment, try them on and get a sense of another's experiences. Readers are invited to walk in my shoes, to read my story about my life with Allison. She has been described as autistic, severely disabled, mentally retarded, dependently handicapped, epileptic and so on. She has been called many things, but we call her Allison. Most importantly, she

is a human being living out her own journey, one that I have been blessed to share with her, as her mother.

Allison's father, Gord, and her brother, Derek, have had their own experiences along the way. I have no doubt that their perceptions, interpretations and beliefs may not mirror mine, nor should they. I honor their right to make their own meaning, to have their own feelings — some that are similar to mine, some that are very different. They have their own stories, but I can only truly know my own. In no way can I even pretend to be able to describe Allison's perceptions of all this. At best, I can only speculate about her personal experiences and what her life as been like for her. However, I do believe that Allison and I are soul mates, and that we have come together in this life to walk the path of destiny together.

Allison has a purpose in this life as well and she is on her own path. She is here to experience life in a very different way, a life without words and a life in which she is dependent on others for her survival. Allison is also a gift to others whose lives she has touched. Her presence in their lives changes them in many different and positive ways. I suspect that she is here to learn and to teach others, and she has done this well. I have to wonder if Allison chose to come to this life autistic, severely disabled, and if so, why would she choose such a difficult life? Perhaps she is much further along in her own personal evolution than most of us. No doubt she has a very strong soul, maybe even a very old soul, tough enough to endure the challenges she has to face. There are no doubt reasons for Allison's disabilities and having autism is part of her destiny. Thinking along these lines makes it easier for me to accept her disability and it provides me with a very different framework, a different lens from which to view our lives. For one thing, I have no need to feel responsible for her disability. I also do not need to feel that I must do everything I can to make this go away, to make her normal, to change her. The focus shifts to one of simply being there for her, accepting her, appreciating her and loving her just the way she is. This philosophy is quite freeing, as it takes away the judgment, guilt and negativity. It also means that I must let her walk her own path, to step back at times and let her get on with her life's work.

I chose the title of the book, *Allison's Suncatchers and Chains: A Journey with Autism,* for specific reasons. Ever since Allison was introduced to suncatchers as part of a sensory stimulation program as a small

child, she has loved and cherished them. Allison uses them as a form of smoke screen or protection. At times she holds one up and appears to looking at it, when in fact she is looking through it or around it and actually assessing or appraising the people around her. It allows her to have indirect contact with people, avoiding the eye contact that is difficult for her at times. Suncatchers have become a form of security blanket for Allison and she seems better able to cope with the world if she has one in her hand.

At the age of thirteen she had a specially trained dog and she was fascinated with her dog's collar, wanting to have it, so I gave her one of her own. Since that time her chain has become another constant companion. It has to be just like her dog's chain, silver in color and about a foot in length and no other chain will do. Allison flicks her fingers and manipulates this chain with great dexterity for someone who is unable to use her hands in other ways. She uses her chain to calm herself down, to help her relax in unfamiliar situations. She wraps the chain around her suncatchers and together they have become her symbols of security. Holding on to these helps her cope with a world that is sometimes frightening to her. To this day we always have chains and suncatchers available for Allison.

For me, suncatchers and chains are also a metaphor for autism. Persons with this disability are special human beings with unique challenges. The chain represents the bondage or tribulations of autism, holding them hostage, trapped in an alien world. People with autism have information-processing problems and many motor and perceptual disturbances that make it difficult for them to interact and interpret the world around them. This causes many of the characteristics of autism and challenges they have to live with every day. Autistic individuals have heightened senses and they do not experience or view the world around them in the usual way. Although their vision may be distorted, some of the visual images may be intensified, allowing them to see and appreciate more depth, more beauty and detail in the environment. Therefore suncatchers represent the bright side of autism, bringing bursts of light that sparkle through the shadows. For me, the suncatchers also represent some of the unique and wonderful experiences I have shared with my daughter that have brought us great joy. Allison has brought light into my life and through her I have had many transformative, enlightening experiences. Like many things in the world, autism is a paradox.

It has its shadow side as well as its light side, positive and negative aspects existing together, the yin and the yang. When I think about Allison, her suncatchers and chains exemplify what autism means to me.

There have been books written about children with autism and some of them are about cures and miracles, but this book is not about that. It is about our ordinary and extraordinary experiences and how these have given meaning to my life and no doubt to all those who know and love Allison. The story of our on-going journey will be told from my perspective as Allison's mother. At the time of writing, Allison is almost thirty years old, so much of the narrative will be a reflection back over the years. This story is about our journey to date and includes the challenges we have dealt with in Allison's early childhood, during her school years, adolescence and in her young adulthood. No doubt there will be more stories as we both continue to age, grow and evolve. The story that will unfold in this book is one of great joy, great sorrow and above all one that comes from my heart. It is my intention to share how I have attempted to meet the challenges Allison and I have faced, some of the feelings I have experienced, the adjustments I have had to make, and how I have tried to cope and give meaning to it all. It is the story of how I have raised my daughter in the best way I knew how, guided by the love and commitment I have for her. Being a parent is something we are not well prepared for. To me there is some irony in the fact that we go to school for years to learn and develop the skills we need in order to be successful in our careers and jobs, but we embark on perhaps the most important career of all, parenting, with little formal preparation. Of course there are resources available to parents, but there are no pre-requisites, particularly for parenting a child with disabilities.

A central theme or thread woven throughout the story will be my attempt to communicate and share the many lessons I have learned along the way. Through my experiences with Allison, I have grown in many different ways and learned a tremendous amount about parenting, autism, who I am and life in general. One cannot have this kind of unique experience and not be changed or transformed. Some of life's lessons are easy to come by and others must be learned through experiences that are difficult, painful and seem downright cruel and unfair. Allison has had a positive affect on each member of our family, influencing the development of our values and providing us with opportu-

nities for personal and spiritual growth. I am not saying I would have wished for this life; in fact, I had envisioned a very different life for myself way back when I was contemplating having children. The process of learning is often painful, but is always enlightening. To learn is to change, to grow.

This is my story, my reality. In the telling I will share a number of my values, beliefs and philosophies that have evolved over the years. Many times I have challenged my personal, religious and spiritual beliefs, asked many questions and I have not found all the answers. In my quest for meaning, I seem to have generated more questions. I believe in a strong interconnection between mind, body and soul. The book will include not only what I have learned intellectually through my experiences with Allison, but will include some of the physical, emotional and spiritual challenges and consequences I have encountered along the way. I do not expect others to embrace my beliefs or my

way of thinking. I only invite readers to hear my story, to listen and try to understand a little about this journey with Allison and autism. Some may gain insights into the spectrum of autism. Others may gain an appreciation and understanding of the ongoing struggles and adjustments facing the members of a family living with a person with a disability. Reading this story may shed some light on how others can help, how they too can gain from becoming involved. Some may

Allison and her mother, Kris Jones.

even be able to develop an inkling of what it may be like for the individual who lives with a disability. Some may be moved and touched by the beauty of Allison and her contributions to our lives. Above all, it is my hope that readers gain an appreciation of those people who are different, people who fall outside the parameters of what we call normal, and can see them as unique individuals, differently-abled, valued human beings.

Part I:
The Early Years

Chapter 1
What is Wrong with Our Baby?

Young couples often dream of having children one day and my husband Gord and I were no exception. We were married in 1968 and delayed having children until Gord completed his Bachelor's degree in education and we had moved to Okotoks, Alberta, a small community south of Calgary. In September of 1970 Gord became the physical education teacher at Okotoks Junior-Senior High School and I was teaching Medical-Surgical nursing at the Foothills Hospital School of Nursing in Calgary. We both had been raised in small towns, and were happy to move from Calgary, even though it meant that I had a forty-five minute commute to work. We were to come to appreciate the value of raising our family in a small community.

A year after our move to Okotoks, once Gord's career was well under way, we started talking about having a family. Unfortunately I had some difficulties with getting and staying pregnant. Over the next year I had two miscarriages and an ectopic pregnancy on an ovary, which required emergency surgery. Gord once said that I had "no problem catching the passes but I kept fumbling the ball." Finally I became pregnant again. There were some tense moments when I had some spotting at about eight weeks, but I responded favorably to hormone injections. Over the next seven months I was healthy, happy and reveled in the experience of having a developing baby in my body and had a normal pregnancy after a precarious start. Of course I had feelings and questions about the upcoming event and prayed that my baby would be normal; in fact I remember asking God to please not give me a baby with mental disabilities. I felt I could handle a physical impairment, but intelligence was so important to me. I suspect that most moms have fears and similar feelings during pregnancy, but in retrospect, I wonder if I was trying to prepare myself for what was to come.

I went into labor at six am on July 14, 1972, my due-date. Gord is never late for anything and I thought this baby will be just like him, right on time and reliable. Our beautiful daughter arrived at just after three o'clock in the afternoon. Both Gord and I were filled with great joy and awe with the miracle of childbirth. Once I set eyes on my new daughter I felt an immediate bond, a connection with this sweet, small,

wonderful little person. I was overcome with love for her – and for her dad. We named our daughter Allison Janelle and she came through the initial assessments made on newborn babies with flying colors. We went home five days later, ready to embark on our new lives as a family. Gord and I were a little nervous about the direction our lives were about to take and we had no idea how challenging it was going to be.

I was successful with breast-feeding Allison and words cannot describe or capture the feelings I had as I held, fed, changed and cared for my baby. I was a very proud new mom and our daughter was so precious. She had fair hair, her eyes were blue and she had such an angelic face. Allison went by many nicknames, but the one that stuck was Alli. We had many visitors and were always happy to show off the new addition to our family. I took Allison to her first ball game when she was two weeks old and had even made her a little shirt to match the team's uniform. Gord was coaching a girls fastball team and Alli became their best fan, although she slept through most of the innings. Gord and Allison had a special relationship right from the start. He loved it when his daughter fell asleep lying on his chest. Her little feet didn't even reach his waist. Gord did not get up in the night to feed our baby, but he usually heard her first and would nudge me, waking me up.

Two of my colleagues in nursing had given birth to babies about the same time as I had that summer. Over the next few months the three of us met for lunch with our new babies, compared notes and discussed all the important things related to babies and child-rearing. When our children were about seven weeks old, I noticed that the two boys were smiling in response to their mothers and making all kinds of interesting sounds. Allison was not responding in this way and I experienced my first twinge of anxiety about her. I reassured myself that soon my babe would be smiling too, but it didn't happen. Oh, she smiled eventually, but not in response to my face or her dad's. Weeks later she even started to laugh out loud, but only in response to her flying mobiles or some other stimuli we couldn't discern. She was not developing the expected social responsiveness and avoided even looking at us. She did not make eye contact and would look away from any human face. Over the next few months my concerns grew as I noticed other delays in her development. She did not use her hands, did not hold a rattle or begin to reach for things. She seemed to prefer to lie on her back, kicking her feet to make her mobiles fly. Over all she was a content baby, especially if we

let her be and did not try to impose ourselves on her. She resisted being held, except when she was being fed. Allison balked any attempts to cuddle her, unless she was held in an upright position, with her looking over our shoulders. The one exception to her aversion to touch was that she loved to be rocked to sleep, but again only if she were held upright. These examples were subtle indicators that something was not quite right with Allison's development and I brought these up with her pediatrician on several occasions. He assured me that she was doing just fine and said that I was expecting too much. The doctor knew that I was taking a university course in child development that winter and he suggested that children develop at their own rate and the norms I was reading about were only guidelines. His advice was to "just love her and she will develop at her own pace." I wanted to believe him, but I sensed that there was something wrong with my sweet, sweet daughter.

I had returned to work that fall on a part time job-sharing basis. Like many young couples with a new family, we very much wanted to build our own home, so I worked in order to save the money to do so. Returning to work so soon was not an easy decision for me; many new moms experience some concerns about leaving their children, and even feel guilty when they choose to go back to work. I knew those first few years in a child's life were critical to the child's development and I wondered if I could ever find anyone capable enough to look after our baby while I was at work. I was fortunate in finding a wonderful baby sitter, Edith Larsen. She and her husband had two teenaged children, a son and a daughter. The Larsens had been fostering young children on and off for years. Edith knew more about babies than I did and I was thrilled when I interviewed her. I liked her and hired her immediately, sensing that she could teach me a thing or two. On the days Edith cared for Allison, she would get up at four in the morning, get all her housework done so that she could devote her day to our daughter. During the day she cared for her, played with her and took Allison out in her buggy for daily walks. I knew Allison was in the capable care of this woman and Allison was receiving a great deal of love and attention. In no time the whole family loved our little girl. Annette, Edith's daughter, took a special interest in Allison and she became her baby sitter if we were going out in the evenings. Annette was very conscientious and I knew I could trust her. Besides, if she had any problems Edith would be there in a flash. Edith's husband, Peder, would hold Allison and found many ways

to make her laugh and their son, John, even took an interest in her.

Over the next few months Edith and I talked when I came to get Allison after work. She always had a cup of tea ready and some cookies or baking, so she was taking care of me too. In many ways Edith eased our journey. She became a tremendous support and always knew exactly what to say and do when we were in crisis. She and I became life-long friends. I have often wondered if I could have coped with my fears and feelings if I didn't have Edith to talk to and to support me. I believe she was meant to arrive in my life at a time when I needed her most and I am thankful for her. Eventually she shared my concerns about Allison because she too had recognized that Alli was different and her behavior at times did not seem to be normal. Often she would have ideas of things we could do to encourage Allison to learn.

In many ways I was thankful to return to work. I loved teaching nursing, found it challenging and believed I had found my niche in terms of my career. I had graduated from a three-year diploma program in 1966, from the University of Alberta Hospital School of Nursing in Edmonton, Alberta. Immediately after graduating from my generic program, I enrolled in a special post-graduate diploma course at the U. of A. In the mid- to late-sixties, there was a shortage of nurses and nurse educators, and the university started this program to entice RNs to continue their education. Students could specialize in either Teaching and Supervision or in Public Health. Upon completion, graduates were allowed five more years to complete their Bachelors of Science in Nursing (BScN), the equivalent to taking another year of university, although this could be done on a part-time basis. Although I had very little experience as a graduate nurse, I was fortunate to be hired as a new instructor by the Foothills Hospital School of Nursing in Calgary. Over the next three decades the requirements for nursing instructors became much more stringent.

In my first years as an instructor, I had to work very hard to stay one step ahead of my students and I spent many hours studying and preparing. After Gord and I were married in 1968, completing my degree in nursing was one of my goals and I had started taking courses at the University of Calgary before Alli was born. I only had two courses to complete and took an evening course in developmental psychology during her first winter and completed my last course the summer of 1973, when Allison was a year old. It was a challenge for me to find a balance

between work, going to university and parenting. I did not have a great deal of spare time and had to be organized and disciplined. However, I believed that it was the quality of time spent with one's child that mattered most, not the quantity. When I was home I was devoted to Allison and I studied and wrote papers when she was sleeping. When I was at work I was engaged in the activities at hand and could put my concerns about Allison on hold for a few hours. Work for me was therapeutic, allowing me a break from my growing alarm about Allison's development. I had complete faith and trust in Edith and rarely worried about Alli when I was away.

My anxieties would surface once again on the drive home from work. I remember praying that Allison had learned something new that day. I know it hurt Edith when she had to tell me that she hadn't. Edith was doing everything she could to promote Allison's learning and was deeply committed to her. Edith took Allison for a check up with the public health nurse when Alli was about seven months old. The nurse noticed Allison's developmental delay and said to Edith, "this often happens when moms return to work leaving babies to the care of baby sitters. Nobody can replace a mother's love." Edith was hurt and angry and when she related this story, I shared her anger and felt that this was such an unfair thing to say, although I felt a twinge of guilt. This nurse had no idea of the situation or circumstances, was being judgmental and in my opinion she had stepped out of line.

In Allison's first year I often felt vulnerable and fragile. Edith was able to be more objective than I was and helped me to keep my perspective. Even on days she was not caring for Allison, I could call on her if I was having trouble with my babe. Sometimes when Alli got fussy I was unable to calm her down. Babies are sensitive to their mother's feelings and I suspect she sensed my anxiety. In these situations all I needed to do was to call Edith and she would be there, calm and caring. She would take Allison into her arms and within a few minutes my upset baby would settle down, stop crying and drift off to sleep, content at last.

With the exception of a few incidents, throughout her first year Allison was a content baby. However, things changed when we took her away for a weekend to visit relatives or friends. She cried most of the time we were away. She would not sleep well and we would all return exhausted. Unless they came to our house, relatives and friends were

seeing a different baby from the one we knew. Even as an infant Allison could not seem to handle a change in her environment. We spent her first Christmas Eve with my family and Christmas Day with Gord's relatives and she howled the whole time. I could not understand what the problem was and I so wanted our relatives to see Allison as the beautiful child that she was, but she always seemed to be upset when we visited. I knew our family members felt sorry, unable to understand what was wrong with her either.

My feelings of concern escalated as the months went on. I was well aware of the developmental tasks children normally go through and Allison was still not progressing as I thought she should. Our child was behind in many developmental tasks and did not follow the expected sequence of accomplishments. She rolled over and was able to stay sitting up when put in that position on schedule, but made no effort to creep or crawl. If she were put on her stomach she would flail her arms and legs, but was not able to get up in a creeping position or get to a sitting position by herself. Gord and I did everything we could think of to help her to learn, providing Alli with stimulation and encouragement. We bought almost every educational toy available. But Allison was not interested in toys. She did not pick them up or even look at them. She had a particular aversion to stuffed animals; it was as if touching them was painful to her. Eventually she would hold a toy if it was placed in her hand, as long as it was not soft or fuzzy. She did not reach for them herself and if one were placed in her hand she held it for a few moments, but she did not play with it in an appropriate way. Toys were just objects that had arrived in her hand. Once she dropped the toy she made no effort to retrieve it and it was as if it ceased to exist. Children usually are delighted to watch a toy drop, reach for it, point at it and demand they get it back. Allison never pointed at anything. Children learn to look for toys if they are hidden. Allison did not. But she did respond to music. She would laugh and make sounds if you played a music box for her or put on a record or tape. She also loved to be read to. At an early age she would listen attentively and turn the pages of a book, well before children are expected to do so.

Knowing deep down that your child may not be normal is an unsettling feeling, one hard to describe, but it tends to gnaw away at the emotions, creating a silent ache that never goes away. I kept voicing my concerns to her doctor, but he just kept trying to reassure me, reminding

me that each child is different and develops at his or her own rate. At one point I even asked if she might be autistic. The doctor seemed horrified by this question and responded by saying, "you don't want to have an autistic child, that is a form of childhood schizophrenia and I do not believe she is schizophrenic." Of course I did not want her to be autistic, or schizophrenic for that matter. I didn't want her to be anything but normal. I was simply exploring the possibility in an attempt to understand and explain her strange pattern of development. I needed some answers, something to adjust to. Alli's doctor was wonderful in many ways, he had a special way with children and I could not have asked for better attention to her physical needs. But for some reason he wouldn't entertain the possibility that there was something wrong with Allison, or if he did he was unwilling to share this with me. I couldn't adjust to the unknown, but I believed that I could handle almost anything if I had something to adjust to. I felt so helpless and his attempts at reassurance only made me feel more desperate. He did concede that perhaps she was "developmentally delayed." To me this was a euphemism, an inadequate explanation that only served to add to my frustration. I really was only looking for confirmation of what I already knew.

Finally a significant event caught his attention. When Allison was eleven months old she had a seizure. I had put Allison to bed for a nap in the early afternoon and I too lay down to rest in the next room. I was awakened from my sleep by a horrible cry coming from her room. I then heard a thumping sound. I leapt out of bed and ran to her side. By this time my baby was ashen in color, was non-responding and looked deathly ill. I picked her up, called her name, but got no response. I had no idea what was wrong but had a terrible sense of dread. I ran to my neighbor's carrying my limp baby and she quickly drove us to the doctor's office in Okotoks. After assessing her, he told me she had had a seizure or convulsion. Her temperature was high and he thought it was a febrile convulsion, something that can happen to any child with a high fever. After checking her throat and diagnosing an infection, he prescribed antibiotics and Tylenol for her fever. We stayed at the clinic until her temperature dropped and she became more alert. The doctor phoned her pediatrician, who suggested that she be started on Phenobarbital along with the antibiotic; an appointment was made to see the specialist in a few days. I remember feeling so helpless, so afraid and rather incompetent because I hadn't recognized that she had a

seizure. The outcry I heard was an epileptic cry, a sound emitted at the onset of a seizure. By the time I got to her she was in the postictal stage, or the period of time following the seizure, and the convulsions had stopped, but I hadn't recognized the symptoms. Things are very different when it involves your own child. I taught neurological nursing, had witnessed many seizures in my career, but when it happened to my child it didn't even occur to me that she had had a convulsion.

Allison recovered from the infection with no further complications and we had our appointment with her pediatrician. Finally he expressed concern about Allison. Because there was no pediatric neurologist in Calgary in the early seventies, he made an appointment for Allison to be seen by a neurologist in Edmonton, Alberta. We had to wait a couple of months and in the mean time, the doctor started her on a combination of drugs: Phenobarbital and Dilantin, medications commonly used for epilepsy. I was relieved that her doctor finally shared our concerns; somehow it validated my feelings. It was a very lonely time for me, and I suspect for my husband as well and I knew he was hurting too. We didn't talk about it very much; it was as if talking about it might make it real. Perhaps our fears were unfounded and if we just waited all our concerns would vanish. I struggled to keep a strong front, but tears were never far away. I know doctors do not like to jump to conclusions and want to stay positive, but distressed, concerned parents need to feel they are being heard. It took something dramatic like a seizure to get the doctor's attention. When parents feel something is not right, perhaps further investigation is warranted. Simply listening to parents' feelings and concerns is important and so appreciated. Besides being listened to, I needed to know what was wrong. I looked forward to our appointment in anticipation of finally getting some answers.

Our concerns were confirmed after our consultation with the pediatric neurologist. I took Allison to Edmonton and the doctor agreed that she was not progressing in a normal fashion at all. He felt she had some kind of brain damage, was likely mentally retarded and susceptible to seizures. He thought it was too early to diagnose autism, and he too seemed uncomfortable with that diagnosis. I was upset, but at least I knew that my concerns and fears had been warranted and having our feelings validated was helpful. Her medications were changed immediately. The neurologist did not give the drug Dilantin to children because of the side effects related to hypertrophy, or enlargement, of the gums

causing serious teeth problems. We were to continue giving her Phenobarb, an anticonvulsant, in order to prevent further seizures.

Although Phenobarb is a sedative to older children and adults, it can have the opposite effect on young children and this was true in Allison's case. She became hyperactive, irritable and slept very little. I admit to having a fear of seizures and believed this hyperactivity was better than the alternative. Sleep became a problem for all three of us, as she slept only short periods at a time, four to six hours a night and rarely during the day. We were all over-tired and Allison was irritable most of the time. Most days she woke up at about four in the morning and one of us had to get up with her. Chronic fatigue and sleep deprivation were added to our problems.

Having a more definitive diagnosis did help in that I was more realistic in my expectations of Allison and no longer watched in anticipation for signs of sudden improvements. I could accept that her progress would be slow and emotionally I was a little less volatile. There were many other examples of impediments in her development. She did not use her hands and even well into her second year she walked with her hands clasped either in front of her or behind her back. She did not pull herself up on furniture to stand, but she had an obvious preference for being on her feet. She allowed me to hold her hand while she took a few

steps until one day, when she was twelve months old, she took her first steps independently. For many months after that I had to put her on her feet and once she was walking, she could stop near furniture and hold on. She was unable to let herself down into a sitting position, so I had to put her down. She was happiest when she was on her feet, but at times she would fall flat on her

Allison at eleven months old.

face. She was unable to extend her arms out to break her fall. I had a special safety harness that she wore in the car and I found this to be useful in other ways too. It had a strap that I could hold on to so if she had her harness on, she could walk by herself. This worked well for both of us because she did not like me to hold her hand. I could "catch" her if she fell, preventing injury.

After several months of doing this I realized that she still was not learning to break her own falls. I had solved one problem only to create another. In order to help her develop this skill, I had to take her outside on the lawn, let her walk, knowing she would likely fall. Sometimes I even had to push her gently, causing her to fall, although this was very difficult for me to do, but falling on the soft grass was better than falling on a sidewalk or hard floor. It took her a long time to discover that if she put her hands out, she could break her fall, but she did learn. I had to be creative in teaching Allison. She did not learn in the usual way and I had to think of different ways to teach her. I have often said that normal children learn in spite of us, but Allison needed special attention in order for her to learn. Learning requires a change in behavior, and Allison resisted change. She therefore resisted learning. I must add that once she acquired a new skill or mastered something new, she never forgot it. Retention of a new skill or knowledge was not the problem; overcoming her resistance to the actual process of learning was the issue.

To keep Allison's level of frustration down, I often tried to make things easier for her. She would pick up a toy if I left a favorite one on a piece of furniture at her waist level. Once she dropped something she didn't seem to be able to even see it, although she would return to the table looking for another toy. We had quite the game going, as I had to ensure that toys were always on the furniture, available to her. If she couldn't find one she would simply wander around with nothing to do, and I felt that was not productive. It wasn't until Christmas when Allison was seventeen months old that my Mom noticed what I was doing. She tactfully told me I wasn't helping her by making it so easy for her. By this time it seemed that Allison could at least track the fallen object, but reaching for it was not in her repertoire of skills. My Mom noticed how rigid Allison was and that she did not seem to be able to bend over when standing. I was still having to put her on her feet so she could walk. She used her hands only to break a fall and had not discovered other useful ways in which to use her hands. Mom had

Allison learning to bend over and reach for her toys.

an idea and asked if she could try something. She removed three cushions from her couch, put them one on top of the other on the floor and put a number of Allison's toys on top. This was at her level and Allison found them immediately. She picked up her favorites and returned to the cushions to find another toy after she dropped it. The cushions remained there for a couple of hours and then Mom removed one. The toys were replaced and Allison found them once again, this time bending over slightly. Then another cushion was removed. By the end of the day Allison was bending right over, picking her toys up off the floor. Not only that, it was not long before she learned to use her hands to pull herself up on furniture and to hold on while getting from a standing to sitting position. Her inability to bend over at the waist was the underlying problem. She was able to put her new skills together and could now get up and down on her own and retrieve those toys that she dropped. To our delight she would even drop a toy on purpose so she could practice this skill. This was another lesson in breaking things down into small tasks when trying to help her learn something new. I was learning to be open to suggestions from others, knowing that sometimes I could not even see the obvious. I have come to appreciate these humbling occasions and welcome helpful suggestions from others.

The development of language skills also follows a natural progression. It wasn't that Allison was quiet, but her sounds were different and

she made no attempt to imitate the sounds of our voices or words. It was as if she had not heard us and we saw no reaction or response to our verbal stimulation. She never engaged in babbling, a stage children go through in the development of language, in which they make sounds that mimic words in terms of inflection and tone, although the sounds may make no sense.

There were other examples of Alli's delay in development, but a most significant factor for me was her lack of response to others, her lack of social skills. From the time she was a baby she would not maintain eye contact; she would not even look at another human being. If we smiled at her, talked to her or tried to connect with her, she gave no obvious response. She would avert her eyes elsewhere, avoiding eye contact, looking right through us. She seemed indifferent and showed no recognition of people in her life. She did not make strange in the usual sense, nor did she seem to even notice my presence when I came to pick her up after work. My daughter didn't seem to recognize me or even to care if I came or went! This hurt, but I just kept hoping that some day she would respond. I had to make a point of going right up to her, picking her up and talking to her before she would even seem to recognize that I was in the room. She might show some minute sign of recognition but quickly resumed what she was doing. She preferred things to people and would rather not be with other people at all. Once she was walking on her own she often escaped to her own room, away from contact with others. If we had company she preferred to leave the room or if she did stay, she seemed to ignore the people around her. She showed no awareness of their presence and made no attempt to interact with others, even other children.

Allison did not engage in appropriate play with her toys. She would drop a toy, pick it up and drop it, again and again. She seemed to enjoy being engaged in repetitive behaviors such as spinning a coaster or bouncing a ball on the table. We tried to share some of these activities with her, to break into her world. We tried bouncing the ball to her, but she would grab the ball and turn away, making no attempt to engage in play or interact with us. She liked noisy toys, although she did not play with them in the expected way. She had a Fisher Price toy, three men in a tub. She ignored the "men," but took great pleasure of taking the tub, which was hard plastic with a spring mast with a bell, into the bathroom and dropping it into the empty bathtub. You can imagine the noise that

made. It was irritating to us, but she seemed to enjoy the horrible sound that it made. She did not play with dolls. In fact, she disliked them, but that is understandable given her aversion to people. She did have one doll she would carry around, but she always held her with the face away from her and often held it by a foot with her doll hanging upside down.

Some of her favorite things were not toys at all. She would carry around an egg carton made of Styrofoam, manipulating it, making all kinds of interesting squeaking sounds. One of her cousins drew her name for Christmas one year and she was delighted to discover that he had given her an egg carton. He could not have picked a more appreciated gift. Often presents she received for various occasions meant nothing to her but she might enjoy the box it came in. The toys that she did seem to enjoy, and play with appropriately, were music boxes. She learned to wind them up and carried them around for hours, playing the same tune over and over again. She did have a child's record player and although she was able to learn how to put the record on the turntable, she couldn't turn the machine on. She learned to take the hand of a person and direct it to the record player, indicating that she wanted the music on. This was a big step for her; she was finally connecting with another person to make her needs known. I later learned that this is called "autistic leading," when a child physically leads an adult to a desired activity or object.

The next year, up until Allison was over two years old, we struggled with the realities of her disabilities, but our efforts to help her to learn were hampered by her frequent infections and resulting hospitalizations. This is common in children with disabilities. It seemed that along with a delay in development she had an immature immune system, lowering her resistance to disease and making her susceptible to infections. If anyone sneezed in her vicinity she would end up in hospital with pneumonia within a couple of days. At one point she was tested for cystic fibrosis in an attempt to explain the frequent respiratory infections, but this proved to be negative. Finally the doctors concluded that she had a form of childhood asthma, the result of an allergy to the organisms causing the respiratory tract infections. Most of the infections were accompanied by high fevers and in spite of the Phenobarb she had more febrile seizures until she was four years old. Each time it happened she had an infection of some kind.

When Allison was hospitalized with her various infections, some

eager resident would always decide to do developmental testing. After all, Allison was an interesting child who was not typical in her development. This always upset me, because how could they expect a child that was ill or had a high fever to perform? Of course she "scored" low on the tests! When she was ill she couldn't do things she could do when she was well and they were making assumptions about her that I considered to be rather unfair. In order for results of tests to be valid they should be conducted under optimal conditions for the child. I knew that the findings would have been very different if the assessment were done at a time when she was well, at home, in an environment she was comfortable in. I had to accept the fact that they did not have the opportunity to assess a child with difficulties like Allison very often and this was meeting their needs, not hers.

Allison's problems of frequent infections and physical illnesses compounded my anxiety and added to the stress I was experiencing. I had thought having a diagnosis would help me to adjust, but it was only the beginning of the adjustment process. Initially my question was "what is this, what is wrong with Allison?" Now the burning questions were "why me? Why this innocent child?" Wasn't it enough that she was retarded? Why did she have to suffer so many infections on top of all her other problems? It just didn't seem fair to her or to me and I constantly struggled with my questions, trying to make sense of this.

I remember sitting in the hospital cafeteria one day with a dear friend who was a resident in pediatrics. Allison was in the hospital with one of her infections and she was down having more tests, so I had taken a break. During our conversation he said something like this: "Kris, you are a wreck! Look at you; you are barely coping. Perhaps you need to consider putting Allison in an institution. I think you would all be better off. It is time you realized how very severely retarded she is and that perhaps you can't help her. You need to get on with your life."

I was aghast. I felt this friend didn't know me because if he did, he would know putting my daughter away in some institution was out of the question and I told him so. After that situation, I realized that I had better get myself together and find a way to cope. I had been wallowing in self-pity, understandable perhaps given my situation, but I realized that this was not serving me well and was not helping Allison. Over the next several weeks I went through a great deal of soul searching in an attempt to coming to terms with many issues. The process took some

time, and has been ongoing in many ways.

I had a fundamental belief that we must accept the consequences of our choices and actions. When my husband and I decided to have children, we made a commitment to parenting, no matter what. We were in this for the long term. In my estimation, the most important thing a person can do in this lifetime is to keep one's word. When I say I will do something, I know it is my responsibility to do it. It relates to personal integrity and honesty, other values of mine. So, I knew I had already made this commitment to parenting and I was prepared to fulfill that in the best way I knew how. But first I had to allow myself to grieve, grieve the loss of the normal child I had expected to have.

I was aware of the writings of many authors about the stress response. Dr. Elisabeth Kubler-Ross had written *On Death and Dying* in 1969. She described the adjustment and grief reaction a person and family members have in response to the diagnosis of a terminal disease. Although the diagnosis was different, I was experiencing a similar adjustment process. This was a crisis for me and I was grieving. Kubler-Ross described various stages terminal patients often go through in coming to terms with death and dying. I had seen patients go through this process and I felt that this process was therapeutic, in fact a form of good grief! In order to accept Allison's disability, I had to find a way to give it all meaning, see the positive in what I had been interpreting as only negative. How could I turn it all around? How could I reframe my experiences, shift my focus from grief to hope?

Through a great deal of further soul searching I came to believe that if Allison was to be disabled, it was meant to be. There must be a reason for this, although for the life of me I couldn't figure out why a loving God would give us a child with such severe limitations. For a while my faith was shaken until I could accept the fact that even though I couldn't understand it, I simply must trust that God knew what he was doing. I went through a whole gamut of emotions in the process of coming to terms with this, including guilt. I must have done something to cause it. Somehow it must be my fault. In the next moment I knew that this idea was ridiculous. Eventually I realized that guilt is a destructive feeling, serving no purpose other than making me feel miserable. Guilt can even be immobilizing. So I had to give it up, quit beating myself up! I had to temper my feelings and come to understand that although I could not change what was, I could change how I reacted to

the realities of the situation. I found that I had a choice when confronted with this difficult, devastating situation. I chose to have some control over my reactions and my feelings. I could shape my responses. I didn't have to like the fact that my daughter was disabled, but I no longer had to feel responsible for her disability. Now that was a major breakthrough for me, freeing me in a sense.

The next issue I had to deal with was my disappointment. My heart ached for the child I believed I deserved. Allison should be perfect in every way. Not only should she be perfectly normal and healthy, she should grow up to be successful, popular, beautiful, intelligent, athletic and famous! I was projecting my standards, values and expectations on this innocent child. In retrospect, I think most parents sooner or later have to come to terms with the fact that their children will not become exactly what they want them to be. I had to come to terms with this realization much sooner than most parents and perhaps the magnitude of my disappointment was different. Because of her disability, she was different from what I had expected and I had the additional pain of knowing that she might not ever have the opportunity to choose for herself.

Underlying all of these negative feelings was fear. Fear of the unknown, fear of failure, fear related to the future. A very realistic concern for parents of children with disabilities is the future, for the child and for themselves. Although I could only imagine what our lives would be like, I had a sense of dread. I worried about how I would manage to care for Allison in her adolescence, in her adulthood. Who would look after her when I am too old to manage her physically? What will happen to her when I die? I had no trouble finding things to worry about. Finally I realized that worrying about possible problems was so unproductive. Worry leads to fear. Fear is another disabling feeling I had to try to set aside and replace with a sense of trust. Trust that I would be able to handle events as they occurred, trust in my abilities to cope. It was important to trust Allison too, trust our relationship. Surely Allison and I would both grow and change through our experiences together, and I had to trust that we would be able to mobilize resources, as they were needed. The best thing I could do was to take one day at a time. I had to try to live in the present moment, focus on the here and now, knowing that the future would look after itself. I had to concentrate on celebrating the temporary, seeing the positive in each day. I realized that

it would be ludicrous to live without planning for the future, but realistic planning is different from needless worrying.

Other feelings I struggled with were those related to my own self-worth. Throughout my life I had expected to succeed and had been rewarded for achievement. Subconsciously I had accepted a formula that equates performance, or achievement, with self worth. As long as I was achieving I was happy with myself. For me to feel worthy, I had to achieve high grades at school, excel in sports and in fact, excel in anything I took on. Failure was out of the question and unacceptable. This philosophy worked until I became a parent. Now what? Was my disabled child my failure? How was this to affect my worth? What about the child? Was Allison less than worthy because she was unable to meet my performance standards? Of course not! In examining other personal beliefs I recognized that I had always striven for perfection. I wanted to be the "perfect" mom of the "perfect" child. I had to question this and recognize how unfair and unrealistic I was being. Perfection, as I defined it at the time, could never be reached and therefore failure was inevitable. I concluded that rather than expecting perfection, it might be healthier to strive to be the best that I could be. As well, that was even a realistic goal for me to have for Allison. As long as I tried to deal with her disability as best I could, my self worth could remain intact. I knew and trusted that as Allison's mother I would always do as much as I could to help her grow and develop. Allison didn't have to become "perfect" either, but together we would strive to help her to reach her potential, whatever that might be. Of course I would make mistakes, but the intention of doing what I thought was best at any given point in time was what mattered. I believed that often our most profound lessons come out of what we learn through our mistakes or errors and I had to allow myself that much. Once again I had to discard old beliefs and assumptions separating performance standards from measurement of worth. This was not without pain as it was difficult to realize that longstanding values were no longer valid and to discard them. I had to replace these with more constructive and realistic values that hold more truth. I came to value both Allison and I as we were, human beings trying to do our best. My values shifted and I realized the most important things in life include loving and being loved. I was committed to providing Allison with a life filled with love and knew that my feelings would be my guide.

When I think
My mind gets in the way.
When I feel
I know who I am.

I emerged from this internal personal exploration intact and in fact stronger. In the process I had to go deep inside my self. I learned that when I was overly stressed and upset I tended to think a great deal. I tried to figure things out intellectually, to rationalize and question everything and my mind became cluttered and full of chatter. My thoughts often interfered with my ability to deal with my true feelings. I had to learn to shut down my thoughts and let my feelings flow, to express them and even release some of them.

There had never been a question about my love for Allison. My love for her became my driving force and I believed we were on this journey together, and that we would both grow and learn. I wasn't expecting it to be easy, but I had finally come to some understanding, some level of acceptance. It was in my nature to be an optimist and my glass was half-full. I had reached a point when I could rely on my own resources, maintain a positive attitude knowing that things were unfolding as they should. I felt increased confidence in myself and my abilities to cope. My focus shifted from one of self-pity and sorrow to a focus on Allison's abilities and the possibilities that we could consider. If this was to be the way it would be, then what could I do to help her, to enhance the quality of her life? Certainly retarded people can learn and my challenge was to assist her in any way that I could. Our journey together had already begun; I had no clear vision as to where we were going, but we were en route and I was committed to giving my all in helping Allison find her place in this world. My mission had become one of providing her with whatever she needed and the challenge was to figure out what that was.

Chapter 2
What Does Allison Need?

My focus had shifted from feeling sorry for myself to figuring out what I could do for Allison. At one point the doctor suggested that Allison needed exposure to normal children because children learn from each other and imitate each other. Well, for one thing she had been "exposed" to other children and had shown no signs of imitating anything. We had tried to have her imitate words, sounds, actions to no avail. She didn't seem to even see others, did not play with or interact at all with other children, but I had to try. I enrolled her in a day care program in Calgary for three days a week. This program was one in which young children with disabilities were integrated with normal children in a day care setting and I liked that philosophy. Well, this day care turned out to be a disaster. Allison was just over two years old and she was put in with infants and babies up to eighteen months and the needs of the younger children took much of the staff's time. Allison did not demand much and she was content to just sit, looking off into space. The individual attention that was promised did not happen. I was disappointed to learn that she had physiotherapy only once a week and the session lasted less than a half hour.

Along with my disappointment about the program itself, Allison had an increase in infections and illnesses. Allison had pneumonia several times while in the program and on one occasion we almost lost her. One morning she woke up with a cough and seemed to have difficulty breathing. She was lethargic and very soon I noticed that her chest was indrawing with each respiration. Breathing was an effort, she began to wheeze and I recognized that she was in respiratory distress. Her respirations were about seventy a minute and her color was poor, almost cyanosed or bluish in color. Gord and I rushed her in to the hospital in Calgary, the one at which I worked, teaching nursing. I had many friends there and knew many of the staff and by this time they knew Allison well because of her frequent hospital admissions for treatment of a variety of infections. In terms of hospitalizations and the care she received I had no concerns.

My main complaint was the necessity of repeating her history each time, sometimes to two or three different interns or residents. I knew

they had to learn and were expected to complete their own histories, but as a parent this gets tiring. I was exasperated because it was taking so long and I knew my daughter was in need of immediate medical attention. After the intern completed her history, he left to write it up and hopefully consult with Allison's pediatrician. We waited and waited until I could no longer stand it so I went to the desk and demanded that I see the doctor in charge, in Allison's room. I turned and walked back to be with her, angry and very upset. In a couple of minutes a senior resident arrived and he said, "I understand we have an upset mom here!" I lost my composure and told him in no uncertain terms that of course I was angry, he only had to look at this child to understand why. My child was critically ill, she was not being looked after. The resident's demeanor changed and he immediately examined Allison.

Things moved quickly after that; her pediatrician was contacted, and came personally. Within minutes Allison was wheeled off to X-ray, accompanied by the resident and her pediatrician. We were told that she was gravely ill and the doctors wanted to accompany her to the X-ray department in case she went into respiratory arrest en route. I wept as they wheeled my baby down the hall, a doctor on each side of her. Gord and I stood there, holding each other. We were frightened and filled with so much love and concern for our little girl. I had wanted to go with them, but the doctors insisted that I wait on the unit with Gord. The X-ray confirmed severe pneumonia and the doctors returned to report the findings. One of Allison's lungs had collapsed and they were afraid that she might not live through the night. They started an intravenous and IV antibiotics and bronchodilators to open her airways were administered. Our vigil began. With two doctors in attendance, constantly assessing and administering medications, Gord and I watched and waited by her side all night, praying for her life, her survival. By morning her breathing had eased and she was showing signs of improvement. The crisis was over and she recovered. After a few days we were able to take her home. Alli had been at the day care for six months and she did not return after this illness. We would have to find other ways to help her.

For the next year we had to deal with Allison's ongoing infections, although the incidence of these was gradually decreasing. Between hospitalizations we worked with Allison as best we could, trying to encourage normal development. Our lives stabilized somewhat and Gord and

I were even able to discuss our desire to have more children. Although we knew we would face many more challenges with Allison, perhaps it was time to entertain the idea of adding to our family and having another baby might help to normalize our lives. Of course we had concerns about the possibility of having a second child with a disability and after discussing it with our doctor and having some genetic counseling, we decided we could not handle the risks and it would be best if we adopted our second child. In the spring of 1973 when Allison was almost two years old we submitted our application to adopt a son. We had decided to request a boy to reduce any comparisons with Allison and the age, race or color didn't matter to us; we only wanted a normal, healthy little boy. After a number of interviews we were conditionally approved as potential adoptive parents, but there were still some regulations regarding housing to be met. At that time we were renting a two-bedroom house and social services insisted that our adopted child must have his own room. We were already in the process of building our first home, but final approval was not granted until they could see that there were three bedrooms. In June of 1974 we moved into our new home and our application for adoption was approved. Once we received our child I would have to quit work and stay home for a year and after a year, if we passed all the " tests," the adoption would be official. We expected a long wait, up to two years, because of the small number of children put up for adoption. We were told that in all likelihood we would receive a new born baby and to plan for this. Gord and I were now expectant parents once again, anticipating the arrival of our son, a brother for Allison.

During the waiting period we continued to concentrate on helping Allison. Edith was very much part of our lives, baby-sitting Allison while I continued to work part time. In the early fall of 1974 another crisis with Allison presented itself. One Saturday evening she was lethargic and not feeling well, so I checked her rectal temperature, finding she had a slight fever. I decided to administer her phenobarb a bit early and give her a bath to cool her down. I sat her in the tub and turned away to pick up one of her favorite toys to give to her. I heard her fall over and by the time I got to the edge of the tub she was under water, convulsing. Although I was panic stricken, I responded automatically. I lifted her out of the tub, lay her on the floor, opened her airway and checked for respirations. She was not breathing so I commenced mouth-to-mouth resuscitation. Between breaths I hollered for Gord

and he came on the run. I had to continue rescue breathing for a few minutes until she started breathing on her own, although her respirations were very shallow. Alli's color was poor; she was pasty-pale and semi-conscious, not responding other than to open her eyes slightly when I rubbed her chest. I checked her temperature once again and it had gone up to 40.5°C, causing the febrile convulsion.

We left immediately for the hospital in Calgary and because it was dark we left the interior light on in the car so I could continue to assess Alli. I could barely hear or feel her respirations and had to watch her chest rise and fall to be sure she was breathing. Allison was seen in emergency and an X-ray confirmed that her lungs were clear, much to our relief. She had not inhaled water into her lungs because her respirations had likely stopped before she went under the water. A severe throat infection was diagnosed as the cause of her fever and resulting convulsion. The doctor in emergency started her on antibiotics to combat the infection and wanted to discharge her. However, I refused to take her home; she was very ill and I feared she would develop further complications. Because we lived out of town we were too far away from medical help if we needed it quickly. After I convinced the doctor to keep Allison in the hospital she was admitted to pediatrics. An intravenous was started to deliver fluids and the antibiotics, Tylenol was given control her temperature and she was put in a croup tent for extra humidity. I stayed with Alli and kept vigil at her crib side and throughout that night and the next day Allison's temperature fluctuated, in spite of the Tylenol. She was still very pale, drowsy and slept on and off. She looked like a limp, rag doll. She was so small, so vulnerable and so very ill.

The next afternoon she became hyperactive, stood up in her crib, began making noises and laughing out loud. She kept throwing her head back and looking over her right shoulder. She was, as I call it, "wired up." The staff interpreted this behavior as an improvement in her condition and they commented on how active she was, how cute. She had been very lethargic and barely responding for hours and now she was awake, noisy and therefore must be getting better. A resident doctor happened to come by to examine her and he too believed that she was rebounding. I did not agree. I had a strange feeling that something was not right and I did not like her behavior or the look in her eyes. I explained to the resident that I was quite certain that she was about to have another seizure, but he shrugged this off. I suspect he was think-

ing that I was just another over-anxious mother. Once again my intuition was correct; her eyes rolled back, her back arched and she went into a major clonic-tonic seizure. The resident had to administer intravenous Valium to abort the convulsion. Once the seizure had run its course and Alli settled and fell asleep, he apologized to me, acknowledged that my feelings about an impending seizure were correct. He admitted that mothers are so often right about their children and he had learned another lesson about listening to parents. Over the next few days Allison did have a couple more seizures that they were able to abort and later on that week she had recovered enough to be taken home.

Convulsions were something I had a great deal of difficulty dealing with and, in fact, I felt a sense of terror when Allison was having a seizure. Perhaps it was because I felt so helpless and I couldn't make it go away. During a seizure I had the feeling that we were losing her, although I knew that they were not usually life threatening. However, repeated, uncontrolled seizures can cause brain damage, and she already had enough problems in her brain. It seemed like one more burden, something else I had no control over. My anxiety persisted for some time and once we were home I did not sleep well, getting up often to check on Allison. Complicating this anxiety about potential convulsions, I had to deal with my feelings of guilt. I had turned my back on my ill baby in the bathtub. I could not have lived with myself if she had not survived, if I had not been able to revive her. On the other hand I was grateful that I knew what to do and was able to respond to the crisis.

As the weeks went by, my anxiety about her physical health decreased and I was able to concentrate on her developmental difficulties. We were in limbo once again and I was in active pursuit of some program that would help her. She was getting further and further behind. She was just over two years old and although she was walking she was still very dependent. She was still drinking from a bottle and made no attempt to feed herself. She could not hold a spoon in her hand and meal times were not pleasant because she showed no interest in food or eating. She did not play appropriately with toys, other than to carry them around, spin the wheels of a pull toy or flick the tail on a toy animal. Most of the things she liked to carry were not toys at all, but were boxes, egg cartons or coasters. She resisted when we tried to teach her anything and seemed most content to wander around aimlessly or

sit and rock back and forth or bounce her head against the cushion on the chair or sofa. Sometimes she would hold a toy up and stare at it for long periods of time, or simply hold her hand out in front of her eyes, flicking or manipulating her fingers. She seemed to be looking right through whatever she was holding and not at it. She twirled and didn't even seem to get dizzy, and she stared at lights. When she drank from her bottle she poked her finger in her eye and I was afraid she would damage her eye. Although she cooperated in getting dressed, she could not even pull on a shirt or put on her shoes. We had not even attempted to toilet train her and she was still in diapers.

Although she made sounds, they did not seem to mean anything and she was not developing verbal language skills. She did not communicate with others and in fact, for the most part, did not seem interested in or aware of other people at all. We had very limited eye contact with her and if she did look at us it was for a fleeting moment. I noticed that if she did look at someone, she usually had her hand up in front her eyes, as if she didn't want us to know she was looking. She seemed to be off in another world, locked up inside herself.

Physically Allison was very attractive. Her hair was blond; she had blue eyes and a pretty face with fine features and high cheekbones. She had fair, clear skin and had a distinctive beauty about her. Although she seemed distant and withdrawn at times, she did not look abnormal, did not look retarded until one noticed and observed her rather odd behaviors. When she smiled her whole face would light up, although we often had no idea what was making her smile. Her exuberant laugh was infectious and one couldn't help but laugh along with her, even if we couldn't always identify the source of her delight. In spite of Allison's obvious disabilities she had many positive, lovable characteristics and attributes. She would laugh at some of the noises her dad would make and seemed happy in many ways.

Allison loved to be outside, to be constantly moving. I had taken her swimming when she was young and she loved the water. She didn't swim but took great delight in splashing around in the water, wearing her water wings, showing no fear. We took her many places with us and she was already a hockey and baseball fan, going to her father's games and the games of the teams he coached and she took great delight in the noise, the cheering and the action. Allison demanded very little from us. She did not have tantrums and I always had the feeling that inside her

there was a delightful, loving little person, wanting to express herself. One could not help but notice her great appreciation for and love of music. She would rock and sway rhythmically, keeping perfect time with the beat. I wrote a poem when Allison was about three years old, which captures something of what I felt about her.

My Daughter

A little girl
Fair and soft
And strong.
Not like you and me
But herself—
Whomever that might be.

She speaks not with words,
Occasional touch and hasty smiles
Communicate her warmth.

Her eyes -
How deep her eyes
Penetrate into my very being.

She brings me joy
And sorrow.
Feelings that exist together,
For what is one without the other?
And what am I without her?

Rare glimpses of her real self
Behind her withdrawal
Spur me on.
She lets me hug
Yet rarely hugs.

And oh her laugh -
How contagious and real!
All her sounds touch my heart.

I hope
Someday she'll let me in
And I will know her person
My daughter.

Someone gave me a book about a program in the United States that promised a cure for children with brain damage. I read it with great

Allison loved to look at her books.

interest and hope welled up inside me. The premise of this program was based on the theory that children with brain damage have fewer functioning brain cells than normal. Theoretically the brain has numerous dormant cells that are not being used and through stimulation these can become activated, replacing the function of the damaged cells and reversing the signs of brain damage. The child could improve and even be cured. The authors believed that in order for the cells in the brain to develop normally, a child must progress through the developmental milestones in sequence. Of particular importance is crawling and creeping, which children usually do before they walk. They had noticed that brain injured children not only do not develop in the normal progression, but tend to skip important developmental tasks. They often do not crawl or creep. The program they designed included activities that supposedly stimulate brain cell development by putting the child through the physical motions of creeping and crawling in addition to exercises and various forms of sensory stimulation.

Although this program seemed rather bizarre to me and I was skeptical given my nursing and science background, I was also desperate and willing to try almost anything that even hinted at a cure. Parents of children with disabilities are vulnerable and I was no exception. We knew Allison was mentally challenged and the neurologist had suggested that she had brain damage. Through further investigation I found out that there was a branch of this program in Calgary, so Gord and I took

Allison for an assessment and the doctor we saw offered us a great deal of hope. His immediate diagnosis of Allison's problems was autism, the result of brain damage. At the time I didn't question the fact that he made his comments based on only a few moments of observations and had done no formal testing. He suggested that if we were willing to devote the next two years to Allison's life she would be normal. Normal! That word was a very powerful motivator. How could we not participate? The program entailed starting an intense home program in which we would need many volunteers. He outlined the details of the program, gave us more literature to read and we went home to consider whether or not we were willing to take on this extensive program. We decided that implementing his ideas was a small sacrifice, given the promise of such positive, encouraging results. In the fall of 1974 I began to make plans to implement this home program. Meanwhile I read a great deal about the syndrome of autism and truly believed that this was Allison's disability.

I was still working part time and because this program would demand my full participation, I planned to resign at Christmas. We had decided to start the program in January of 1975. I invited a few friends to my home to explain the program and see if I could recruit some volunteers. I asked them to bring any of their friends who might be interested and was thrilled when more than thirty people showed up. At the meeting I explained as much as I could about autism and outlined Allison's unique problems. A couple of women volunteered to help me with the details in organizing the schedule. I was overwhelmed with the response of the people of our community and was encouraged by their enthusiasm and willingness to help. I still had some final preparations to make, some supplies to purchase and we were almost ready to go. We were optimistic and anxious to get on with the program.

However, things did not go exactly as planned. We had another crisis, another stumbling block to deal with. On my last day of work, December 17, I was sitting in the cafeteria at coffee time with some of my colleagues celebrating my retirement. I heard my name being paged over the intercom, which was not unusual, but this time it was Gord on the phone. Allison had fallen on the floor furnace at Edith's house and had suffered serious burns. Gord did not take the time to provide me with many details other than our family doctor was there and they were on their way to the Emergency department and I was to meet them

there. The next forty-five minutes were just about more than I could bear. The pediatric unit had been alerted and the staff was making preparations for Allison's admission, setting up a burn unit. I waited in the emergency department expecting the worst and was numb with fear. Soon Gord and Edith arrived with Allison. Edith was obviously upset, carrying our baby in her arms. Gord looked pale and drawn. Allison was conscious and crying, but her crying was music to my ears. Although I had not known many of the details before she arrived, I had expected her to be charred, disfigured and barely alive. I had imagined that her clothes had caught on fire, causing serious burns over much of her body. I quickly assessed her and was relieved to discover that the extent of her burns was not as serious as I had imagined. Indeed the wounds were deep, but the surface area was not as extensive as I had anticipated. She had patches of burns on her left forearm and down the outside of her left leg, thigh to ankle and on the sole of her right foot. The hot grates of the floor furnace had left their imprint, leaving deep, but narrow burn wounds, in the pattern of the grates. Apparently Edith had just taken Allison's clothes off and was about to give her a bath in the tub when the phone rang. While she was on the phone, Allison got up and wandered around the living room. The main source of heat in Edith's home was a furnace in the floor in the hall between two bedrooms and in front of the bathroom. The cover, a metal grate, got very hot of course, and Edith and all of her family members had been very careful in keeping Allison away from this heat source. Usually the hall was blocked off from Allison, but Edith had removed the gate with the intention of carrying Allison directly into the bathroom, until she was interrupted by the ringing telephone. Before Edith could stop her, Allison went into the hallway and stepped on the floor furnace in her bare feet. Her immediate reaction was to recoil and she tried to step off the hot grate but she fell, landing on her left side. Edith ran to her rescue but the damage had been done. I know Edith felt responsible and there was little I could say or do to reduce her feelings of guilt. I knew it was an accident and assured her that I was in no way blaming her. I knew she loved Allison and this was not supposed to happen, especially on her last day as Allison's baby sitter. Edith and I held each other for a few moments, crying together, sharing our pain. Emotional agony was no stranger to me as I knew all about guilt and I could feel her despair. Hugging her was the best I could offer; words were inadequate at a time like this.

Allison was admitted and her burn wounds were cleansed and covered with antibiotic cream and dressings. The standard treatment for third-degree burns was administered over the next several days. Her wounds remained clean and the healing process had begun so on December 23 the pediatrician decided we could take her home.

Although the burn was an unfortunate accident, I had little difficulty dealing with the situation. Allison's burns turned out to be much less serious than I had anticipated. Furthermore, I was able to help, to do something. I did not feel helpless like I did in the case of seizures. By doing her dressings and applying the tensors I was able to participate in and facilitate the healing process. It was not a life-threatening condition and I wasn't even worried about scarring. Even if she did have some, that seemed pretty minor to me. We saw no reason to delay the program we had planned to initiate in January and in spite of Alli's setback, we made the decision to carry on with our plans.

We were about to begin a new phase with Allison and although the future was not clear, we were moving forward. Just keeping Allison at home and loving her, as we had been advised, was not working, was not enough. We recognized that she was not able to learn on her own, she needed us to force ourselves into her world, to rescue her from a life of isolation and loneliness. This program was to be the first of many in our attempt to make her life better. Maybe it reflected my need to be proactive, to be involved, but I simply could not sit back and watch her become more and more disabled without planning some interventions. Our home program started the first week of January in 1975. We were expected to work with Allison eight hours a day, in one-hour blocks of time. It took three people working with her in each time frame so I needed two volunteers for each hour. That meant that each day I required sixteen volunteers. We developed a schedule and the volunteers signed up. We worked with Allison for three hours each morning, had a break for lunch and a nap and started again at two o'clock in the afternoon, working with her another three hours. After dinner, we had two more sessions.

The main component of the program involved manually putting Allison's body through the motions of crawling. This was called "patterning" and it required three people to work with Allison. She was positioned on a mat on our kitchen table, lying face down. I stood at the head of the table and held my hands on either side of her head, over

her ears. To establish a cadence, I used the rhyme, "one, two, buckle my shoe, three, four shut the door…" and so on, turning her head from side to side. There was a person on either side of her, holding her wrists and ankles. As I repeated the rhyme, they moved her arms and legs into the positions used in crawling. When her head was turned to the right, her right arm was extended and moved up parallel to her face and her right leg was flexed at the knee and her thigh moved to a right angle of her hip. Simultaneously, the person on her left extended her left arm down along her body and straightened her left leg. This is difficult to explain and it may help if one visualizes the motion used in crawling. Allison resisted initially but soon was able to tolerate the procedure. She actually seemed to enjoy the repetition and the rhyming.

After ten minutes we moved her to the floor and had her creep, moving across the floor on all fours. The only way we could do it was to have one person in the same position perched over Allison so she could not stand up. A second person pulled one of her favorite, noisy pull toys in front of her, enticing her to creep forward. We had to try to make this fun so we sang, laughed and generally encouraged her. Both the patterning, which mimicked crawling, and the creeping along the floor was supposed to stimulate those dormant brain cells. We had Allison creep several times throughout the hour because she would not cooperate and do this for ten minutes at one time. After a few minutes, we would sit her in a chair, apply earphones to her head and play sound effect records. She really liked this activity and would listen intently to the sounds. One person sat in front of her, trying to engage her in eye contact. After ten minutes we got her back on the floor and off we went to her room for tactile and light stimulation. In stimulating her sense of touch, we would rub the exposed parts of her body with various materials including such things as a brush, pieces of material of differing textures, ice cubes, fuzzy toys, wooden blocks, a metal ball and a warm, moist face cloth. Sometimes we blew warm air across her skin using a hair dryer. We also stroked her and tickled her. We had to be creative and think of various sensations to provide. This was not a favorite activit;, Allison did not like to be touched, but eventually she was able to tolerate this physical stimulation of her body. We discovered that she was able to tolerate a rather firm touch much better than light stroking of her skin. Once this tactile stimulation was completed we started light stimulation. I had a black-out blind installed on her window and we

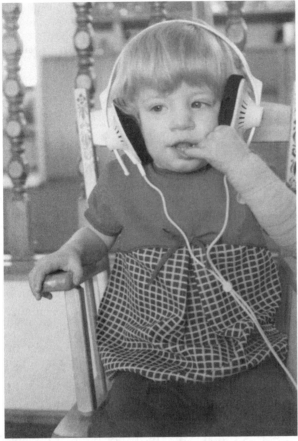

Allison during sound therapy.

spent ten minutes shining a flashlight through transparent, colored paper, making various images on her wall, ceiling and around her room. As well, we had a variety of colored Christmas lights strung around her room that blinked on and off. The tactile, light and sound therapies were used to stimulate her senses in an attempt to normalize her perceptual problems. When the ten minutes was up we were back on the floor, creeping down the hall to the dining room. At that time we had very little furniture in that room, only a cabinet for storing our dishes and crystal. The next activity involved hanging her upside down for ten minutes. I had designed ankle straps that I had to have made out of leather to hold her feet. These were attached to a jolly jumper spring that was hung from the ceiling. Allison would hang there, twirling and swinging herself back and forth. Her face would turn red but she loved this and squealed with delight. According to the specialists, this was done in an attempt to increase the circulation to her brain.

This rather strange program certainly provided structure to Allison's day. We were expected to do this program seven days a week, eight hours a day. We had monthly appointments with the doctor supervising our program so he could assess Allison' progress and discuss any concerns or issues we might have. After the first month we had decided to work with her six days a week, realizing that we needed some time off from this hectic schedule. The doctor strongly recommended that we continue doing the program daily. We held firm to our decision in spite of the fact that he told us that it would mean continuing the program an extra six months and that reducing the time we worked with her would delay Allison's progress.

This program was an exhausting undertaking, although Allison was much more tolerant of it that the rest of us were. We were literally consumed by this and had little time for anything else. The volunteers were wonderful, always showed up and were very devoted to Allison and this potential "cure." In addition to working with Allison, some of the volunteers would stay behind after their session to wash floors, do laundry and generally help out with the housework. I never had to ask for anything, they would just go to work while I continued to orchestrate Allison's program. One woman brought us a batch of freshly baked muffins and cookies every week. Other times a volunteer would bring us supper already prepared. It is impossible to explain how much this meant to us, having so many people willing to give of their time to say nothing about the chores they did and the treats they brought us. This truly was an example of how people in a community can rally to help others in need. They asked nothing in return. Their rewards came in knowing they were providing a service, giving something to others. Giving as they did was incredible and their commitment to us and to Allison was overwhelming. Most of the people helping were women, although I did have some teenage boys and girls involved. These young people were remarkable and Allison responded favorably to their giggles and sense of fun. Gord too took his turn working with Allison, especially on the weekends and in the evenings. Edith, our former babysitter, was instrumental in the program, working with us several days each week and her teenagers volunteered as well. We had a woman of sixty-five volunteer and she was even willing to get down on all fours and creep with Allison.

I must say that this experience was one of mixed blessings. We were

grateful for all the help we received and the community support. People we didn't even know offered to help once they found out about it and ultimately we had over forty people volunteering. Nevertheless, this program was a strain. Gord and I had little time together and when we did we were too tired to do anything. We rarely went out, other than to get groceries or conduct business. Every waking moment was devoted to Allison, and although we had made a commitment to this process, our relationship did suffer. I believe that in order for a relationship to grow and flourish, it must be nurtured, and we had no time to attend to our individual needs, let alone the needs we had as a couple. Nevertheless we continued on, willing to risk everything for our daughter.

In early February I got a call from a professor in the psychology department at the University of Calgary. She had heard about us through a mutual friend and wanted to talk to me. She had a graduate student taking his PhD in psychology and he was looking for a family with a disabled child to work with on a project. He was majoring in developmental psychology and was interested in doing some research in which behavioral techniques, behavior modification to be specific, were to be used to help children learn. I was interested, but I explained that we were already involved in a home program. I agreed to meet this young man and we set up an appointment for him to visit us in our home one evening. We met John and he seemed very interested in Allison and offered to help us. We agreed that we would continue with the program under way, but we would try and incorporate some of his ideas into our days. Sometimes I think I must have been insane to take on another project given that I was already stretched to my limit, but he enticed us with his ideas. He wanted us to work on some very basic skills with Allison, such as toilet training, increasing her eye contact with others, fine motor skills, and the effective use of her hands in feeding and dressing herself to name a few. In behavior modification the intent is to teach a new skill by modeling the behavior, prompting the child and randomly reinforcing successful attempts. For example, in working on eye contact, we were to sit directly in front of Allison, and say "Allison, look at me." If she responded appropriately, she would be rewarded with a smartie or M and M candy. We incorporated some of his suggestions into the existing program. For example, we started a program of scheduled toileting, which we did throughout the day. Between

sessions I would take Allison to the bathroom, sit her on her "potty" and if she voided, I would praise and reward her. Sometimes I used food or smarties and sometimes social reinforcement, saying "good girl." In no time she was scheduled, although not independently toilet trained. She did not initiate going to the bathroom but did go when I took her, which we were very pleased about. I must add that John tried to discourage us from continuing on with the other program, but accepted the fact that we wanted to give it more time.

As destiny would have it, another unexpected event occurred. I received a call from social services near the end of March. They had a boy for us. This call came many months before we had expected it. "Delivery" of our son was premature, although it had been nine months since we had started the adoption process. We were invited to come to the office in Calgary to meet this little boy in two days and we were told he was fourteen months old, another surprise because we were expecting to adopt a new-born baby. March 26, 1975, is a day we will always remember. Gord, Allison and I went Calgary to meet this little boy. The social worker met with us first, explaining that we did not have to make the decision to take this youngster home, but that she wanted us to at least meet him. The boy's mother had given him up for adoption and the baby was placed in a single parent foster home and had been with the same woman and her eight-year-old son ever since he was eight days old. The reason he wasn't put up for adoption right away was related to legal issues and the case had to go before the courts. Our main concern about adopting a child of fourteen

Derek in 1975.

months was related to where he had been for that period of time. We were quite relieved to learn that he had been in only one foster home. I wanted to be sure that he had been loved and not moved from one home to another and we were assured that that was the case. She told us that his biological mother had named him Nathanial Wesley, but his foster mom and brother had called him Wes. After giving us a few more details, she brought this boy in for us to meet and left us alone with him. Gord and I were nervous, but the minute we saw this little boy, we knew that he would become our son. He was a big boy, weighing over thirty-two pounds and he walked into the room and even came over and sat on my lap when I reached out to him. Here was the perfect brother for Allison. He had the same coloring as Allison, was a blue-eyed blond and actually looked a lot like her, except his bone structure was larger. He even said a few words and although he seemed rather shy, he appeared normal in every way. After a few minutes the social worker returned to take the boy and leave us alone to discuss the situation. Gord and I looked at each other and Gord said, "We couldn't have done better ourselves!" There was no question; our hearts had been won over and after completing the necessary paper work, we left with our new son. We were not really ready for this so we were in a mild state of shock to say the least. It was a good thing that his foster mom had sent a few clothes and his favorite toys, because I had nothing ready. When we got home I read a letter written by his biological mother and another that his foster mom had written. His biological mother wrote a lovely letter explaining her sorrow in giving her baby up for adoption but she stated that she did not have the resources, financial and otherwise, to raise this baby. Her only hope was that a good home would be found for him and that he would be happy and well cared for. The foster mom provided some information about his likes, dislikes, his personality traits, outlined his daily routine and provided a brief medical history. At the end of the letter she said that he had developed a strange diaper rash within the last day or so, but otherwise was a healthy, happy baby. Both letters were precious and our son still has these.

We cancelled Allison's program for the rest of the week in order to have some time together as a new family. It felt rather strange, to say the least. I had experienced an immediate bond with Allison when she was born, but this was different. Here was this toddler, our son, and we didn't even know him. We changed his name to Derek Todd right away and

he became one of the Jones boys. Our first problem became evident right away. The first time I changed him I discovered this diaper rash was in fact chicken pox, and it had already spread to his stomach and chest. By that time Allison had been exposed and I just knew that she would have chicken pox within eighteen days, the incubation period. This was a concern because of her health history and I had been enjoying the fact that she had been well since Christmas. I was disappointed that social services had not checked this out before calling us, but Derek was with us now and we just had to cope with whatever happened. I felt sorry for him too. Here he was, suddenly uprooted from the home and family he had come to know, sent to a different home with strangers and unable to understand what was happening. To make it worse he was covered with a rash. Derek was amazing in spite of all this. He adjusted quickly, settled in and soon found out that our house was filled with toys. He did not get very sick with the chicken pox and only had a slight fever along with the rash. I had already prepared his room, so this was not a problem, but we had to go out and buy him some clothes. Ever since we had applied to adopt I had dressed Allison in red, blue, yellow and green, thinking I would be able to hand these clothes down to our baby boy. Although he was eighteen months younger than Allison, he was already bigger and none of Allison's clothes fit him. Things did go quite smoothly, although we all had an adjustment to make. Allison seemed rather unaffected and she essentially ignored him although she did tend to follow him around. Derek seemed comfortable with Allison and did not seem to notice her disability, but of course he was still very young. He certainly liked her toys and she didn't seem to mind sharing them.

Once Derek's rash was gone, we resumed our home program with Allison. At first it was a bit overwhelming for Derek, but he soon got used to having people come and go and he participated in the program as best he could. My life changed considerably and I was very busy, but soon we had a routine and I was actually enjoying having another child around and in no time I grew to love him. He brought us so much joy and pleasure. His happy disposition was like a breath of fresh air and Gord and I took delight in playing with him, watching him and enjoyed his so very normal behavior. He was sociable and very different from Allison. Of course nothing could change our love for our daughter and we soon found we had enough love for both of them. Gord has a wonderful way with children – he does not impose himself on them but lets them gradually become comfortable with him. He took his cues from Derek and very soon they had become friends. I took great pleasure in watching my husband and son develop their own relationship. Derek called Gord "daddy" sooner than he called me "mommy" and this was likely because he hadn't had a dad before.

Allison did get the chicken pox and developed pneumonia as a complication, but we were able to manage to care for her at home and she did not require hospitalization. Her program had been interrupted by Derek's arrival and then her pneumonia and it was becoming more and more evident that continuing was causing too much strain on our family. We persevered for a few months longer, but by the end of June, we were convinced that we could help Allison in different ways. The psychology student was still helping us with Allison and he was very supportive when we told him of our dilemma. He felt all along that this program was not the direction we should be taking. He was well aware of the theories behind the techniques, but did not agree with them. He had indicated to us on several occasions that other doctors had not been able to replicate the results of the program although he had respected our need to give it an honest try. Allison's pediatrician had the same feelings about the program, and he was concerned about us. He felt we were being consumed with all the responsibilities and he worried about all the stress we were under. He had suggested we abandon the program several times as well.

We had many factors to consider in deciding whether or not to continue this program. Our philosophy had always been such that once we started something we were committed to finishing it. We were not quitters, but we were not convinced that the program was doing what we had expected it to do for Allison. I was near exhaustion and was having trouble juggling all my responsibilities. Both Gord and I felt we needed more time to engage in more normal, constructive family activities. We had to question whether or not this was a healthy lifestyle for Derek. Allison's time was almost totally occupied with the activities of the program and we had little time left to teach her the skills we felt she really needed. We felt some urgency to work on self-help skills with her. On the other hand, were we going to be able to live with knowing that Allison was being denied the possibility of a cure? We definitely had ambivalent feelings, but finally came to the decision to discontinue this

program. We had an appointment with the institute and needless to say they were disappointed. This was not an easy meeting. They urged us to continue; in their opinion we hadn't given it enough time. If we quit we were taking away Allison's chance for a normal life. We stood firm, knowing that we would have to live with the consequences. The circumstances had changed and we believed we were making the right decision. I admit to having some feelings of guilt and wondered if we were in fact hurting Allison. In my heart though, I knew we were not giving up on Allison. The program just wasn't right for us any more. By this time I wasn't convinced that there could be a cure. We acknowledged that we had seen some improvement in Allison's behavior and that she had benefited from the structure and many of the therapies. Some of her repetitive behaviors had disappeared. She had stopped twirling, but perhaps that was because her time was so structured that she didn't have the opportunity or time to spin. She had also responded well to the sensory stimulation, but we could continue to provide that. We had no regrets about trying it in the first place, but on the other hand we also had no regrets about stopping the program either. In different circumstances perhaps this program did have merit, but we had to find another way to help Allison. I was grateful that we were able to try this program and just as grateful that we were strong enough to know when it was no longer serving our best interests.

The arrival of Derek into our family added a new dimension and the needs of our family changed. By shifting the focus to maintaining a strong family life, each member could be valued and everyone would benefit. I found that living only for one child was not healthy and could be damaging to a family. Concentrating on Allison's needs to the exclusion of those of the rest of us was beginning to cause more harm than good. We realized that we were all becoming stressed and our relationships were beginning to show signs of strain. Gord and I had been drifting apart. Derek's arrival had brought us to this understanding. Our new son had needs too and we could not sacrifice these. The integrity of our family was at risk and this certainly would not help Allison. It's all about balance and honoring the needs of each individual family member. Making the decision to discontinue the program was something we had not taken lightly. We weighed it out carefully, considering all the consequences. In the end I did not feel guilty, I felt relieved. Somehow we would find a way to help Allison without sacrificing our

Allison and Derek, 1975.

family and our relationships. I had to believe that it would not hurt Allison and that our reasons were valid and justified.

The many volunteers who had been devoting their time and efforts to Allison and the program were most understanding and supportive of our decision to discontinue the program. They had witnessed some of the strain we were under and were aware that we were considering altering our plans for Allison. Some of them were getting tired too. Although their direct involvement in Allison's program was drawing to a close, their interest in Allison and her progress would continue. Allison now had a whole group of people who knew and cared about

her and we all had many new friends. No doubt our volunteers had gained something at a personal level through their involvement and experiences with Allison. Knowing that you are contributing and helping others is fulfilling and they knew that their efforts had been appreciated and valued. Through their participation in this program our volunteers had developed an expanded awareness about the challenges of disabilities in general and autism in particular. The spirit of the community had been strengthened. The people of our community had come forward and embraced our family when we needed them and we were grateful for that.

Chapter 3
Characteristics of Autism

We knew that Allison's disability was autism and I needed to learn as much as I could about this syndrome, so I read everything I could get my hands on in an effort to increase my understanding. In the seventies autism was poorly understood and even in recent times we do not know a great deal more, particularly in relation to possible causes.

Children with strange, unexplainable, unpredictable behaviors have likely caused confusion and baffled people for a long time. At one time it was believed that these children were possessed. Later on children with the characteristics of autism were believed to be completely insane and beyond any hope and they were locked up in insane asylums or mental hospitals. Leo Kanner, a psychiatrist at Johns Hopkins Hospital in the United States, was the first to coin the term autism in 1943. He defined autism as a mental disease, a form of psychosis with a psychological basis. He believed that the cause could be reduced to the fact that parents of autistic children rejected them, causing these babies to be autistic. He put forth the theory that these children were the result of "refrigerator parents" and more specifically, "refrigerator mothers" (Kanner, 1949.) He suggested autistic people be treated with psychotherapy, but the prognosis was regarded as pessimistic at best. Both the child and the mother required extensive therapy. The mother didn't even know she was damaging her child.

My reaction to this theory was not positive. I could not understand how any civilized professional, or any sane human being for that matter, could possibly believe such absurdity. Fortunately many more enlightened people challenged this damaging theory and it was essentially disregarded and abandoned in the sixties. Much was written in the next few decades. In the sixties attempts were made to differentiate childhood schizophrenia, mental retardation and autism. Often the diagnosis overlapped and was muddled. Many doctors and psychologists believed that autism was not a psychiatric problem, not due to some unknown devastating psychological trauma. Many doctors were suggesting that it might have some physical or organic basis. Perhaps the source of the problem was in some malfunction or damage within the brain itself.

Over the years there have been many theories on the cause of autism. Research has suggested that in all likelihood there are some organic, biochemical, genetic or physical factors causing this disabling syndrome, although a single definitive cause has yet to be identified and is still a mystery. However, we now have more technology, sophisticated diagnostic equipment, and tests such as Magnetic Resonance Imagery (MRI) and CAT scans to help in the search for answers. Through relatively recent neurological research, abnormalities in the brains of those with autism have been identified and several different areas of the brain seem to be affected. Some areas are smaller than normal and there is a reduced number of particular type of cells in some areas of the brain. Along with structural abnormalities some studies have implicated neurochemical dysfunctions or alteration in the chemistry of the brain. The brain is responsible for so much of human functioning, no wonder autistic persons have so many serious problems. There have been many other theories as to the cause of this disabling disorder, but they remain theories. Further research in the neurosciences may ultimately shed some light on the cause or causes. I have always held the belief that Allison's autism is the result of some unknown brain dysfunction.

Because there is a wide range of problems and severity in this syndrome it has been called a spectrum disorder. Many symptoms have been described and each individual with autism demonstrates a unique combination of these. Autism usually has an early onset, before the age of three, and diagnosis is based on several characteristics. In the seventies it was considered extremely rare, and I was told it affected one in ten thousand children. Now the incidence is considered to be a great deal higher and I can only speculate on the reason for this increase. Autism is much more common in males, with a ratio of males to females at five to one. I personally would define autism as a disabling, life-long developmental disorder. The cause remains an enigma, but these children have neurological, motor and perceptual abnormalities resulting in developmental, physical, social, language and behavioral problems. Autism has no racial or ethnic boundaries and there is no known cure, although some treatments and therapies have some degree of success. Treatment goals revolve around helping these children reach their potential, whatever that may be.

In the literature the prognosis of autism is regarded as pessimistic

and guarded. Although there have been a few cases in which children improve remarkably and are able to live relatively normal lives, many are destined to live with severe limitations requiring special educational programs and supervision throughout their lives. They have a normal life expectancy, although usually require ongoing care and supervision. Allison is severely disabled and will require care throughout her lifetime, but her future is not necessarily pessimistic.

Approximately seventy five percent of children with autism are diagnosed as mentally retarded. Accurately assessing the cognitive skills of individuals with autism is very difficult if not impossible. I have found that intelligence testing, or any testing of skills, is not accurate and the results are not reliable in children with autism. In my experience Allison was unable to demonstrate what she did know or could do and such testing was always frustrating for both Allison and me. Children with significant communication impairments cannot be tested using conventional methods or standardized tests. A small percentage of persons with this disability are autistic savants, which means they possess extraordinary talents juxtaposed with severe restrictions in their ability to perform daily activities. Some savants have exceptional mathematical skills and there are many stories of otherwise handicapped individuals who are able to create magnificent works of art or play complex classical music on the piano, without ever having special training or music lessons. Others have extraordinary engineering skills. I once heard that the famous musician and composer Beethoven might have been mildly autistic, given his dislike of socializing with other people and his tendency to isolate himself. If that is true, he would be an example of a savant. It is important to understand that although some persons with autism may have special talents or abilities in some areas, they still may have serious limitations and may be unable to care for themselves. The genius they have in an area may not be very useful to them in their daily lives. The movie *Rainman*, starring Dustin Hoffman, has done much to increase awareness of autism, although after seeing that movie, many assume that all autistic persons are savants like the character of Raymond, who had amazing mathematical abilities. In fact only ten percent of people with autism are savants. When people learn that Allison is autistic they often ask about her special talents. I simply explain the incidence of this phenomenon and say that Allison is not a savant, or if she is, we haven't yet discovered her area of genius. I often

refer to a quote I found in *Son Rise*, written by Barry Neil Kaufman, the father of an autistic boy, in answering the question about Allison's special talents. "In each of us is a specialness that is a gift to others" (Kaufman, 1976). Indeed Allison's specialness is her gift.

Based on their behaviors, autistic children are sometimes thought to be deaf or blind. Again, reliable testing is difficult. I remember when Allison had her hearing tested, the person conducting the test told me to have Allison drop a small bead into a cup when she heard the sounds in the ear phones. Allison did not have the fine motor skills to even pick a bead up let alone drop it, nor was she was able to comprehend or follow the instructions. After I explained this, the woman asked me to drop the bead when I thought Allison showed signs of hearing the sound. This was not particularly accurate, given that I would be guessing. Although at times Allison did not respond to spoken words and appeared to be deaf, at other times she would turn around abruptly in response to the sounds in her environment. We had a similar experience when she went for vision testing and the doctor was only able to examine the interior of her eyes. Allison could not read the vision chart or indicate what she could see. Through our observations of Allison we knew she could see and hear, but what she perceived was another matter. One only had to watch her response to music to know she could hear. We knew she could see, but we could not know what she saw and whether her vision was distorted, although we knew she had difficulties with depth perception.

In the mid-seventies there were five categories used in the diagnosis of autism and in order to be labeled autistic the child had to exhibit problems in each of these. These characteristics or categories included: Speech and language deficits, developmental discontinuity (which means they do not develop skills in the normal sequence and may even skip some developmental tasks), perceptual disturbances, problems in relating to others and bizarre behavioral patterns. To my knowledge, the diagnosis is still made based on similar categories and a specific test for autism does not yet exist. Diagnosis is based on the child's history and behavioral patterns.

Individuals with autism may exhibit various combinations of some or all of these signs and symptoms: laughing or crying for no apparent reason, little or no fear of real dangers, insensitivity to pain, a dislike of being touched (often referred to as tactile aversion), sustained odd play,

inappropriate play, spinning objects, little or no eye contact with others, a preference for being alone, inappropriate attachments to objects, lack of effective speech, acting as though deaf, resistance to change in routines, difficulty or inability to interact with other children, uneven development of skills, marked physical overactivity and/or extreme passivity.

At the age of three, and even before that, Allison had difficulties in all five categories used in the diagnosis of autism and she displayed many of the above symptoms. Earlier I described the odd pattern of her development. She had what was described as developmental discontinuity, or uneven progress in acquiring developmental tasks. She was delayed in the development of fine and gross motor skills, language and speech, and social skills. However, she was normal in her physical development. She did not relate to other people in a normal way; she preferred objects to people and had poorly developed social skills.

There is a wide variation in speech and language deficits in autistic children from being mute to having some functional communication skills. High functioning autistic children may be able to talk and use language skills, although their speech is often monotone in nature and not expressive. They have difficulty in articulating abstract concepts or emotions. Few individuals with autism are able to carry on meaningful conversations with others. Other children have more limited abilities, and although they may be able to speak and make the sounds of words, it is in the form of echolalia. They repeat exact words, phrases or even complex sentences that they have heard using perfect pronunciation. However, the words are spoken out of context, mean nothing to the child and this may even be delayed, spoken hours or even days later. With speech therapy and intensive training, children with echolalia can be taught a degree of functional speech and echolalia can be shaped into effective language. At the other end of the spectrum are those with severe autism and they are often mute, like Alli, having no effective expressive speech. Lack of the ability to communicate effectively is likely related to the perceptual problems so evident in autism. For some reason they have impaired auditory processing; they can hear speech and words but cannot perceive the meaning of sounds nor can they duplicate the words they hear.

Allison did not talk and had no effective verbal language skills. Being mute did not mean she was silent, but her sounds were often

uttered without any obvious meaning. She was not able to speak and she did not seem to listen. I was able to distinguish her happy sounds from sounds of distress, so she did have a rather primitive, vague means of communicating, although I am not sure it was intentional on her part. Often her sounds were made in response to something rather than attempts to knowingly "tell" us something.

Perceptual disturbances, another characteristic of autism, are the most difficult aspect of autism to explain and comprehend. We can only speculate about what goes on in the brain of such an individual. However, I believe this is the key to understanding autism, as it may be the root or source of many of the other deficits. The problems these children with autism have in relation to language, reaching developmental milestones, relating to other people and even their tendency to engage in odd, repetitive behaviors may be the result of perceptual abnormalities. The neurological system and the feedback mechanisms are very complex. The environment provides us with various stimuli through our senses and the messages are carried to the brain for interpretation. Our brain receives the messages through our nervous system and makes it possible for us to interpret and respond to the various sights, sounds, tastes, smells and sensations we encounter. In all likelihood, autistic persons do not perceive the world in the same way that people with normally functioning brains do. For example, their senses may be intact, they are able to see, hear, feel and so on, but somehow what they see, hear or feel is distorted. It was my belief that the structural brain abnormalities created the perceptual problems. I thought that Allison was unable to sort out all the information coming to her brain and that her brain was likely in a chronic state of overstimulation. Most of us are able to be selective and direct our attention, or tune into those things coming in through the senses that are meaningful to us. At one time when I was teaching nursing, we had classrooms without doors and walls. Room dividers or movable walls separated the classroom spaces. During class students could hear noises coming from many different sources – the classrooms on either side, students and faculty walking by and people talking outside the area. They could smell the odors coming from the food service area or hear the sounds coming from near-by offices such as telephones ringing, the sound of secretaries typing, photocopying and so. The challenge for me was to get and keep my students' attention and the challenge for students was to try to

ignore all these distractions so they could attend to the lecture. They had to tune out the extraneous noises in order to pay attention in class. Although the noises were still present, most students were able to focus their attention. No doubt sometimes students paid more attention to the activities and stimuli around them, but even then they were capable of tuning out the sound of my voice so they could listen to whatever they chose to hear. Our senses are continually being bombarded but we can be selective in directing our attention. Maybe a person with autism can't do that; can't filter out all the "noise" or all the information or stimuli bombarding the brain all at once. They are overwhelmed with all the incoming sounds, sights, smells and sensations. Imagine how confusing and disturbing this would be. The brains of autistic children may be chronically over stimulated, constantly on overdrive. No wonder they seem to withdraw; this may be an attempt to shield themselves, to turn off all the "noise." Engaging in repetitive, rhythmic behaviors may have a calming effect on them, a way to block out all that unpleasant stimulation.

An example of Allison's inability to filter out all the stimuli became more evident to us the first time we took her and her brother into the city to go to a Walt Disney animated movie. We went in the middle of an afternoon and it was a hot day. When we got out of the car, Allison became upset and was almost frantic. Her senses were on overload. There were all the sounds of traffic, sirens in the distance and the street was crowded with people. The air was hot and we could smell the pollution. I carried her and spoke to her calmly, trying to comfort her. We didn't want to disappoint Derek, so we had to try to get to the movie. Once we got into the theatre she settled down almost immediately. It was much quieter inside the theatre, the lights were dim and she could handle the environment and Allison and Derek both enjoyed their first movie. In fact, Allison had a great time. Her noises did not seem to disturb the other children in attendance and some of them were noisy as well, so her behavior was acceptable. We did have to deal with her anxiety and negative reaction once we left the theatre, but at least we were able to anticipate her response. Because we lived in a small town she was not familiar with all the sensory stimulation of the big city and we had not even thought about the fact that she might not be able to handle it.

Characteristically autistic children have abnormal reaction to sounds and Allison was no exception. She seemed to ignore the human

voice, although she would sit for long periods of time listening to music. She showed no reaction to the noise of the vacuum cleaner, but would wake up in the night to the noise of the furnace coming on. Allison had many indicators of perceptual problems. She had little interest in food and perhaps this was due to distortions in taste or smell of foods. However, she would eat things that we normally consider inedible, such as plants and dirt, if we didn't stop her. At the same time she was quite selective in her tastes. She only drank one kind of apple juice and refused to drink an alternative brand.

As a toddler she had problems with depth perception. I had to block off stairs to prevent her from falling down them because she didn't seem to notice the change in depth. She would climb up on the bed and jump up and down, but we had to watch her carefully because she did not seem to see the edge. When outside walking she would stop when she came to a change in the surface. Going from the sidewalk to grass was difficult for her and she often required assistance. In the day care she attended there was a long hallway made up mainly of white tiles but a row of black tiles was interspersed every fifteen feet or so. She would walk down the hall until she came to these black areas and then she would stop. Once I took her hand she would carefully step over the black area. It was as if they appeared to be holes in the floor to her and she was avoiding falling into them. Allison walked on her toes, a common feature in autism. I thought this was due to her perceptual problems as well and perhaps she was trying to find her center of balance. I also wondered if this was another indication of tactile aversion, she was avoiding contact with the ground because of a perceived unpleasant sensation.

Allison's obsession in florescent lights was a mystery too. Her behavior would become strange when exposed to environments with such lighting. She would look up at the lights, poke her finger in her eye, twirl, laugh and become overexcited. Was she able to hear the high-pitched sound coming from them? Was the bright light somehow triggering her behaviors?

It was difficult to ascertain whether Allison's perceptions were the result of heightened sensitivity or decreased sensitivity to stimuli coming to her brain and we saw evidence of both, or mixed reactions. She seemed overly sensitive to soft, fuzzy toys and yet liked hard, solid toys with clearly defined edges. She didn't like being touched but seemed

insensitive to pain. Sometimes she seemed to see, hear and feel too well and other times she seemed insensitive to events and things in her environment. She would sit quietly staring off into space and appeared to be listening to something we couldn't hear or she would laugh out loud for no apparent reason. Was she listening to some inner sounds? Could she hear her own heart beating or her digestive tract? It seemed that a times her sensory system was short-circuited and the least bit of input would activate the system. At other times it appeared that the sensory channels didn't allow enough information to get to her brain, making her insensitive to sensory input. The stimuli in her environment must have been very confusing to her. Allison also engaged in self-stimulating behaviors. She seemed to be obsessed with stimulating her own senses, particularly her sense of hearing and the noises she created seemed to be pleasurable to her. She would lie in her crib and scratch repeatedly at the mattress, listening to the sound it was making. She seemed enthralled with the noises she could make herself, and took great pleasure from dropping things and listening to the noise reverberating around her, especially things dropped in the bathroom. She loved noisy toys, enjoying the sounds long after they had become irritating to the rest of us. Visual stimulation was something else she engaged in. She poked her eye and that certainly causes distortions in vision. She would hold her fingers up in front of her face, watching carefully as she manipulated them in different configurations. She liked to sit and stare at the sunlight streaming in through the windows and she would tilt her head or flick her fingers, watching the light move. She loved to hold up her suncatchers, watching the light filter through or the rainbow of colors that were reflected off them. Shadows were fascinating to her and she would create shadows using her hands, hands she didn't like us to touch, hands she didn't use in functional ways. She took great delight in endlessly spinning objects, watching them intently. Further to her preoccupation with and attachment to objects Allison seemed to have a compulsive need for routines in her life. Any change in her routine or rituals caused her to become distressed. Her bizarre behavior patterns and insistence on sameness seemed to me to be connected to her abnormal perception of things in her world.

Allison had many of the characteristics of autism. She was withdrawn, living in a world of her own. Our attempts to bring her into our world, to connect with her and to teach her seemed to cause her distress.

I can't even imagine the frustration, confusion and isolation she must have felt. My only wish was for her to be normal. I longed to be able to free her from this autism, make it go away. Her pain was my pain. I too felt isolated; this autism was isolating her from me. I couldn't know her feelings nor could I perceive the world as she perceived it and I was unable to understand what was going on in her head. At best, I could only guess how terrifying the world must be for her. I have written the following poem in an attempt to describe what Allison might have experienced as a young child when she was three years old:

Can You Imagine What It is Like to be Me?

Try to imagine what it would be like
To be living in autism like me.
You can't understand the sounds that you hear
Or make sense of the sights that you see.

Bewildered and frightened by your perception of things
The world doesn't make any sense.
You don't like to be held or even be touched
The pain that results is intense.

Eye contact is something you cannot maintain
You can't even look at your mom.
You stare right through the people around
As if they aren't in the same room.

The feelings you have you cannot express
You aren't even able to talk.
Unable to relate or to socialize
Connecting with others you balk.

It's lonely in here, you have no friends,
You don't even know how to play.
You sit on the sidelines confused and alone
Afraid you might get in the way.

You have no idea who you might be
You have no sense of your self.
And all those toys put in front of you
Might as well have been left on the shelf.

Your development is slow and out of sync
You don't learn in the usual way.
You resist any change, it's distressing to you
Routines help you make it through the day.

Although you walk your gait is unbalanced
And you often walk on your toes.
You cannot feed or dress yourself
You can't even blow your own nose.

Your behaviors are bizarre and stereotyped
You twirl and you poke your eye.
And when you are stressed you bite your hand
You aren't even able to cry.

Obsessed with things, you know not why
You hypnotically spin a block.

Or stare blankly at lights or particles of dust
Or sway to the ticking of a clock.

You are trapped in this world, alone and afraid
You desperately want to be free.
Imagine my world, put your self in my place
Can you imagine what it's like to be me?

Chapter 4
Other Programs for Allison

After we abandoned the patterning program in the spring of 1975, we replaced it with a home program using behavior modification techniques. John, the psychology student from the University of Calgary, continued to provide assistance and he saw us weekly, sometimes in our home and sometimes at the university.

In behavioral techniques the child is taught a new skill using a procedure in which the skill is first modeled, or the therapist shows the child what he or she is expected to do. The child then is encouraged to do the task and often hand over hand assistance, called prompting, is provided. Initially any attempts the child makes at doing the skill are rewarded, or reinforced. Food is considered to be a primary reinforcer and is commonly used in teaching youngsters with learning problems, particularly when these techniques are first introduced to the child. It is hoped that ultimately social rewards such as praise or approval from others will be reward enough for the child. As the child becomes more competent in accomplishing the task, the level of proficiency required is increased before the child's behavior is reinforced. Furthermore, once the child seems to understand the process, the reinforcement is provided randomly when the child performs the expected task, which supposedly encourages the child to keep trying.

We had to adapt or modify the behavior modification methods in Allison's case, taking the characteristics of autism into consideration, because these would impact the effectiveness of the techniques commonly used in behavioral therapy. Allison had very little eye contact and did not pay attention so modeling was not too effective, so first we had to work on increasing her eye contact and getting and holding her attention. Using primary reinforcers such as food was an issue because Allison really had very little interest in food and it was not particularly rewarding for her. Smarties and candies like M & M's worked, but we had to cut them into quarters because she would seem to get "full" or tired of them quickly. Praising and providing social reinforcers might not work with an autistic child. We had to examine each step of the process to try and determine what might or might not work with our child. Her individuality, her preferences and her autism all would

impact on our success in teaching her new skills.

To increase her ability to maintain eye contact with me I started by sitting her in a chair directly in front of me so we were face to face. I would say, "look at me" and at the onset of this if she even glanced in my direction I popped a Smartie into her mouth. I would have about ten sessions with her throughout the day and in each session I repeated the command many times. Gradually Alison's ability to make eye contact improved and she was able to sustain this for a few seconds. Eventually she was compliant even with social reinforcement such as praise or smiling at her.

After I was getting more and more eye contact from Allison, we decided to work on getting her attention and eye contact from different people and from further distances away. John, Gord and I would sit in various places in our living room and call out her name or say, "Allison, look at me." If she did, we would reward her by using liquid soap and a wand to make bubbles. She loved bubbles and watching them move through the air! She actually enjoyed this "game" and would whirl around and look at us when we called her name, knowing she would have bubbles floating around her when she responded to us.

Over the next period of time we had to be creative in finding things that Allison liked, things that would be positive reinforcers for her. Once again we had to use our imagination in selecting things that she would respond favorably to. Social reinforcement was not something she relished because of her dislike of human contact. She did, however, seem to respond to words such as "good girl" or "great work," especially if this was said with gusto and enthusiasm. Music was always rewarding for Allison but we discovered that music was useful in another significant way. Because of her perceptual problems and the difficulties we were having in getting and sustaining Allison's attention, John suggested we try putting earphones on Allison when we worked with her. When Allison wore these and some soft classical music was playing, she seemed to be more focused, more able to pay attention to us. It was as if the music blocked out some of the distractions, allowing her to better attend to the task at hand. This was a form of music therapy that proved to be helpful and after a while we only needed to put on the record player and have music in the background. Eventually she learned to pay attention even without the aid of music.

Now that we had a means of getting Allison's attention through the

use of music and she was able to establish and maintain eye contact, we were ready to start teaching her specific skills. An example is the process we used in teaching her some fine motor skills, such as picking up a specific shaped block and placing it into a hole. We had a large, simple wooden puzzle that had four blocks. The blocks were in the shape of a red circle, a green triangle, a blue rectangle and a yellow star with matching holes or places for the various shaped blocks in the base. We were trying to teach her to pick up a specific block, find the appropriate hole for it and place it into that hole. The round one was the simplest but she did eventually learn to manipulate the other shapes as well. This procedure took two people at the start. One would sit facing her and Allison would be in her high chair, so she couldn't leave and go away. The second person would stand behind her, ready to physically prompt her. Allison often held her hands up in front of her face watching her fingers as she moved them through the air. This was one of those stereotype behaviors that kept her off in her own world, distracting her and keeping her from paying attention. We had to first get and focus her attention. John was often the one facing Allison and he would start by saying, "Allison, hands down." I would take her hands and put them down in her lap. Then he would say, "Allison, look at me" and reward her if she was compliant. He would ask her to put the red circle into the hole. He picked up the block and showed her where to put it, talking to her as he demonstrated. He then said, "you do it." Then I would take her hands and prompt her, helping her to pick up the block and moving it to the appropriate hole in the piece of wood. Once she dropped the block, she received the reinforcement. This sounds easy enough, but it took us months before she was able to follow the commands and carry out the task without prompting. Eventually she was able to learn to pick up the block that we asked for by color and put it where it belonged.

We used a similar technique in teaching Allison many fine and gross motor skills. We encountered many problems and stumbling blocks but we persevered and eventually her rate of learning increased. One of the main problems was her resistance to learning anything new. She would cry, refuse to cooperate and try anything she could to get out of the task. In behavior modification, if a child is non-compliant or has a tantrum, the method used to stop that behavior is called "time out." The child is removed from the situation and put in a quiet place until the child settles down and is ready to cooperate. Although this may work with normal children, it certainly did not have the desired effect with Allison. Being autistic, she did not like contact with other people and she preferred to be left alone in her room, so this time-out procedure actually reinforced her resistance. Ultimately we had to simply try to ignore her outbursts, crying and noise and push through her negative reactions to learning. This was not pleasant and it would have been much easier to let her go, let her be alone, but that would sacrifice her learning. After a session with Allison, I often felt exhausted and my energy was spent.

Teaching her self-help skills was a challenge as well. It was as if she had no strength or ability to utilize her hands in performing these tasks. It did not make sense because she was physically strong in so many other circumstances. One only had to try and take away a toy she wanted to know she could hold on tightly to something. When it came to holding on to a spoon or putting on her clothes, her hands and arms became weak and ineffective. Not only that, she strongly resisted any touching of her hands making physical prompting difficult. Teaching her to feed and dress herself continued to be something we had to work on for many years and in fact, she still needs help in these areas, even as an adult. She did eventually become very cooperative in dressing and feeding and became accepting of assistance from others. We continued with the toileting schedule and took Allison to the bathroom regularly and she was cooperating well, although it would be years before she was able to initiate going to the bathroom on her own. Perhaps she did not recognize the sensations of a full bladder or her need to have a bowel movement because of her perceptual disturbances.

Some of Allison's odd behaviors, referred to as stereotype behaviors, were interfering with her ability to learn. Although her twirling had decreased considerably when we were doing the last program, she had started to do this again, although less frequently. When she was twirling, staring at an object or lights or engaging in repetitive behaviors, she was off in another world, out of contact with us. Poking her finger in her eye and biting her hand could cause injury and was harmful to her. In autism these are often referred to as self-mutilating or self-destructive behaviors. The challenge was to extinguish these behaviors in order to prevent injury. Once these self-stimulating behaviors were stopped, Allison was more responsive and attentive. Ignoring negative or undesirable behaviors is one of the techniques used, but for obvious reasons this would not work well because Alli preferred to be ignored.

We had to be careful that the method we used didn't actually reinforce the behavior.

At the time, in the mid-seventies, even respectable clinics and many professionals had begun using aversive techniques in treating children with self-mutilating behaviors. Utilizing this extreme method meant stopping the child from engaging in these behaviors by applying an aversion, something unpleasant, to the child. The aversion may be in the form of slapping or hitting the child and some even promoted use of techniques such as electrical probes or shocking the child in order stop the behavior. Others suggested using physical restraint or holding the child down to break the pattern. The whole idea of using aversion was objectionable to me. Although the "experts" did not believe this was punishment, I certainly regarded it as such. The belief was that these children were unable to stop themselves and we, as their caregivers, had to apply this external restraint or aversion in order to help them, to prevent injury and to bring them into the real world.

John strongly encouraged us to use aversion for Allison's eye poking. There was considerable risk that she would damage her eyes and cause visual and structural impairment. This meant we had to slap her when she poked her eye. Because I was concerned about the risk of personal injury to Allison, I reluctantly consented to hitting her on her bottom when she poked her eye. This did not work. I was told that I would have to smack her hand, the one she used to poke her eye with. I must say that this was the most difficult thing I have ever had to do. I used this aversive technique only once and I am sure that it hurt me more than it hurt her! It did stop her eye poking at the time, but I simply would not ever hit her again. We would have to find another way to extinguish this problem. Then I took a closer look at the situation. I realized that she poked her eye when she drank from her bottle. It was a whole lot easier to take away her bottle than hitting her and this stopped her eye poking. We did have to teach Allison to drink from a cup and although this was not an easy task, I believed this method of using aversion was archaic, unacceptable and objectionable. In deciding on an approach to use we would always be guided by our love and respect for Allison and find some gentle, kind way of extinguishing self-injurious behaviors or changing inappropriate behavior. The use of aversion was never again in our repertoire of techniques.

We found that stopping Allison from engaging in the behavior was

often enough, particularly if we were able to divert her attention to something else. When she was biting her hand I would take her hand away from her face and initiate some other, more acceptable activity. I tried to make no reference to her hand biting, trying not to bring any attention to the behavior. Allison would often poke her fingers in and out of her ears, stimulating her sense of hearing, I suspect. Sometimes it was effective to merely take her hands away from her ears. If I could figure out what was causing the behavior or discover what was triggering her actions, I would remove that stimulus, or take away the cause. Sometimes she would poke her ears in response to sounds, noises in her environment and even music. If I removed the source of the sounds or turn off the music, her behavior changed and she would stop the behavior. Her love of music was obvious and she soon learned that she could listen to music only if she did not poke her fingers in her ears. Here I was using a natural consequence. There were times when simply removing Allison from the situation, or avoiding environments that seemed to trigger these inappropriate behaviors worked, as was the case when she stared at bright, fluorescent lights.

It appeared that Allison was off in her own world or withdrawn from us when she was doing these self-stimulating activities and the very act of drawing her attention back to us, back into our world, was effective in stopping her from performing these potentially injurious behaviors. Not all of these behaviors were physically harmful, but they were perpetuating her isolation, her withdrawal. It appeared that Allison was receiving reinforcement from these actions from the sensory or perceptual effects she was creating. She was not doing these things to get attention from us because drawing attention to herself would not be particularly rewarding to an autistic child who preferred to be left alone. These behaviors may have been her attempt to stimulate her impaired senses, a way she could deal with her perceptual disturbances. Therefore we continued with some of the sensory stimulation techniques we had used earlier, believing she needed that kind of stimulation. It was more appropriate for us to be providing it in a safe and acceptable way rather than letting her possibly injure herself. We would sing and dance with her, twirling her around believing that this was better than letting her twirl endlessly by herself. Playing a xylophone or drums with her was better than letting her endlessly drop a noisy toy into the bathtub. Now the behaviors became a social activity, rather than a way for Allison to

withdraw further into her self. We continued with the tactile stimulation of her hands and she eventually came to actually enjoy having us "play" with them. She even tolerated being hugged, but did not often initiate this. In fact, initiating anything was identified as a problem for Allison. She also seemed unable to stop doing something once she got started. This is a characteristic in autism and engaging in repetitive, stereotype behaviors is an example of perseverance. This means that once started, the child is unable to stop the activity without intervention from others. Being unable to initiate an activity and to stop something once she got started, continued to be issues we had to work on for many years with Allison.

I happened to read a book written by a father of an autistic boy and he outlined the extensive program he and his wife had developed to help their son. The book was *Son Rise* by Barry Neil Kaufman (1975). This father wrote the story about how his son was cured. Cured from autism! In order to help this small boy emerge from autism, they started by joining him in his world. They would imitate the child's stereotype behavior and eventually the child responded to this. Kaufman described this as an act of love and respect for the child, showing him that they were willing to meet him in his withdrawal, wanting to understand his world.

During the time I was reading the first book, one day I noticed that Allison was bouncing a small ball on the coffee table. She had that distant look in her eyes and I knew she was off in her own strange world. Derek got himself another ball and started to imitate her, bouncing his ball on the same table. Allison stopped what she was doing and looked directly at Derek. She started to laugh and was once again in touch with reality. This was amazing to me so I joined them. The behavior that was once strange and inappropriate had become a game and Allison joined in bouncing the ball along with us. Even in other situations, if we attempted to join her in that alien world, she would stop what she was doing and respond to us. Copying her strange behavior actually seemed to be an effective way of stopping her from doing it or at least it was turning her withdrawal into appropriate play. We found that when she was sitting on the couch and banging her head on the cushions, if we joined her, sat beside her and bounced off the cushions too, she would stop. Often Allison would hold up her hand and stare at it, manipulating her fingers and making different configurations, twisting her wrist or flapping her hand. If I sat down beside her and did the same things

with my hand, she would drop her hand and watch me. I had no idea what was happening, why this was effective in stopping her stereotype behaviors. Perhaps I was breaking through into her world, thereby bringing her attention into the real world. Maybe somehow I was showing her that I was accepting her world and was willing to even join her there. This technique was never met with approval from many of the "experts" in child psychology, but I learned a long time ago that the so-called experts don't necessarily have all the answers. Those who disagreed with this process of joining the child in his or her private world, discouraged the use of this technique. It was believed that in doing so, withdrawal and isolation would be reinforced, perpetuating the child's problems. I was discovering that often this resulted in the opposite effect. To me, it seemed that by joining Allison in her world I was communicating my total acceptance of her, loving her as she was. I was not judging and demanding her to change. I was showing her that I was appreciating her, wanting to know her and join her wherever she was at that time. Allison became more responsive to us as a result and actually seemed to need to withdraw less.

We continued working with Allison at home with John's assistance and guidance and Alli continued to show progress, although it was painfully slow at times. I had to structure in time to work with her and Derek loved to be involved with his sister and her program. He taught us a great deal about unconditional love. He didn't seem to even notice that Allison was different, or if he did it didn't matter to him, and he did not hesitate to break into her world. We celebrated Allison's achievements and Derek was often the one to tell his dad what she had learned that day. We were all involved with Allison's program, but it was not consuming our lives.

In the fall of 1975, when Allison was three years old, John recommended that we enroll her in a program at the Alberta Children's Hospital in Calgary. This was a six-month program for children with disabilities, called the Language and Behavior Program and it was designed to assist parents and their children in managing difficult behavior. The program also incorporated speech and language therapy. Through John's referral, Allison was accepted into the program. For the several months I drove Allison to Calgary. The techniques were mainly behavioral in nature although the staff soon found that some of their approaches had to be modified to meet Allison's unique needs. Allison

soon developed a special relationship with her main therapist, Bob, and they worked well together. Bob truly cared about Allison and was devoted to her. Allison was in the program from nine in the morning until noon, five days a week. Derek and I would leave Allison and we joined a swim and gym program for moms and tots. Derek went to a play program for an hour following and I was free to swim lengths. I had been a lifeguard and competitive swimmer in my youth and welcomed this opportunity to get back into shape. Parents of children with disabilities tend to make little time for themselves and their health and personal interests are often sacrificed. I recognized that in order to take care of Allison and the rest of my family, I had to take care of myself too. It is all part of finding a balance, and caring for and loving oneself is an essential ingredient in being able to care for and love others.

In the program Bob worked with Allison on motor skills, speech and language, self-help skills and compliance to name a few. She did have testing occasionally and this was always frustrating for me, and for Allison. The psychologist who did the testing was not too successful in working with Allison and the results were always disappointing. Allison did not seem to like this psychologist. She was completely non-compliant with her and would not even do things I knew she could do. At one point she said, "Allison is the most stubborn, difficult child I have ever met!" She had no idea as to how we could help her. Allison's test results were dismal and on one occasion I suggested that she might get more accurate results if she were to test Allison in our home, in an environment in which Alli felt more comfortable. I volunteered to conduct the test once I had the directions and the psychologist could watch and record her observations. The woman was willing to give this a try and we set up an appointment.

Upon her arrival at our home, the first thing the psychologist did was put her coat on Allison's counter; but of course she had no idea that this was a space reserved for Allison alone. Allison abruptly threw the coat on the floor and the power struggle was on. I explained to the psychologist about the counter, that this had been designated as Allison's special place and we all respected that by leaving it free of our belongings. Allison would sit up on this counter and watch me when I prepared meals or was working in the kitchen. We left her favorite toys there so she could always find them. The young woman would not accept this explanation and she indicated that no matter what, Allison's

behavior was inappropriate and she should not be allowed to throw her coat on the floor. Allison must learn to respect others and their belongings as well. She proceeded to make Allison pick the coat up and put it back on the counter. Allison looked her right in the eye, picked up the coat & put it back on the counter, but moments later she pitched it off again on to the floor. The two of them repeated this procedure several times until I finally had to intervene. Both of them were being stubborn and nobody was winning the battle. It was a stalemate. I had Allison hand me the coat and I hung it up in the closet where it belonged. The psychologist was not pleased with either one of us, but I felt we had to get on with the testing, the reason she came in the first place. Needless to say Allison was much more compliant with me and in spite of the earlier battle, this young woman did get a better perspective about Allison's abilities. I never had the nerve to tell the psychologist that Allison disliked her, but I suspected she could sense this. I was actually pleased with Allison, in a left-handed sort of way. At least she was reacting to another person, she was showing her feelings, and even though they were negative, she was definitely not indifferent towards this woman.

Even the results of this testing session were not encouraging, but Allison never did well at any of these intelligence tests anyway. I had already learned not to worry too much about the results, believing that it was impossible to accurately test a child like Allison and the results were not particularly reliable or even useful. I knew Allison was much smarter and had more abilities than she could demonstrate on any standardized tests and I conceded that the specialists were required to conduct their business, complete their paper work and do this testing. They would draw their own conclusions, but I did not have to get too disturbed with their findings. I was content just to recognize that Allison was making progress and I could be grateful for the evidence that she was learning and her behavior was improving.

Allison's health had shown improvement that fall as well and she had only a few more incidences with serious respiratory infections. In spite of having been immunized, she and Derek both developed a strain of whooping cough that fall. During the day both of them would cough, whoop and even had episodes of vomiting because of the violence of their coughing spells. The doctor had prescribed antibiotics and expectorants and we had humidifiers going full tilt. During the day

both children were able to move the secretions up out of their throats and expectorate them, but this became a serious problem for Allison once she went to sleep at night. Fortunately I was sleeping in her bed with her because the first night I awoke to discover that Allison had stopped breathing. I opened her airway and tried to initiate mouth-to-mouth resuscitation, but could not get any air in. Her airway was obstructed, so I had to pick her up, put my arms around her waist and performed the Heimlich procedure. It took several abdominal thrusts to clear her airway, but eventually I was successful and Allison started to breathe on her own again. A mucous plug had obstructed her airway and she had not even attempted to cough, she just quietly stopped breathing. I slept very lightly the rest of the night, listening to Allison's breathing. Her respirations ceased four or five more times and I had to repeat the maneuver.

The following morning I called her doctor and both of us spent much of the day on the phone trying to locate a suction machine I could borrow or rent. I was afraid that I might not be able to remove the mucous plugs that were obstructing her airway using the Heimlich maneuver and having a machine would provide me with the means to suction the mucous out. No such machine or suitable apparatus could be found. Allison had to be admitted to the hospital once again and she was in a croup tent with wall suction readily available. Gord stayed home with Derek and once again I took up my vigil at Allison's side. She required suctioning on several occasions and I was very glad that I stayed with her because there was not enough nursing staff available to have someone assigned to stay with Allison. Because she would stop breathing in her sleep, she required constant supervision, so I became the nurse that provided that specialized care. Naturally I was becoming sleep deprived and after a couple of days in the hospital the doctor and I agreed that I could safely take her home. At least there I could get some sleep by lying down beside her and there was no question that I would wake up if she got into trouble; I knew I would. Somehow I had developed a special kind of intuitive sensitivity to Allison and I had come to trust this.

Upon Allison's discharge I was given a hand-held manual suction, one in which I could use in an emergency by creating suction using my mouth over a connecting tube. Once home I constructed a home-made croup tent by putting a card table over the head of Allison's bed, cover-

ing it with a sheet, with a humidifier on each side of the bed pumping cold droplets of moisture into our "tent." At bedtime we both crawled into this contraption and during the night I had to revert back to the Heimlich procedure to clear her airway when she obstructed, because this suction apparatus was not effective. Fortunately her secretions were not as thick and sticky and I was much more confident in clearing her airway of the mucous. After a few more days both children recovered without further complications and Allison returned to her program at the Children's Hospital after missing about ten days.

At Christmas that year, when Allison was three and a half and Derek almost two, we were with Gord's family at the farm in Ponoka. The whole family had gathered on Christmas Eve so there were quite a number of people present. One man, fondly known as Uncle Fritz, a brother of Gord's sister's husband, was there with his family. For some reason Uncle Fritz and Allison quickly developed a special relationship and he held Allison on his knee and tickled and played with her. Every time he laughed she too would burst out laughing. She loved his hearty, boisterous laughter and the sounds of both of them carrying on was entertaining to all of us. I was so happy that she was having such a good

Allison and Santa.

time and everyone was impressed with how aware she was, how responsive she was to this man. She was even maintaining good eye contact with him, looking directly at him. She would reach up and touch him, encouraging him to laugh again. It was a special moment for all of us and he was thrilled. He knew she did not like to be around other people and realized this was unusual for her to be so connected with another person. Arrangements had been made for him to dress up like Santa Claus and to arrive with gifts for all the children, so he left to make his preparations. When "Santa" came to the door, all the children were excited and gathered around him, all except Allison. Once again she seemed unaware of his presence and was on the periphery of the activities. Then he started to laugh. Allison whirled around, looked at him and burst out laughing herself. She had a knowing look on her face; she recognized this man and knew who he was. Fritz might have fooled all the other youngsters with his Santa costume, but this little autistic child had figured him out. She sat on his knee, kept looking at him and laughed out loud. Once again she was the center of attention, something that was so unusual and so special. Allison was beginning to be able to make connections with others and this evening was indeed memorable.

Over the winter Allison became more tolerant of physical contact with her therapist in her program at Children's Hospital and they became friends. Along with the other things Bob was working on with Allison, he was determined to teach her how to go up and down stairs independently. She had great difficulty with depth perception and stairs were an ongoing problem for her. We had been working on teaching Allison to crawl up and down stairs and she was able to master going up, but coming down was another story. It was as though she could not accept that anything existed behind her back and she would not even turn and look over her own shoulder. She could not grasp the concept that she could turn around and go down stairs backwards, one step at a time. If anything she wanted to go down headfirst, which did not work well because she would take a nosedive down the stairs. She only tried this a couple of times and after she avoided stairs or when she came upon them, she would stop and stand there, waiting for assistance. She would do stairs if someone was holding on to her hand, but even then she did not alternate using her feet. Bob made it his project to teach Allison to hold on to the hand railing and walk up and down stairs on

her own, alternating her feet in the process. He did not want her to stop on each step and always lead with the same foot.

Bob had used a soft, rubber, noisy turtle as a reinforcer in teaching Allison other things and he believed she might be motivated to go up stairs in order to retrieve this turtle. They had a set of wooden stairs with hand railings on either side and a platform on top that was used in teaching children to maneuver stairs. Bob would prompt Allison by putting her hand on the railing and then physically moved her legs through the motions of walking up the steps. Someone else was at the top, squeaking the toy and that enticed her to cooperate. The process worked well and in no time she was walking up the stairs independently and she even began to alternate her feet in the process. We were all thrilled about her accomplishment, but going down the stairs was another issue. Allison simply would not or could not do it. Even the favorite turtle would not entice her to try. She would stand at the top of the stairs and refuse to go down. We were coming to the end of the program and Bob was determined that she would learn this skill. He negotiated an extension of her program and he even convinced another therapist to assist in this venture. So for six weeks three of us worked with Allison for two hours every week day morning, trying to overcome Allison's obstacle with the stairs. One of us would hold her hand on the rail and the other two would move her feet, alternating the steps. Allison was not happy with this and she howled most of the time but we were determined to persevere so we ignored her protests and pushed on.

This time we were using the stairs that went down to a landing and a door that led out of the building. At the end of the six weeks, our time had run out and we were prepared to admit defeat. Alli had shown no progress and could not manage the task of walking down stairs. On the last day Bob and I were standing at the top of these stairs talking about it and lamenting the fact that Allison would continue to need assistance with stairs. We had failed, but it wasn't for lack of trying. Before our very eyes, without any hesitation Allison walked to the edge of the stairs, took the handrail and walked independently, alternating her feet on the steps down the stairs, walked across the landing and out the door! She never looked back and if she had, she would have seen the looks of astonishment on our faces and seen our tears flowing. Of course we had to run to catch up to her and I am sure she couldn't fig-

ure out why we hugged her and made such a spectacle out of this. She gave us a look as if to say, "What's the big deal? Of course I learned to do the stairs and I met the deadline too! Now let's get out of here."

This story is an example of how teaching Allison can be so difficult. She was absorbing our cues all along, but could not show it and in fact she had to hide her learning by protesting vehemently. Our persistence had paid off and even when she resisted and we assumed we were not accomplishing anything with her, she was taking it in, learning and absorbing the necessary steps. There were other examples of this strange sequence of events that Allison went through in the process of learning and this example reinforced my need, as her teacher, to be persistent. I had to trust that she was learning and in due time she would be able to demonstrate what she had accomplished. Autistic children are often resistant to change and learning and they seem to want to maintain sameness in their environment. Psychologists have defined the learning process as synonymous with change in behavior or a change in the meaning of an experience. Any change was likely perceived as threatening to Allison, compounding her resistance. Her resistance and fighting back was a demonstration of her need to protect herself, to avoid change.

In teaching anyone, disabled or not, it is the student's responsibility to do the learning and the teacher is only a facilitator. In teaching an autistic child, the process of facilitating is just more challenging. Allison was not reacting to me personally, but was resisting change. It helped me to frame Allison's reluctance to learn in this way: it wasn't that she didn't want to learn, she was afraid of change. Having to learn created a sense of insecurity and anxiety for her and somehow we had to move her through this fear until she could assimilate the lesson and appreciate the benefits of acquiring new skills and information. Once Allison mastered something new, her fear was gone and she became comfortable and secure once again. It was worth the battles we all had to endure because sooner or later we did get positive results. This usually happened quite unexpectedly and one day she would just do what ever we had been struggling to teach her to do without any resistance. There were times when we waited a long time for this to happen, but we knew that eventually something that seemed difficult for Allison to do would become easy for her. Once she accomplished a task she never forgot it, so we had to be persistent, knowing that in spite of her reactions,

progress was being made.

We were disappointed that the program at Children's Hospital was coming to a conclusion, but they had a policy that dictated that a child could only be in it for a short period of time. It was designed to be an interim program in which behaviors were to be changed and language encouraged in preparation for integrating the child into other programs with higher functioning children. In our eyes Allison had done well, in spite of the psychologist's opinion. Her scores on the testing procedures may not have increased, but Allison was more compliant, had an increased ability to pay attention and she had mastered the stairs. In spite of further speech therapy, she was not showing progress in developing language skills, and we had to accept that. The staff had provided us with more tools in working with Allison and encouraged us to continue with our home program. By this time we all had agreed that Allison was autistic and would continue to require individualized attention and special interventions. They suggested I visit a school for autistic children in Calgary for more ideas and that I might even consider enrolling her in the program they provided for such children. This was the first I heard about this school, and I was willing to look into it further.

Chapter 5
More of Allison's Preschool Programs

I made arrangements to visit the school for autistic children in Calgary in the early spring of 1976 when Alli was almost four and before she had to leave the program at Children's Hospital. The school provided both a day and residential program for autistic children and children living in Calgary were a priority. Because we were not residents of the city, Allison was not likely to be accepted for a very long time and the waiting list was long. They consented to see Allison and do further testing and offered to assist us in planning a home program. Autism was confirmed as Alli's diagnosis after she was assessed. I found the woman who was in charge of the school rather abrasive and I was offended by some of her comments. She said that it was unfortunate that we had not known that Allison was autistic previously, because early intervention was the key to helping such children and she implied that we had lost valuable time with Allison. She assumed that we had done little to help her without even asking us. Right away I did not have a positive impression of the director. One would not call her supportive. At one point she said, "Allison needs KA Therapy." I didn't know what she meant, so she explained that this was "Kick Ass Therapy." I was beginning to feel grateful that Allison would not likely be a candidate for this program.

Nevertheless, I spent a couple of weeks at this school observing so I could get some ideas about teaching autistic children. I soon discovered that they used aversive techniques, although they did not call them that. If a child began to engage in stereotype, repetitive behaviors, the child was removed from the situation and restrained. Sometimes this meant holding the child down on the floor. The child would often scream, cry and fight back, but the restraint was continued until the child settled down and was quiet and this often took a long time. I witnessed this on several occasions and was most uncomfortable with the technique. In fact, I found the whole scenario upsetting. In explaining the theory, they told me that autistic children were unable to use their own internal discretion in stopping such behavior and they were providing this external restraint to help the child. We had been working for years to help Allison accept touch and physical contact and in no way was I about to allow anyone to turn touch into punishment. They objected to me using the word punishment, but that was how I interpreted the techniques used. Some of the staff could see my reaction and went out of their way to assure me that it had helped many children and the behavior of these children had been altered dramatically by using such techniques. Perhaps this was true, but they would never find out if it worked with Allison because I had vowed earlier that she would never receive aversive treatments. She was just beginning to be able to tolerate others holding and touching her and I was not prepared to risk losing that. I knew I could find more acceptable ways of managing her inappropriate behaviors.

I was also concerned by the fact that because this was a specialized school, all the students were autistic and I questioned whether this was wise. Autistic children do not relate well to others and perhaps it would be more advantageous to integrate these children with others who were not autistic. Autistic children usually ignore each other and being in such an environment might perpetuate their isolation and tendency to withdraw. Of course the teachers would be there to interact with and help these children, but it had been my experience that often other children got more response from Allison than adults did. Allison could not initiate contact with other children but she almost had to respond to them. Children are quite comfortable in demanding attention and they are often unaffected by the fact that another child in their presence might be disabled. They don't know or care that the other child might be autistic and uncomfortable with human contact and they are not inhibited in approaching them, disabled or not. Certainly Alli's brother, Derek, had been able to invade her world and she could not ignore him. I believed that it was healthy and beneficial for Allison to be around other children, particularly verbal, outgoing youngsters who seemed to have the ability to draw her out. These concerns, along with my inability to accept some of the therapies used at this school, indicated to me that enrolling Allison in this school was not the direction I wanted to take with her and even if she had been accepted into this program, I would not have enrolled her after all.

So once again we were left with having to plan and develop a home program for Allison. I designed a program using many of the behavioral techniques we were already familiar with and our next home program was launched in the late spring of 1976 just before Allison turned four years old. We worked on fine and gross motor skills, attending skills,

following directions and self-help skills. I tried to incorporate speech therapy, although I had little experience in this, but I encouraged Alli to make sounds and tried to teach her to shape these into words, with little success. Working with Allison could be trying at times, but I knew I had to be persistent and work through her resistance to learning. I tried to be positive and encouraging with her. We would often sit on the floor and I tried to help her learn to play appropriately with her toys. Some of the program was structured and I set aside time each a day to work with her on a one-to-one basis. We used our home as the classroom and the activities of our daily lives as the curriculum.

I was feeling somewhat overwhelmed and finding it difficult to be all things for Allison: her mom, caregiver, teacher and therapist. It was trying at times. I felt like I was losing sight of who I was as a person. As well, I had Derek's and Gord's needs to consider and did not want our family to get into the same state of complete absorption with Allison's needs as we had in the previous home program. After discussing options, Gord and I decided to apply for a nanny and we made arrangements to have a young woman from Scotland, Linda, join our family. We had just moved into a new house and were able to convert our den into a bedroom for her. Once Linda came, I found that I was happier and actually had time for everyone in our family, including myself. I taught Linda how to work with Allison, but for the most part I continued to do most of the one-to-one sessions with her.

Once we made the arrangements to have additional help, I discussed another issue with Gord. I had not been working for a year and a half and I missed nursing and teaching adult students. I discovered that I really wanted to resume my career as a nursing instructor. I had received a telephone call from a faculty member at Mount Royal College in Calgary who was looking for part time instructors to teach medical-surgical nursing students. This community college had a two-year nursing diploma program and one of my former colleagues had recommended me to this woman. I believed that I could handle returning to work on a part- time basis and Gord and I agreed that I would return to my profession on a trial basis. Returning to work was very healthy for me, giving me more balance in my life and I continued my career in nursing for many years. I worked two and a half days a week for four years teaching and supervising students in the clinical area, or the hospital, as well as teaching some lectures and seminars. In 1979 a

full time faculty position became available, and although I hesitated, I applied and was hired. Returning to work was a decision I have never regretted. There were times when found the demands of fulfilling my responsibilities at home and work to be somewhat overwhelming, but overall, I knew I was emotionally healthier and my life was more fulfilling when I worked. I felt whole again, felt like I was contributing to nursing education as well as to my family. Of course I had to be very organized and Allison taught me a great deal about that. I always had a back-up sitter for the children and would have my lectures prepared well in advance. In the college setting there was considerable flexibility and this was perfect for me. I had to be in the classroom and in the hospital at specific times, but I was free to develop my lectures and do much of the preparation and marking at home. I had a job to do, but because of the philosophy at the college I was able to juggle my time and meet my responsibilities to both my family and career without compromising either. This position as a nurse educator came at a very opportune time and like other things in my life, I believe it was meant to be.

Things generally went smoothly for the next year. Our nanny Linda was very helpful and her presence in our home allowed me to consider the possibility of returning to work. She enjoyed planning and cooking meals and for a year we enjoyed sampling various recipes from Scotland. She took a special interest in both Allison and Derek. Linda was a very tidy person and this was a small problem for a while. She was constantly putting the children's toys away and I had to ask her to leave them out during the day. Allison in particular needed to have things readily available to her. I told Linda that we could tidy up in the evening and putting the toys away became a bedtime ritual in our house. I was successful in juggling my roles as wife, mother and teacher, thanks to having our nanny. Both Linda and I worked with Allison and she continued to show signs of progress. Allison no longer had frequent infections and seemed to have outgrown her febrile convulsions. She was becoming more responsive to others and to her environment. Her eye contact was increasing and she even allowed us to hug her. If I asked for a kiss she would lean forward and turn her cheek, able to at least receive my affection. She did not initiate contact, but she did not reject it and in fact, was responding to us more and more.

She loved to watch television, especially children's shows. Sesame

Street, The Elephant Show and the Muppets were her favorites and we made a point of watching these with her. She was captivated by the music and most of the characters were not really people but puppets. She liked to sit on the floor near the TV, although she did not face it directly. It appeared that she had better peripheral vision or perhaps it was just too stimulating to look directly at the television. Sometimes she would get up and leave the room for a short period of time, even during her favorite shows, and after a short break she would return and resume her seat in front of the TV. Again, I don't think it was because she was unhappy, but she needed a break from the stimulation, at times it was just too overwhelming for her. During these programs she seemed completely absorbed in watching and reacting to the events on TV. She often laughed out loud appropriately, clapped her hands and showed signs of enjoyment. She always knew when her shows were about to end and she would object. When the final song came on she would start to cry and great big tears would roll down her cheeks. She was able to recognize that the program was almost over and she wanted it to continue. At these times she would look at me as if to say, "please don't let it end." Allison did not like endings, particularly when she was engaged in something she enjoyed and although I felt badly that she was upset, I was pleased that she was able to show her emotions. Some 'experts" believed that autistic children were incapable of having emotions, let alone showing them, but I had a different opinion based on Allison's reactions and these examples that provided evidence that she indeed had feelings. She couldn't tell me directly what was wrong, but her actions spoke loudly, reflecting her feelings.

Derek thrived and was a normal, healthy little boy with lots of energy and he was helping to normalize our lives. The siblings of a disabled child have unique needs and we had been trying to ensure that three-and-a-half-year-old Derek was getting his share of attention. In the summer of 1977, Linda returned to Scotland and we were all adjusting to life without her. Fortunately we were off work and on holidays and both Gord and I were able to devote some time during the week to Derek. In spite of this, Derek was well aware of all the attention Allison was getting and one day he said to me, "I wanna be artistic too – just like Allison." I knew he was likely feeling a little jealous of the time and attention Allison was receiving from us. Derek and I talked about his wish and I told him he could have his own special day in which he could

be autistic. I made arrangements for Allison to go to a sitter one day and Derek's day as a boy with autism began. I talked to him, just like I did with Allison, and told him I was getting his breakfast ready and was making porridge. Derek said, "I don't like porridge. I want cheerios." I had to remind him that he was autistic just like Allison and he could not talk. He could not tell me what he liked or didn't like and he would get the same breakfast Allison got. He had no choice. Then I picked him up and put him in Allison's chair and started to feed him the cooked cereal. Now he was getting frustrated and said, "I can feed myself," to which I replied, "but you can't feed yourself, you are autistic, remember, and I have to help you hold the spoon and bring it to your mouth."

Derek did try to get into the role-playing for a while but had some trouble in performing his part in the "play." He kept talking to me, he couldn't help it, and I had to repeatedly remind him that he could not talk. I gave him a bath in the tub and began to dress him in some clothes I selected. Derek liked to pick out his own clothes and certainly did not like having to be dressed. The phone rang in the middle of this process, so I left him to answer the telephone. We had just got to the point where he had his underwear on when I left him, so of course he carried on with the task. Once I got back to him I reminded him that he couldn't dress himself and he had to wait until I was ready to help him. Once we had that settled, I picked him up and told him we were going to read a story. We sat in a rocking chair and I held Derek on my lap and I started to read to him. Derek kept interrupting, like he normally did, to fill in the story and talk about the pictures. Again I reminded him that he couldn't speak and he had to sit there and listen. I ignored his comments about the pictures and continued reading, which did not please him.

We carried on like this for most of the morning, but Derek was losing interest and was having difficulty handling his new limitations. He certainly did not like me making all the choices about what we would do and rebelled when I told him we were going to work at Allison's little table, doing puzzles and practicing some of the skills Allison was learning. Then the doorbell rang and one of Derek's little friends was at the door. He asked if Derek could come out to play and I told him Derek was having an autism day, so he could not go out. I also explained to both of them that autistic children don't usually have

friends and nobody ever called on Allison. Derek burst into tears, told me he didn't want to be "artistic" any more and asked if he could please go out to play with David. Derek's friend could not figure out what was going on, so I sat down with both of them and we talked about the events of the morning. Derek told David all about what it was like to be autistic and he kept emphasizing that he couldn't talk and he had to do what I wanted him to do. Both children expressed how hard it must be for Allison and they were very glad they weren't like her. Needless to say, that was the last time Derek ever said he wanted to be autistic like his sister. Through this experience and just by his association with Allison, Derek was to become very kind and sensitive to his sister's needs and feelings. He had an extraordinary way of accepting and loving Allison.

In the fall of 1979, Derek started nursery school and we were able to integrate Allison into the program as well. They were in this program each week day morning. Edith, my friend and Allison's former babysitter, was the nursery school teacher and she was most amenable to having Allison in the class. Because she knew Allison well, she was able to explain her disability to the other children and their parents. Once again the community came forward and accepted Allison, welcoming her into the nursery school program. I was able to hire a friend, Beryl, a woman who seemed to have a connection with Allison, to work with her in the nursery school on the mornings that I was at work. She and Allison spent some time with the other children and for an hour they would go off to another room and work privately, continuing to work on Allison's special needs. On the days I worked, she looked after both children until I got home.

One day when I came to get Derek and Allison, Beryl told me of her upsetting morning at school. The morning had started as usual and she and Allison spent the first hour with the class as a whole. However, Allison was especially irritable and generally uncooperative, so this woman removed Allison from the classroom and attempted to work with her individually. The whole morning was a disaster and she couldn't figure out what was wrong. She knew, however, that Allison could be difficult at times, so she made Allison continue in spite of her obvious distress. When it was time to go home, she bent down to put Allison's boots on and she found a tack stuck in Allison's foot! Allison had been in stocking feet, had stepped on a tack and it had been impaled in her

foot all morning. No wonder she was upset. My friend was in tears as she related this story and I had to reassure her that it was not her fault. This was an example of Allison's reaction to pain. This time she did feel the pain, although she was unable to localize it or tell anyone about it. She reacted by being fussy, making unhappy sounds and being non-compliant. Even her response was non-specific, offering no clues as to the source of her distress. Once again we learned from this experience. When Allison is upset and not cooperating, we need to assess her further rather than simply assume she is having one of her difficult days.

The next year we were able to duplicate this concept of partial integration, but the setting changed. She and Derek started the kindergarten program in the elementary school. We were able to access special funding, called a category A Grant, which allowed us to hire different people to be involved with Allison. She would have a classroom aid, like before, but a speech pathologist and physiotherapist were hired to work with her as well. Each morning she had speech therapy for half an hour, followed by physiotherapy. The physiotherapy was particularly beneficial because the therapist taught us various exercises to help Allison with mobility and flexibility. Allison, like many children with autism, walked on her tiptoes much of the time. As a result of this she had heel-cord shortening and the therapist gave us exercises and movements to do with Allison to help lengthen these tendons. She also provided a series of other exercises. Allison liked physiotherapy and was very cooperative. Once again we tried to make it fun and would sing songs to her throughout the session. The speech therapy was not quite as successful, but the therapist worked hard at trying to help Allison develop effective language skills. Teaching Allison to use words in communicating was something we continued to have great difficulty with.

Once again I participated in the program when I was not working, but having a classroom aid for Allison made it possible for me to be a helping mom for Derek too. In kindergarten mothers frequently attend with their children, bringing snacks and helping the teacher. Because Allison was looked after, I could be there for Derek when it was his turn to have his mom as the helper for the morning.

Through Allison's involvement in the nursery and kindergarten programs the children her age in the community and their parents got to know about Allison and her special needs. We never had any complaints about her integration and, in fact, it was encouraged and sup-

ported. I attended parents' meetings and was asked to provide presentations on autism and Allison's problems in particular. The teacher asked me to come and speak to the children as well, and Derek and I did this together. We found the children to be very accepting and most interested in learning about Allison. Derek was especially effective in explaining that although Allison did not talk, she could hear and she liked it when you talked to her. He told his peers not to talk about her when she was in the room, because she could hear everything they said. He reminded them that Allison had feelings too and it was important to remember that. He explained all this without me even telling him to and I was filled with pride and love for him. Already Derek was becoming an advocate for his sister. Once these children had a better understanding about Allison's difficulties, they treated her with respect, knew she did not like to be touched, and spoke to her often. Many of them took it upon themselves to look out for Allison and help her as best they could.

Another situation presented itself that was an indication that Derek needed some assistance in coping with having a sister who was disabled. One day when he was just over five years old, he was obviously troubled and brooding about something. When I approached him and asked him what was bothering him, he started to cry. He sobbed and blurted out, "When you and dad die, I can't look after Alli all by myself. I don't know what to do. How will I go to school?" This caught me by surprise. The first thing I did was reassure him that he would not be expected to look after Allison and it was not likely that his dad and I, or both of us, would die in the near future. I realized that children at this age often begin to think about death and needed help in understanding this whole concept, so we talked about life, death, heaven and God. I tried to keep my explanations simple in answering his questions, and he had many. I was honest and realistic with Derek as we discussed death and did not pretend that it would not happen. I didn't need to explain about wills and arrangements we had made to ensure that our children would be looked after in the event of our deaths, but he did need to know that he would not be alone. He finally seemed to understand and his fears about our imminent death decreased. He seemed comforted when I told him that he was not going to have to take our place and be responsible for Allison. I told him that all he really had to do was to love her and be her brother. Once he understood that he was finally able to put

his worries aside. His outburst and concerns reminded me to be alert and sensitive to his needs and to be available to him when he was worried about something. Even as a small child Derek felt responsible for his sister and we wanted him to know that loving her was all we really expected him to do.

We assumed that Allison would start school in the fall of 1978, when she was six years old. The school superintendent in charge of special needs programs came to visit us in the spring of that year. He told us that the school act stated that children with severe disabilities did not have to be sent to school. Parents could choose to keep them at home. It was the law that parents of normal children had to send them to school until they were sixteen, but the rules were different for handicapped children. Before we could indicate that we wanted Allison to attend the elementary school in our school division, he told us that the school board interpreted this act to mean that they were not obligated to take these children. He had come to tell us that there would not be a place for Allison in this school system! He conceded that she did qualify for a category A grant for another year and she could attend the kindergarten program another year, until she was seven years old. This man was trying to be kind and he suggested that we consider moving to Edmonton, Alberta, where there was a program for such children. He said that if Allison were his daughter, that is what he would do. He assured us that we didn't have to rush into this, we had a year, and in the meantime Allison could continue with her special program in kindergarten.

Gord and I were crushed. We did not want to uproot our family. The community we lived in was perfect for us; Allison was well accepted, Gord taught in the junior-senior high school and had been promoted to vice principal. His career was going well. I had found the perfect job situation and did not want to give that up either. This was our home and we did not want to leave this community. We had many friends and they had come to love and appreciate Allison. On the other hand, it was clear that Allison's needs would not be met in this school system so we knew we had to consider different alternatives. We decided to wait until the fall and then begin the process of finding a solution to our problems. Fall came and Allison returned to the kindergarten in the school and we were grateful for that. We did consider moving to Edmonton after all and began the process of looking for jobs. In the late

seventies there were not many opportunities for teachers, either in the school system or in nursing education, so we were quite discouraged. By mid-November we were getting desperate. Our community, or at least the school division, was abandoning us and we did not know what we would do. At the height of our anguish about our situation, the same superintendent called us and made an appointment to visit us again. This time he had a different story. Apparently the school act had just been changed and the school division was now obligated to take children with disabilities into the schools. He did say that there was no special education program in place yet, but they were prepared to develop a program for Allison and other children with severe disabilities by the following fall. This man still believed that Allison's needs would be best met in Edmonton, but he was prepared to make the necessary arrangements if we decided to remain in this community. In our minds there was no question; we would stay. And so the decision was made and we were about to embark on the experience of integrating our child with autism into the public school system.

Part II:
The School Years

Chapter 6
Allison in Elementary School

Throughout Allison's school years she attended various Special Education classes in the Foothills School Division. For the first year, starting in 1979, she had to take a school bus to High River, a town a few kilometers away, because there was not a class in Okotoks. A Special Education Class was established in Okotoks, our hometown, in the fall of 1980 when Allison was eight and she spent the remainder of her school years in Okotoks. She left the school system in the spring of 1991 just before turning nineteen.

In all phases of Allison's schooling she was fortunate to have caring, competent teachers. Of course, Allison always had a teacher's classroom aide working directly with her and once again these people tended to

Allison and Derek, elementary school, 1981.

stay with her the whole time. Each teacher and aide got to know Allison and her needs well and having so few teachers helped provide the consistency Allison needed. Alli's first teacher, Karen Irvine, was in the Okotoks Percy Peglar Elementary School and Alli was in her class for six years. This young woman was experienced in special education and had the credentials, although she did not have experience with autistic children. She was very committed to the children in her class and went out of her way to learn about autism. I spent time with her explaining the disorder and outlining what we had been doing at home to help Allison to learn. We both attended workshops. Of particular interest was one featuring Dr. Ivor Lovaas from the University of California, Los Angeles. He had been using extensive behavioral interventions with autistic children which were not unlike the techniques we had been using. Allison's teacher incorporated many of his techniques in working with Allison and some of the other children in her class. I was particularly impressed with Dr. Lovaas' philosophy of using non-aversive interventions and creating a positive learning environment for disabled students.

The number of students in Alli's first class varied from four to five and the teacher had an aide in the classroom. The children had different disabilities and Allison was the only one diagnosed as autistic at that time, although all of the children had high needs or required extensive programs. One day in the fall of Allison's first year in Okotoks, the superintendent came to the classroom to notify the teacher that, because of the high cost of the program and cutbacks throughout the school division, she was going to lose her classroom aide. He came on the perfect morning to deliver his bad news. The woman assisting had taken Allison and another pupil to the bathroom. She had been helping the other child and when she turned around, Allison was gone. After not finding Allison in the bathroom, she ran back to the classroom to tell the teacher, who went into an immediate state of panic. Allison required constant supervision because she had a tendency to wander away. She had to be accompanied particularly when she was outside, because she had no sense of fear or danger and was oblivious to cars and other potential dangers. When the superintendent entered the classroom, the little boy who had been in the bathroom was crying and very upset. This child was very nervous anyway and he sensed the teacher's anxiety and he promptly threw up on the superintendent's shoes.

Another boy, who was later diagnosed as autistic, had become extremely hyperactive and climbed up on a desk and was flapping his arms and making loud noises. The teacher explained the situation quickly and stated that she and teaching aide had to leave immediately to search for Allison. This poor man was left with four very upset, disabled children for over an hour.

The search was on for Allison and soon the Principal of the school asked as many teachers as could to leave their classrooms and join in the hunt. Derek was in the school at that time and he too left his class to look for Allison, but only after he ran over to the Junior-Senior High School across the schoolyard to find and tell his dad. Gord was the Vice-principal of this school and he too joined in the search. For over an hour there were about thirty people looking for Allison. Calling her name was not effective because she could not answer, so they combed the school, the schoolyard and neighborhood around the school. Allison was found about three blocks away from the school sitting on someone's lawn, off in her own world staring at her fingers. Fortunately no harm had come to her. Once the crisis was over and Allison was safely back in her classroom, the superintendent did not ask the teacher to decrease her staff after all and in fact he said he would make arrangements for another classroom aide to be hired immediately. He had experienced first hand how demanding it was to be in this classroom and recognized the need for more staff, not less. I was at work in Calgary at the time and I heard about all this after Allison had been found. I too was relieved to learn that there would be more help in the classroom.

We had similar situations in which Allison wandered off from home as well. We had to keep our front door locked at all times because Allison would check periodically and if it was not locked she would open the door and leave. It was quite a challenge for all of us to always remember to lock the door. Derek had many friends call on him during the day, so we had to teach them to check the door as well. If they were going outside, they had to let me know so I could ensure the dead bolt was on. She didn't "run away" very often and when she did our neighbors were always helpful. They knew her well and would bring her back if they saw her outside alone or help us search if she did get away. We had neighbors a couple of doors down that were especially fond of Allison. This was a family with five children and they had a special relationship with us. Lynn, my friend and the mother, often invited Allison and I over to visit and she truly loved Allison. Most times when Allison wandered off she would go to their house and stand on the steps, waiting for someone to let her in. We lived on a quiet cul de sac and their house was on the same side of the street. If they didn't notice or hear her, Allison would then wander off further from home. One time she did get a few blocks away and a friend was driving by in her car. She saw Allison and said to herself, "There is Allison out for a walk." She continued driving a few seconds and then it dawned on her that Allison did not ever walk alone, so she stopped her car, got out and brought Allison home.

Another time when Allison was about thirteen years old she and I were home together and I thought the door was locked. I was busy doing something and suddenly realized that I couldn't hear Allison. I searched the house looking for her, but could not find her. I checked the basement, the garage, all the closets, every room, but she was not to be found. In a panic I called the neighbors and we started the usual fan out. Soon several neighbors were searching the streets with me. I couldn't figure out how she got away because I was certain the door had been locked and I returned to our house for another look and I found her. Allison was in the garage, the one I had checked, but she was sitting behind the wheel in the car. To my knowledge she could not open the car door let alone close it after she got in. I had not thought to look in the car.

Getting back to the school program, throughout Allison's school years the main techniques utilized in teaching Allison were behavioral. The philosophy of the school in the eighties was to provide separate, special education classes for children with disabilities. Over the years more and more integration with normal children was included. For example, some of these children joined the "normal" classes for some courses, such as physical education, music or whatever was appropriate for the child. Because of Allison's high needs and "low functioning" she was not integrated a great deal, especially when she attended the Elementary School, although there was a degree of integration when she was in the Junior and Senior High Schools. We were very fortunate in that Allison had one-to-one teaching throughout her schooling. The Foothills School Division honored her need to have individual attention. Autistic children do not do well even in small groups and need programs with their own teacher working with them individually in

order for them to learn. Allison's program focused on self-help skills, compliance, attending and cooperating, which was a continuation of what we had started in her pre-school years. Motor skills were also an area we all worked on with Allison. Her difficulties with depth perception persisted and she also continued to walk on her toes and we found it helped if she wore good shoes, mainly running shoes, with a large enough heel to keep her whole foot in contact with the ground when she was walking.

She had poor fine motor skills and did not use a pincher grasp in picking up objects. Rather than using her thumb and forefinger to pick up small items, she used her fingers in a raking motion to get the object into the palm of her other hand. This is the precursor to the development of fine motor grasp and very young children normally do this. The teachers worked with Allison in picking up small objects to help in this area. Naturally her curriculum did not include the normal reading, writing or mathematical skills, but was tailored to her individual needs. They tried to teach her to draw, and Allison objected and resisted. Eventually she could hold a pencil in her hand and draw circles but it was not an activity she liked. Play dough was used to help with finger movement and manipulation, but she found the texture and feel of the dough objectionable and finger painting was met with the same resistance. Allison was not particularly cooperative in the development of her artistic side, although we all persisted in trying to teach her these things. Time was spent in the gymnasium helping her with gross motor skills and she received some physiotherapy as well. Overall we were very pleased with her school program and at home we tried to reinforce those things she was learning at school, to be consistent with the expectations.

Consistency is a huge issue in special education. Allison's teacher, Karen, encouraged us to be involved in the program, and ensured that we were well informed about her school activities and Allison's progress. Karen often gave us homework to do, things to work on to supplement Alli's school program and this was a fair expectation. However, I often fell short in meeting this expectation and was not always able to do it all. Karen was able to understand that parents were thrown into this role of being special education teachers. This was not our chosen vocation and we did not necessarily have all the right skills. We had a to deal with our disabled children each and every day and had other issues to contend with. It therefore behooves the professional to remember that when they get impatient with parents or are disappointed with our efforts. Being consistent is important, but as a parent this is not always easy. I had trouble with consistency when I was sleep deprived. Sleep disturbance is common with autistic children and Alli had poor sleep habits, sometimes sleeping only four or five hours a night for weeks at a time. She was up for long periods in the middle of the night and required constant supervision. Often I struggled with just getting through the day, let alone with being consistent. As well, my emotional state sometimes would get in the way. It was difficult for me to be firm enough with Allison and I found her resistance very difficult to manage and it was wearing on me. I was not particularly good at forcing her to do something she obviously did not want to do, even though I realized that it was for her own good. I recognized that I wasn't always the best person to work with Allison. I had no problem reinforcing a skill she had acquired, but struggled with the demands of teaching her new ones, particularly when she was not cooperative. Allison's teacher was very considerate of parents and she understood my dilemmas and point of view and was forgiving when I was unable to meet her expectations. Karen was very empathetic and was able to appreciate my struggles and we were able to compromise. The key was to communicate, particularly when I was feeling overwhelmed or stressed, so she would know when to temper and limit the homework expectations.

Derek attended the same elementary school as Allison did and he was exceptional in his relationship with his sister. He did not hesitate to try and explain her disability to his peers and was proud of his sister. Gord would drop them off at the school in the morning and Derek took Allison to her classroom. He got to know all the students in Allison's class and would often drop in at recess to visit them. The school Principal, a friend of ours, called me on more than one occasion to tell me something Derek had said or done. At Christmas one year, he stopped Derek in the hall and asked what he wanted for Christmas. Derek replied, "All I want is for my sister to learn to talk." On another occasion Derek went to the Principal's office to tell him that we had a "Smarties Party" the night before because Allison had counted up to four! Derek was developing sensitivity to persons with disabilities at a tender age and one day, during physical education class in grade three, they were outside playing soccer. He noticed that a young girl with cerebral palsy, who was about eleven years old, was attempting to cross the

street in front of the school. She had fallen down and was struggling to get up and gather up her dropped books and crutches. Derek left the game and went out on the street. He helped her up, gathered her belongings, and assisted her in crossing the street. Once she was safely on the sidewalk, he returned to his game, saying nothing about it. Needless to say the teacher was touched by his actions and upon hearing about his kindness, I was a proud mom! Of course, sometimes he was the brunt of teasing, and some of the school children would make fun of Allison, but we had talked about that possibility. He realized that words could not hurt either him or Allison and he was able to ignore it for the most part. I knew it wasn't always easy for Derek having a disabled sister but I also knew and trusted that he was strong enough to deal with any negative comments or teasing from other children.

Throughout Allison's life we have tried to provide her with opportunities to become involved in various activities. We took her almost everywhere with us and made a concerted effort to integrate her into the community. In no way was she going to be isolated or hidden away. Gord was a hockey player and coach and in the summer he played on a local slo-pitch ball team, so we were his fans and went to many of the games. We also supported the teams he coached at school. Derek too became involved in sports and played T-ball and hockey. Allison and I spent many hours in arenas and ball diamonds supporting her brother and her dad. Because of Allison's love of the outdoors, we also walked many kilometers together. She was never able to run very well because of her problems with coordination, but she did walk at a good pace. I believed that walking and getting exercise might just help her to sleep better, so going for a walk became one of our evening routines. She enjoyed watching skating, so when Allison was about six we got her a pair of bob skates with double blades that attached to her boots and she was able to skate too, which she loved. She wore a helmet and elbow and kneepads and she would scoot around the ice, laughing and having a wonderful time. Once her feet got too big for these strap-on-blades, we had to abandon skating because she was never able to handle regular skates, although we tried. Her perceptual problems and poor balance made even standing up on skates impossible.

Gord, his brother and sister started a summer hockey camp in the early eighties in Ponoka, the town he had grown up in. Hockey was Gord's main passion in sports and he not only had played himself at the

Junior and University levels, but had been involved in coaching at various levels, including University, Senior Men and at the minor hockey level. Derek was a hockey enthusiast as well, so the two of them would spend a couple of weeks at this hockey school. While they were engaged in their favorite sport, for a couple of summers I took Allison to a family camp in British Columbia. I invited a friend who had worked with Allison in kindergarten and she and her two daughters accompanied us for the week. Having them along allowed me to participate in a course called "Body and Soul" in the mornings while Jo worked with and supervised Allison and her daughters attended their programs. We spent the afternoons at the beach and Allison and I enjoyed swimming in the lake and wandering around the area. There was an evening program and because it usually involved music and singing, Allison was in her element. She was allowed to go right up on the stage with the musicians and she would clap her hands and dance to the beat of the music. Everyone at camp accepted this and appreciated Allison's love of music. She had a birthday while we were there and the musicians gave Allison a harmonica and although she was not able to learn to blow into it, she did inhale with this held to her lips, so was successful in making some of her own music.

Sports and recreation had always been an integral part of our lives and I was intent on teaching Allison to swim. I had taken her to swimming lessons when she was a baby and she loved to be in the pool from the time she was an infant. She had no fear of the water but was not swimming either, so she required vigilant supervision. This was difficult because she did not like to be touched, so we provided her with water wings when she was little. The summer she was seven years old, we visited Gord's brother and his family in Toronto. He and his wife had three children who were a few years older than Allison and Derek, but they loved to play with their young cousins. They had a swimming pool in their back yard and I was anxious about the situation because I knew Allison might walk right into the pool and she was at risk of drowning. I worried that we would be unable to keep the back door locked at their house and she would likely wander out to the pool on her own. We solved this by getting her a life jacket as soon as we arrived, which she wore most of the two-week period of time we were in Toronto. As soon as she woke up in the morning we put the jacket on her to ensure her safety. That way we didn't have to worry about her and all of us could

Allison in the pool at six years old, 1978.

relax somewhat. She enjoyed the freedom and indeed she did go into the pool several times on her own, although someone quickly joined her.

Allison was unable to take swimming lessons with other children because of her disability, but I took her to the pool often. I had been a lifeguard in my youth and a competitive swimmer so we shared our passion for the water. Once she had the life jacket she enjoyed the fact that she did not have to be held. She would float around the pool, splashing and enjoying herself. I had become friends of the lifeguards at the pool in Okotoks and one of them approached me one day. She had noticed how much Allison enjoyed being in the water, especially once she had the life jacket. However, she also noticed that Allison was not using her arms to move herself at all and the jacket interfered with her arm movements. She had an idea she wanted to try, so the next time we were at the pool she had the apparatus she had designed for Allison. She had taken a belt and added three styrofoam cylinders. Once Allison had this around her waist the cylinders on her back allowed her to float, leaving her arms free. She looked like a diver wearing oxygen tanks. She had to move her arms a little to keep her face out of the water and she pulled both arms down together. Although she never learned to alternate her strokes, she was able to propel herself through the water. She couldn't kick in the usual fashion either, alternating her feet, but was successful in learning a modified dolphin kick, using both feet together.

Her new-found talent in swimming thrilled Allison and soon she was traveling all around the pool with me swimming beside her and we had a great deal of fun together. She did not like to put her face in the water and this motivated her to keep moving. After a few weeks, we removed one of the cylinders, which meant Allison had to do even more work to keep her head above water. We continued the process of removing one cylinder at a time until she was swimming independently, wearing only the belt. Amusingly, if I removed the belt, she sunk, although eventually she realized that she didn't need it to swim. In the period of transition, before she was able to swim independently, I only had to put my finger on her hipbone and she could swim with her head above the water, but if I removed my finger, she would sink. We all laughed about this and eventually Allison learned to swim on her own. Her technique and style were unique, but she was swimming. Eventually I was able to teach her to sit down on the edge of the pool and fall in, and she would go under the water, surface and start swimming. She learned to hold her breath and go under the lane ropes as well, so she became comfortable going under water for a short period of time. Allison later became strong enough to swim some lengths and this was quite an accomplishment, because her unusual stroke is difficult and tiring. I tried to swim like she did and realized how physically taxing it was. I always swam beside her and if she got tired she would hold on and ride with me.

Sharing our enthusiasm and passion for swimming was something normal and positive and the exercise was good for both of us. The whole process of teaching her to swim took a long time, years in fact, but it was one of those challenges we endured with such positive results. Allison would swim freely in water that was over her head, but as soon as we got to the shallow end she would stand up and walk. I could persuade her to go back to the deep water to swim again but in her mind, she only needed to swim when she could not touch the bottom. This made sense when I thought about it. One day another lifeguard observed this and came up with a suggestion. She gave us some flippers and Allison responded well to them. She was thrilled with her new-found speed and she started to swim lengths without standing up. It was very difficult for her to maneuver the flippers standing up, so she just kept swimming. Eventually she was able to swim more than twenty lengths of the pool wearing her flippers and to this day swimming is part of her routine. This was another example of how breaking a task

into small parts was facilitative in teaching Allison. Swimming and exercise in general had always been important to me and I believed disabled persons needed to maintain a level of fitness just like the rest of the population. I was proud of Allison's tenacity and endurance in learning how to swim.

Besides participating in community activities and sports, we had holidays each summer and in Allison's early years we avoided trips and vacations away because of her disability. It was easier to stay home. The summer Allison turned six and Derek was four, friends of ours loaned us their truck and camper and we took our children on a camping trip to Disneyland in California. Allison was a great traveler and would sit up in the front seat with her dad, watching the sights go by. The motion of a moving vehicle always seemed to soothe Allison and she could ride for hours. Derek was like most young children in a vehicle and we had to make frequent stops for him to go to the bathroom, stretch his legs and have a break from traveling. This trip was a great success and we found camping was a way we could take Allison on holidays. We had tried to take Allison away from home, but she never slept well either in someone else's home or in motels. Because she was so sound sensitive, any slight noise in the night would wake her up, so we had actually avoided trips and weekends away. However, in the camper, she always slept in the same bed and the noisy fan of the air conditioner seemed to block out the noises and she actually slept quite well most nights. This camper had limited cooking facilities and we ate out for most meals other than breakfast. This was not always pleasant because Allison did not behave appropriately in restaurants and would not eat well, if at all. However, I would take a doggie bag for her and feed her back in the camper where she was comfortable.

Disneyland was the perfect destination and Allison discovered her favorite place in this world. She loved the music and most of the attractions. We avoided the fast-moving rides, leaving them to Derek and Gord, but Allison and I had many returns trips to attractions such as America Sings, It's a Small World, Tiki Tiki House, Pirates of the Caribbean and the Haunted House. Derek was spooked with the Haunted House because at one point, if you look in the mirror, you can see a ghost sitting on your shoulder. He kept checking his shoulder for days after, looking for that ghost. Allison was able to handle the long line-ups because there was always a band or some characters walking by to capture her interest. She was in ecstasy when we rode through It's a Small World and I swear that she could hear that music from anywhere in the park. She would head off in the direction of this attraction every chance she had, so we toured this one several times. Allison enjoyed the parades as well because of the music and action, so most evenings we stayed to watch the Electric Parade. We spent four full days in Disneyland and we all fell into bed exhausted but happy at the end of each day after watching the fireworks from our campsite. While in California we took the children to Knotts Berry Farm, Universal Studios and Sea World in San Diego. This was a fabulous family vacation for all of us and Disneyland and Sea World were the favorites. We would return to California several more times over the next few years.

In 1982 we purchased a motor home and this was the perfect vehicle for us. It had an air conditioner with a noisy fan so Allison slept well. We used this for two more trips to California and Disneyland and various other camping holidays. We even took our motor home when we visited friends and relatives and camped in their backyards. This way there was a good chance that Allison would sleep. Autistic children need routines and are resistant to change, so holidays can be a problem. Our motor home became her home-away-from-home and she was able to tolerate traveling because she always had the same bed and the motor home became a comfortable environment for her. She always sat up in the front seat beside her dad and Derek and I could sit at the table and play games and we could even nap en route. Eating out had been an ongoing problem and Allison's behavior was unpredictable. She did not usually do well in restaurants and was often noisy and sometimes upset and crying. Having a motor home solved that problem because we had kitchen facilities and could have our meals "at home." We all enjoyed camping and found that most campgrounds had pools and children's play areas. We spent our evenings outdoors, which Allison enjoyed, and we were able to walk and swim. We found out that Allison was a trouper when it came to traveling in our motor home and camping made it possible for us to have family vacations.

In the spring of her eleventh year, Allison was beginning to develop breasts and the time came for her to be wearing a brassiere. In my wisdom, I purchased her first bra with a front closure believing that some day she might even be able to fasten it herself. One day after work I went to the school to pick her up and the teachers were in stitches. Gord

and Derek had brought Allison to school as usual but when lunchtime came and the teacher opened Allison's lunch kit they found a brown paper bag. Inside this bag was Allison's bra with a note attached. Gord had written, "Please put this thing on Allison. Both Derek and I tried but we could not get this sucker on her. Neither of us could figure this contraption out! Thanks, Gord." The teachers and I had a good laugh about Gord's note and his incompetence and after that I bought a normal bra for Allison and in fact put it on her at bedtime so Gord would not have to wrestle with it in the morning.

In the spring of 1984 when Allison was almost twelve, I was invited by a colleague in nursing education to attend a three-day personal growth workshop in Calgary. This was open to the general public, although most of the people who registered were professionals in the teaching field. The facilitators were two medical doctors. Both physicians were interested in alternative healing and practiced acupuncture and other non-conventional therapies.

The aim of this workshop was for the participants to deal with issues and problems that were perhaps blocking our energies and keeping us stuck or unable to fulfill our potentials. At that time I was feeling positive about my relationship with Allison and our lives were going quite well. I didn't believe I needed to be at this workshop and thought that I was quite well adjusted, but I was always open to personal growth and improvement.

Although I was not convinced that I needed any help myself at the time, I found that I still had issues to deal with and was outgrowing my need to try and change Allison. Up until this time my focus had been on providing programs for Allison and doing whatever I could to help her overcome this diagnosis of autism. My goal had been to make her well, to make her normal. I had been intent on finding the magic key that would release her from her disability. In examining my life, goals and emotional adjustment during this workshop, I realized that I about to go through another emotional transition, and make another personal adjustment. Through the counseling I received at the workshop, I recognized that a cure for Allison was not going to happen. After all, she was almost twelve years old and was still very much autistic. Certainly she had improved and many of her stereotype behaviors had been extinguished, but she still was not talking, and would sometimes become withdrawn into her world of autism. Coming to terms with the reality of the situation was not nearly as traumatic as it was when I had to first deal with the fact that Allison was autistic. I had already resolved many of my issues and feelings and was able to accept her diagnoses. I was emotionally stronger and had many positive experiences behind me and I did not have the intense grief and disappointment to wrestle with. In the environment of this group I had a great deal of support. The facilitators were skilled and the other participants were understanding and compassionate, so the transition was much more gentle and healing for me.

One evening, after a day at this workshop, I was at home with my family. We were sitting in the family room and had been discussing a little about the day's events. I explained some of the insights I had gained. In my heart I had realized for some time that Allison was not likely to be cured of autism, but I had always had a personal need to have a reason for things and was looking for new meaning to explain Allison's autism. Sitting there with my family I started to write a poem. Often writing helped me to sort things out and clarify my feelings. I felt a sense of peacefulness and a special connection with Allison that evening. In fact, as I began to write, I believed that I was receiving some sort of inspiration from her. She sat on the floor beside me for a couple of hours as I wrote. It was unusual for her to sit for that long a period of time without getting up and leaving, but she stayed right there at my side. I would pause and read what I was writing out loud. When I got stuck and couldn't find the right words, I sensed Allison's support and presence and the words I was searching for suddenly became clear. I wrote the following poem as if Allison was speaking to me, explaining her reason for being.

For You

I am a free spirit
Put on this Earth
For a special purpose.
I have nothing to prove
And nothing to learn
For I already know it all.
I am responsible to no person
As I am of God
And indeed, God is wise.
And in his wisdom

He created me
So that you can learn.

To learn is to live
To live is to feel
And I help you identify feel-
ings.

I am different and difficult
And sometimes strange
So you can understand
imperfection.

I am distant
And seem closed
So you can experience close-
ness.

I withdraw so you cannot,
I do not talk
So you can learn to commu-
nicate.

Allison at age twelve.

I teach you to give
And let you receive
When you ask and know your own needs.

I draw back from your touch
To test your persistence
And help you to become sincere.

I make it difficult
For your eyes to meet mine
So you can appreciate depth.

To love music is to love me
As I become part of music
And you love when you listen.

I value your love –
Love that is unconditional
For I meet no conditions.

I make you cry
And I make you laugh
So you can be honest and whole.

My reason for being
Is to help you to grow
As we share our triumphs and failures.

Believe in me
And your God in me
And you'll learn to forgive and be free.
           Love, Allison

Through writing this poem I was able to construct a new meaning and got further answers about what my life with Allison was all about. I no longer believed that that I must change her or search endlessly for a way to draw her out of autism. Allison was meant to be autistic and was perfect just the way she was. This did not mean I had given up hope, but I no longer had to be driven to find a cure, it would happen if it was meant to be. I was able to forgive God for giving me a disabled child, to forgive myself for anything I thought I might have done to cause her disability and to let go of any responsibility I felt for her problems. Forgiving and letting go is important in the process of personal growth and transformation. Now I could honestly and sincerely give thanks for the marvelous gift of my daughter. I learned a great deal about unconditional love that evening. This didn't mean I would no longer work with Allison and try to help her, but my goals had changed. I was able to accept and love her exactly the way she was. All I really had to do was to love her, to be there for her and to provide for her as best I could. I could see my role in her life with more clarity; it was simple, although it would not necessarily be easy. I was able to acknowledge that she was here for us too and I recognized that she had already taught all of us so much through her autism. The poem explains what we were meant to learn. The words in this poem were not meant only for me personally, but were meant to give meaning to anyone who had a relationship with Allison. The process of writing this poem was a profound spiritual experience for me, a revelation. At this point in time I was not consciously aware of the concept of life's work or that we might be on a particular path in this life, but I was awakening to the true meaning of my life and that of my daughter. I realized that Allison, in her disability, was here to teach us and her autism was meant to be, part of a greater Divine plan.

Chapter 7
Allison's Friends:
Her Canine Companion and Elke

Allison's program at school was going well and she was improving on many levels. In the fall of 1984 when Allison was twelve, Karen, Allison's teacher read a story in an American magazine about the use of specially trained dogs for people with various disabilities. She was very excited about the concept. She approached us, and the parents of one of Allison's classmates, Kyle, who was autistic as well, wanting to explore the possibility of us getting dogs for our children. None of us were overly enthusiastic initially, believing that we already had enough to deal with and having dogs, even ones that were specially trained, would just further complicate our lives. Karen finally convinced us to think about it and provided us with the article she had read.

The program was called Canine Companions for Independence, or CCI, and it was a non-profit organization in Santa Rosa, California, that bred, raised and trained dogs for people with disabilities. A woman psychologist founded CCI after seeing animals used for people with severe physical disabilities on a visit to the Middle East and this inspired her to start the program in the United States. CCI's mission was to serve the needs of people with disabilities through the love and assistance of dogs called Canine Companions. Charles Schultz, the author of *Peanuts* and creator of Charlie Brown and his friends, lived in Santa Rosa and was a supporter of this organization. His wife, Jean Schultz, became the President of Board of Directors in the nineties. There were some similarities between the training of these dogs for people with disabilities and Seeing Eye dogs for the visually impaired. At CCI they had three types of specialty dogs: service dogs for people with physical disabilities who were often confined to wheel chairs, signal dogs for persons who were hearing impaired or deaf, and social dogs that were used mainly to visit people confined to nursing homes and institutions. A teacher in special education had been given a social dog that he brought into his classroom to be with children with special needs. After learning more about the concept of using such dogs for people with disabilities, both families consented to making an application, so Karen contacted the officials at CCI to find out whether or not we would be able to bring two social working dogs into Canada. Taking the dogs out of the country was not a problem, but historically social dogs had remained with the teacher or in a long-term-care facility and at first they were reluctant to consent to these children receiving dogs of their own. Karen was able to convince them that they would benefit from each having their own Canine Companion. Our application was approved and we were about to embark on a unique and most remarkable adventure.

The process involved attending a two-week extensive training program in Santa Rosa, California. CCI insisted that the teacher and her staff who were regularly involved with these children take the training program along with Allison and Kyle and their family members. Allison and I planned to go and Kyle was to be accompanied by his mom, dad and his younger sister. Karen and one of her teaching assistants, Lorna, who worked directly with Allison, were registered as well. The course scheduled for May of 1985 and we began to make the appropriate plans. First we had to get approval from the School Board to be able to bring the dogs into the classroom and this was granted after they researched the legal aspects and the necessary arrangements had been made for insurance. Because autistic children do not like to be touched and neither Kyle nor Allison had been around dogs a great deal, Karen brought her dog Sunny, a Golden Retriever puppy, into the classroom for several weeks prior to our trip. Initially Allison and Kyle were not thrilled about having a puppy jump all over them and definitely disliked the dog licking their faces, but both children were eventually able to tolerate this animal and would even pet Sunny when asked to. This turned out to be a very sound idea in preparing Allison and Kyle, because when the time came for them to receive their own dogs, they were comfortable with physical contact from an animal. The United Way and several other service organizations funded CCI, so they provided the dogs free of charge although they were valued at over five and a half thousand dollars each. We had to absorb the costs of traveling to Santa Rosa, and pay for our meals and accommodations. The school, the communities in which Kyle and Alli lived, and many friends helped in fundraising to help cover some of our expenses and we were grateful for the support.

The teachers, Allison and I went by airplane and Kyle and his family traveled to Santa Rosa by car. While we were finally at CCI headquarters we learned more about the organization. They used several

breeds of dogs including Standard Poodles, German Shepherds, Golden Retrievers, Black and Golden Labradors, Dobermans and Border Collies to name a few. These were the service and social dogs. The signal dogs were Welsh Corgis. After the pups were born, they were placed in a Puppy Raising Program, sent to live in homes with children for their first year for socialization. The puppy raisers were expected to attend basic obedience classes and begin the process of training the puppies in a family environment. The dogs were returned to CCI after a year for extensive training and preparation with the experienced dog trainers at the facility. The dogs were taught eighty-eight commands and became very well disciplined and capable of assisting people with various disabilities.

Canine Companions all wore blue and yellow backpacks that had been specifically designed for them. The packs were worn to identify them as working dogs and were useful in carrying items that might be needed throughout the day. They all carried plastic zip lock bags for "pooper scoopers" and it was an expectation that the clients would clean up after the dogs. These animals were so well trained they only went to the bathroom on command! The backpacks also had a handle on top and people in wheel chairs could hook their hand through it and the dog was trained to pull them in their chairs. Service dogs were not only trained to pull the wheel chairs, but would fetch and retrieve items, push elevator buttons, push and hold doors open, and turn on and off light switches, to name a few of their skills. They could open fridge doors and retrieve their client's lunch and even helped with paying for things in stores. They would take bills in their mouths, put their paws up on the counter and "hand" the money to cashiers.

Signal dogs really acted as "ears" for the hearing impaired. They were taught to respond to environmental sounds and alert their owners. For example, when the alarm clock rang in the morning the dog would jump up on the bed and wake the person up. They could alert their owners to the ringing of timers on ovens and microwaves, doorbells and telephones. Some individuals with a hearing impairment had children, and their signal dog was taught to come and get them when their babies cried. Deaf children could be given more freedom and could play outside, having a signal dog there to alert them when their name was called. Out on the street, these dogs were taught to be aware of traffic sounds and helped keep their owners safe. They were taught many of the same

commands as were service dogs, but learned to respond to sign language as well as verbal instructions so that people who were unable to speak could command and communicate with their dogs.

Up until this time Social Dogs had been mainly used as companions and to provide stimulation and friendship to the elderly and people in nursing homes or institutions. This was already recognized as a form of pet therapy. CCI was just beginning to utilize social dogs for mentally challenged individuals or children with autism, like Kyle and Alli, and these children were the first to be receiving such companions. They did require that recipients of the dogs be at least eight years old and that parents of severely disabled children had to take the training as well, as we were doing. We could appreciate that these specialty dogs had changed the lives of those people who received them, allowing disabled people to become more independent. People with Canine Companions received many other personal benefits as well by having a constant companion.

Upon orientation we learned that this training was fondly referred to as "Boot Camp" and we found out that it was indeed much like a military training camp. The demands were extensive and we had to write and pass daily exams, as well as become proficient in working directly with the dogs. The requirements for graduation were stringent. This was an exhausting training period of two weeks and we worked twelve to thirteen hours each day, with only one Saturday off. There were eighteen disabled people, mostly adults, in the program. Sixteen of them were physically disabled, in wheel chairs, and were there for service dogs. Allison and Kyle were the only ones that were ambulatory and there to receive social dogs. For the first three days we worked with a number of different dogs on a rotating basis. The trainers and staff observed our every move and were watching the relationships between the dogs and participants, trying to find suitable matches. These capable animals were already well trained and we were the ones in training, so we could acquire the skills necessary to command and work with the dogs.

Allison and I worked with several different dogs each day and sometimes this was a challenge. I was the one commanding the dog and had to keep Allison on task as well. Allison was a small person for a girl of almost thirteen years in age, weighing about eighty pounds, and some of these dogs were bigger than she was and intimidated her. The

Doberman Pincher they had took us for a walk and I had very little control over him. At noon on the third day the staff gathered us all together and began handing out specific dogs for each participant. The trainers had been in a meeting to discuss their observations and decide who would be assigned to what dog. They tried to match each person with the dog they felt was best suited to the individual's needs and personality. Kyle was assigned a beautiful German Shepherd, named Unity. My anxiety was escalating as we were getting to the end and Allison had not yet received a dog. When all the dogs had been assigned and Allison had been left out, I was in a state of panic and heart broken. We had come all this way and I imagined that they had decided that Allison would simply not be able to handle having a Canine Companion. One of the trainers stood up and said as much, but when she noticed tears welling up in my eyes, she decided she had better stop joking. Apparently they had discussed Allison's situation at length and decided that of all the dogs we had worked with, none were really suitable for her. To solve their dilemma of finding a dog for Allison, they decided to try bringing in one of their signal dogs, a Welsh Corgi. This dog had been trained for and assigned to a deaf person, but because of some problems, the dog had been returned to CCI. One of the trainers escorted a little tricolored corgi named Quality into the room and on first sight I knew she was going to be the perfect dog for Allison. She had a gorgeous face, large friendly eyes and Allison responded favorably to her right from the start. She seemed much more comfortable with a smaller dog and she even put her arms around this little dog. Quality had been taught most of the same commands as the other dogs with the exception of those related to pulling wheel chairs, but she would not need these in her relationship with Allison anyway. By the end of this day each participant had their own dog and we were to keep these animals with us for the next eleven days. We had already obtained permission to have the dogs stay with us in the motel, although that was not really an issue because in California they already had a law allowing working dogs access to public places.

That evening I was talking to Allison and saying "Alli has a doggie." To my complete surprise, she repeated that statement back to me, and her words were perfectly articulated. I immediately called the teachers and they came to our room to witness this. We all kept saying it and Allison would smile and repeat it back, over and over again. She must

"Alli has a doggie!" Allison's Canine Companion Quality.

have said it dozens of times that night. I called Gord and Derek, told them about our day and Allison's new dog, Quality, and put Allison on the phone. With encouragement she said it to Gord and at first he didn't know whom he was talking to. He was surprised, overwhelmed and thrilled when I told him that it was his daughter. That night we all celebrated Allison's first sentence. The next day she repeated this statement several times, but within four or five days it was gone and Allison no longer said these words. This is not unusual in autism and although I was disappointed, I will never forget the sound of her voice as she gleefully exclaimed, "Alli has a doggie!"

We spent the next week and a half learning how to command and handle our dogs in many different situations. We had a double leash set up for Allison and I. Allison had Quality's leash in her hand, but it was attached to a second one that I held. If Allison dropped her leash, I still had control of Quality. Of course I gave the verbal commands. We had to work on having Allison hold the leash and had to teach Quality how to get them untangled when they got all wrapped up in the leash. As a group we went to various parks, shopping malls, grocery stores and restaurants and up and down escalators and elevators, practicing the commands and management of the animals. We all went to a pizza place for lunch one day and it was amazing. There were over twenty people in our group and eighteen dogs and nobody would have even known there was a dog in the place. They had been taught to go under the table, lie down and be quiet. We also took the dogs to the movies and to a live theater. We had been warned that there was going to be the sound of a gun being fired during the play and it was expected that none of the dogs would react. When it happened, Quality was the only dog that barked, but I pretended it wasn't her. Fortunately there wasn't a trainer sitting with us and she only let out one small bark!

By the end of Boot Camp we all had become proficient in commanding the dogs and had learned all about the care of these animals, including how to de-flea them, trim their nails and brush their teeth. We had lectures from a veterinarian, the director of CCI and many lessons from the trainers. All the tests had been written and passed and we were almost ready for graduation. For our final test, a practical examination, we had to go to a shopping mall and perform several tasks. We had written instructions and were informed that there would be a "spy" watching and evaluating us. Not only were they assessing our skills in commanding and handling the dogs, they were looking for evidence of rapport, love and respect between the person and their dog. For over an hour Allison and I went through the mall with Quality knowing that someone was observing us closely. We walked, made some purchases, had a drink in a snack bar, rode the escalator, took an elevator and followed all the instructions we had been given. By the end of the day we had passed all the requirements and prepared to attend our graduation.

Graduation included a banquet and a formal ceremony. Each graduate was awarded a diploma and the person who had been the dog's Puppy trainer presented the Canine Companion to each of the graduates. It was an emotional event, a night for celebration and time to say good-bye to our new friends. As a group of participants we had become very close, having worked together and experienced so much throughout our two weeks at Boot Camp. Allison and Kyle received the first social dogs that would come to Canada and the first such dogs assigned to individual children. We flew back to Calgary the next day and had received permission from the airlines to have Quality ride in the airplane with Allison. Seeing a dog wearing a backpack on board and sitting in the front seat on Alli's lap piqued the interest of many passengers, so I had the opportunity of informing people about Canine Companions. Allison and her new friend were both exhausted after all their hard work at Boot Camp and both of them slept all the way home.

Although the formal training was over, we still had a great deal to accomplish and do once we got home. Canine Companions for Independence would always own the dogs and Quality was actually on loan to us. In order to keep her, we had to comply with the regulations and were expected to represent CCI in a positive and professional way. Each month we had to submit written reports of our progress. We had a veterinarian in Okotoks who volunteered his services and provided care for both Quality and Unity for the duration of their lives and his medical reports were submitted to CCI regularly. Normally someone from CCI made home visits and evaluations, but because we lived so far away, this was not required. We had gotten Derek a kitten just before we went to California to get Quality to help prevent him from feeling left out and this proved to be wise. For the first month after we came home, nobody but Allison and I were to touch or talk to Quality and she was to be on leash at all times. It was very important that Allison and Quality develop a close bond, so Alli was the only one who could ever feed Quality. I would prepare the food, hand the bowl to Allison and she put it down in front of Quality. This little dog loved to eat and quickly associated her meals with Allison. Quality particularly loved cheese, so we would try to hide cheese in Allison's pockets for Quality to find. The only problem was that Allison loved cheese too, so often they shared the find. Allison learned to hold small bits of dog treats, in

Allison snuggled up with Quality.

a pincher grasp, and give them to Quality. Allison and I would sit and brush the dog together and she actually learned to do this herself. Soon they became close friends. I continued to put Quality through her paces with the commands. Quality preferred to be with Allison, because she made no demands on her dog. After working with Quality I would say "release" and Quality would run to Allison's side, knowing she was free for a while. Once the bond between Alli and Quality was clearly established, I began teaching Gord and Derek and they too learned to work with Alli and Quality.

Quality and Allison were constant companions and her dog was with her twenty-four hours a day, accompanying her wherever she went. When out in public Quality was required to wear her backpack to help identify her as a working dog. She would sit on the deck at the pool when Allison went swimming and when we ate out, Quality accompanied us into restaurants. We were able to get permission allowing us to take Quality into shopping malls, theaters and other public places. Out of courtesy we often would phone ahead to ensure they knew we were coming although the laws in Alberta were eventually changed to allow service dogs access to all public places. When we went to the zoo, we had some limitations and they asked us not to go near the large cats, the lions and tigers, and they provided us with a guide. Quality and Kyle's dog Unity went to school with the children and the dogs were integrated into the program. The other students had been informed about the dogs and were told that they were working dogs, not pets. Part of our responsibility in obtaining these dogs was to inform the public about the program. We had to remind people that these were working dogs and ask them not to touch them, but after a few months, with permission from CCI, I was able use my discretion in allowing others to pet Quality. This unusual, cute little dog wearing a pack naturally brought us a great deal of attention. If someone came over to us and asked about the dog, I would tell them about Quality's role and explain about Canine Companions. Quality was bringing people into contact with Alli in such a positive way and this was most encouraging. I granted permission for people to pet Quality, especially if they made an attempt to talk to and include Allison in the interaction. Quality actually diverted the focus away from Allison's disability. People noticed this gorgeous little corgi first and often didn't even realize that Allison was disabled.

The benefits both Kyle and Allison received from having Canine

Allison with Quality, teacher Karen Irvine, and Kyle with Unity, 1985.

Companions were immeasurable. In caring for Quality, Allison now had many responsibilities. Although she required supervision, she had to feed her dog, walk her and brush her. It also gave us all something so very normal to do with Allison as we took Quality for walks and helped Alli care for her companion. In holding the leash Allison could not flap her arms or stare at her hands, so she was much more normal in her appearance when out in the public. Alli became more aware of the environment because she had to pay attention to her dog or they would get all tangled up in the leash. This special animal provided a certain constancy in Allison's life, something autistic people needed. Allison was resistant to change and always having Quality with her helped her deal with change and unanticipated events. At least she could always count on Quality being there and Allison became more calm and more accepting of changes in her routine. Perhaps the most significant benefit was that Quality provided Allison with unconditional love. Quality didn't even notice or care that Allison was different or autistic, she loved her just for being there. She would enter into Allison's world, preventing her from withdrawing because she demanded attention and would not be ignored. Allison was responding to her dog and as a result of us work-

ing with the two of them together, she was more responsive to people too. Quality slept right up on Allison's bed with her and Alli seemed to sleep better with her dog snuggled up against her at night. Quality sat under Allison's chair in the kitchen and she particularly liked meal times. Even though we had to help Allison with eating, to Quality's delight, Allison would often drop bits and pieces of food and these would barely reach the floor before Quality would snatch them up. Sometimes I swore Allison dropped things on purpose for her dog. We nicknamed Quality "Hoover" because she was like a vacuum cleaner and I rarely had to sweep the kitchen floor. Quality and Allison had a unique connection that was difficult to explain. Sometimes there didn't seem to be much going on between them that was obvious to others, but they were very comfortable with each other and were constantly together without us having to encourage this. Quality would sit on Allison's lap or right beside her and Allison would often reach over and pet her dog. If Allison were lying on the floor, Quality would rest her head on Allison's back. This autistic child was able to tolerate and accept physical contact with Quality, which was amazing given her former dislike of anything soft and furry! Allison's life had changed because of the positive effects she received from having Quality. This Canine Companion was aptly named; she brought a unique kind of quality to Allison's life.

Kyle benefited from having his dog, Unity, in many ways as well. He had always had some speech, but it was echolalia, and after getting

Unity he was able to use words more effectively because he learned to command his dog. This made him so proud and he became so much more confident. He rode his bike with Unity running along side of him and playing with his dog brought him great joy. His parents no doubt could tell many stories about how Unity enhanced Kyle's quality of life too.

Gord and Quality had a special bond. Gord had grown up on a farm and had always had a dog as a child but he didn't believe a dog should be left at home alone all day. Because we both worked, having a dog was not something he agreed to until we got Quality. This was acceptable because Quality was not left at home. Admittedly all of us in our family became very fond of Quality and she enhanced our lives as well. There is something so very dear about having a dog around and we all realized some of the benefits of pet therapy. Quality was always excited to see us and would bound up to us when we came home from work or school. No matter how we felt, she was always affectionate, bringing us all joy and pleasure and providing us with the same uncon-ditional love she had for Allison. Quality was to be part of our lives for many years and becoming involved in the Canine Companions for Independence and receiving Quality had a positive impact on not only Allison, but on all of us in our family.

Ever since Allison was about three, when she finally started to hold objects, she preferred to have something in her hand. She liked to hold on to small objects such as rattles, hard plastic toys or even boxes. Over the years suncatchers had become her all-time favorite toys. True stained glass suncatchers were too fragile, but I had found some that were made of hard, transparent pieces of plastic or acrylic. These were much safer for Allison, although I had trouble finding suitable ones. When I did see them, I bought all I could not knowing when I would see them again. I gave Allison one at a time and hid the rest away for later. She tired of some of them after a while and it was advantageous to have a good sup-ply on hand. Her love of suncatchers originated during the first home program, which included light therapy or visual stimulation. Shining a flashlight through a suncatcher in a dark room produced a variety of interesting images on the wall. After this program had been abandoned, Allison found some suncatchers in her toy box and discovered that she too could produce a variety of images by holding these up to the light. I had found that she preferred a small suncatcher with irregular edges

and if it had some holes in it that was even better because she could poke her fingers through these. Maybe these provided both visual and tactile stimulation for Allison.

Her love of suncatchers was an example of how autistic children often develop an attachment to objects. Allison also had many toys she liked to carry around, especially squeaky ones, but it became evident that the colorful suncatchers were her favorites. I liked small ones too because I could easily carry one in my pocket or purse when we were out. If she seemed to need it, it was readily available to her. She did not have the same interest in round, smooth suncatchers and generally ignored these. As a young child Allison not only liked to hold these up to the light, but she used them to hide behind. She often held one up as if she were looking at it. If I watched her carefully I found that she was actually looking through or around it. This way she could check out things and people around her without having to make eye contact. Allison did not always need to have a suncatcher in her hand, but if given a choice of toys to carry around she almost always selected a suncatcher. Allison had difficulty in new environments and we had found that if she had a familiar suncatcher, she could cope with the stress better. When we took Allison out to a restaurant or other public places, she would often get quite upset, become noisy and start making unhappy sounds. This was unpleasant for us and often disturbed other people around us. We found that if we had a suncatcher for her she could pay attention to it and was less upset with the sensory stimulation around her. Her suncatchers provided her with a sense of security and proved to be quite useful. I didn't care whether or not this was socially acceptable, especially as she got older, because I felt her behavior was certainly more appropriate if she had her familiar suncatcher. If having one reduced her anxiety, I was willing to provide one for her. Sometimes people would stare at her but I had learned a long time ago to ignore the curiosity of others although sometimes I offered an explanation for her behavior.

Some time in the first year that Allison had Quality we noticed that Allison frequently wanted the choke chain that Quality had around her neck. I gave her a chain of her own one day and Allison did not like to be without it. She could manipulate it with great dexterity in her fingers, using either hand. Allison was just as particular about her chains as she was about her suncatchers. It had to be a dog chain, just like

Quality's. She did not like gold-colored ones or fine, delicate chains; they had to be authentic dog choke chains. Allison did not abandon her suncatchers. She would wrap her chain around her suncatchers and together they became a source of pleasure and comfort for Allison. Allison now had her dog as well as her suncatchers and chains and all of these provided Allison with a sense of security. She was not allowed to play with her chain and suncatcher when she was walking Quality or attending to her responsibilities in caring for her dog, but these were available to her during breaks and free time.

In addition to her dog, suncatchers and chains, Allison was soon going to have a real friend, a person to whom she would become very close. In the summer of 1985, just after Allison received Quality, one of Gord's hockey friends called us from Germany. He knew a young German girl who wanted to come to Canada to work on her English language skills and wondered if we were interested in having her come and stay with us for a year. She was willing to come as a Nanny and after thinking about it, we decided it would be a good idea. Elke arrived in August and we were pleased to know she spoke English quite well and she had been informed about Allison and her disability before she came. I don't think she really knew what to expect and she was quite shy and reserved at first. This young girl was turning eighteen in September and had not been away from home before. She had a return ticket that was effective for a month and after that she would be committed to staying for a year. She was very homesick and overwhelmed with being in a new country and staying with a family with a child with a disability and didn't completely unpack her bags for the first four weeks. She was a lovely girl and seemed to like Allison, but was undecided about staying until she talked to her boyfriend on the telephone one night, just before the month was over. We honestly thought she would return to Germany right away, but after her conversation with her boyfriend she came downstairs and announced that she intended to stay. He had told her that if she left, she would be giving up an opportunity of a lifetime and he had helped her make her decision. She unpacked her bags that evening and soon became part of our family.

Elke was another one of those special gifts that had arrived in our family. She was lots of fun, had a great deal of energy and fit right in. I had to teach her to work with Quality, but this was not a problem because she liked animals and was amazed with the whole concept of

Allison and Elke, during a visit from Elke in 1998.

Canine Companions. She had to take all the written tests that we had completed in California and soon was able to take Allison and Quality out on her own. Elke was a great help with Allison and after getting her ready for school in the morning she, Allison and Quality walked to school together. She often stayed in the classroom with Allison as a volunteer as well, and because she was interested in learning about the school system in Canada, she would sometimes go to Gord's school and attend his math class. She also volunteered to help in the library in the Junior High School, so she found lots of different things to do during the day. Although she was quite young, she had a spirit of adventure and did not hesitate to try new things. She loved to go to the city, so often I would drop her off at a shopping center on my way to work and she would spend the day exploring Calgary, taking the bus everywhere. She was one of the few women I knew who could spend the whole day shopping and spend only a few dollars!

Elke took a special interest in Allison and they soon became good friends. Like Allison, Elke loved to be outside and to walk, so they took Quality out often. She talked to Allison all the time, sang her songs and seemed to know just what Allison needed and wanted. We took a few weekend trips in our motor home as a family to show Elke around Alberta and she too enjoyed camping. She especially loved the Rocky

Mountains, so we spent several weekends camping in the mountains in Alberta's Provincial and National Parks west of Calgary, including Kananaskis Country and Banff.

There was a special lodge and campgrounds in Kananaskis called William Watson Lodge that had been built and designed for persons with disabilities. Along with the buildings there was a campground with hook-ups and facilities for those that had recreational vehicles or campers. There was a network of paved pathways throughout the whole area that extended for kilometers, allowing those in wheel chairs access to the wilderness. The paved trails were useful for us too; Allison had trouble hiking on ordinary trails because of her problems with depth perception, limiting her opportunities to walk in the mountain parks. The lodge had been built to provide facilities for the disabled, allowing them to enjoy the outdoors and the mountains. This site was reserved for disabled individuals and groups and their family members and the fees to stay there were very low, making it most affordable. Guests only had to supply their own bedding and food. Allison's class in junior high were to stay in a cabin at this lodge on a couple of occasions and these school outings were very successful. There were some structured events and evening singsongs around a fire pit and those staying there could venture out on their own at times and had the added benefit of attending the planned get-togethers. Because it was such a popular site, one had to book months in advance to stay in a cabin, but we were able to obtain a campsite without problem. We wanted Elke to experience camping at this wonderful, unique site in the mountains.

The whole year Elke was with us was wonderful and she became like a second daughter to us and a big sister to our children. The following summer Elke's mother came to stay with us for six weeks before Elke went home. We took them to the Calgary Stampede and they witnessed their first rodeo and enjoyed the hospitality Calgary is known for during Stampede Week. Once again we ventured out in our motor home and all six of us went on a trip to southern California. We drove through Yellowstone National Park, went to Salt Lake City and made our way to Las Vegas and spent a couple of days there. Of course our ultimate destination was Disneyland. When we got there we had to put Quality in their kennel for the first time. They certainly would have allowed her into the park, but she would not be able to go on the rides and into the attractions with us, so we decided that she would be fine

in the kennel. After dropping her off I wept when I was walking away; she looked so sad and abandoned. The following day I simply could not repeat the procedure, so we left Quality in the motor home with the air conditioner on and Gord went back to our campsite at noon to check on her. After going to Sea World and a few other attractions, we made our way up the California coast taking in more sights, including San Francisco, which Elke and her mother loved. This was a fabulous vacation and we had fun showing Elke and her mom various parts of North America. Although we were somewhat crowded in the camper, we enjoyed being outside in the evenings. Elke's mother did not speak English, so Elke had to translate for us all. Elke's mom was very friendly and we all got along well. After supper she and I would be in the motor home doing dishes and cleaning up while Elke took Allison and Quality for a walk. She would chatter away to me in German and I did not understand a word she said, but I talked back to her. It was a riot carrying on this strange conversation neither of us could make sense of, but we became friends in spite of the language barrier. We stopped for a day in Santa Rosa and visited Quality's birthplace and went to the new buildings of Canine Companions for Independence. If they couldn't make a home visit, we were willing to bring Allison and Quality to them. They carried out an assessment of our skills and relationship with Quality and we were given a positive report.

Elke and her mother thoroughly enjoyed this vacation and greatly appreciated being able to visit various places they had heard and read about. When we arrived back in Alberta, we made one more trip to Ponoka for a Jones family mixed slo-pitch ball tournament and Elke's mother was able to meet our relatives and experience this event. This was not a particularly serious tournament and we all dressed up in costumes and Elke and her mom called us the "Crazy Canadians." Our year with Elke had come to an end and it was with great sadness that we took her and her mother to the airport and sent them home to Germany. It felt like we were losing a daughter and Allison was losing her best friend. We all had to deal with our loss, but in spite of the pain of having to let Elke go, we knew it had been worth it. Elke had enriched and brightened our lives. She had established a close friendship with our daughter, something Allison had not experienced before, and we all received so much from her presence in our family. Fortunately we were able to maintain our relationship with Elke and she returned to

visit us for two months the following summer and has been back on three more occasions since 1985. Gord and I met her in Europe on a school trip to Portugal and Spain and she came along on the tour with us with a group of grade nine students. Elke too considered herself to be part of our family and I trust that she always will be, even if we don't see her often. The whole year had been full of exciting events and new experiences and we were about to enter another phase with Allison that fall. She was to move from the Elementary School to join a special education class called Junior Pre-Employment in the Okotoks Junior High School and would be taught by another remarkable teacher.

Chapter 8
Allison in Junior High School

In the fall of 1986 Allison and Quality started at Okotoks Junior High School and she was in the Junior Pre-Employment Program in that school for three years, from the time she was fourteen until she was seventeen. It was a rather unique situation because Gord, Derek and Allison would all be attending the same school for this period of time. Gord was the Vice-Principal and was therefore an administrator in the school. There were a number of changes in Alli's life that fall, including changing schools, a new teacher and Elke's return to Germany. Joan Burke, the classroom teacher, was new but she turned out to be another one with exemplary skills in working with children with disabilities. There were more students in this class and the focus was on teaching these young people some of the skills they would need in the future. It was not an academic focus, but rather one in which the strengths of each one of the students could be developed further. Of course learning social skills and teaching them appropriate behavior were part of the curriculum along with self-help skills.

By mid October it became evident that Allison was losing weight and at times was becoming more and more withdrawn and this concerned us. She had dropped to just over eighty pounds, and although she had always been thin, this was unusually light for her. She seemed lethargic and uninterested in things around her and even Quality was not able to draw her out. She would lie on the couch, looking very sad, thin and pale and gazing off into space. I became alarmed and wondered if she was depressed. Likely there were many factors contributing to her depression, including the change of schools, the loss of her first teacher with whom she was very close and the loss of Elke. To her Elke was gone forever, had ceased to exist and her grief was profound. We even telephoned Elke and had her talk to Allison on the phone and although her face lit up when she heard Elke's voice, her gloom returned soon after. Because of the gravity of the situation we took her to a child psychiatrist who looked after children with disabilities and he confirmed the diagnosis of depression and prescribed an antidepressant, Elavil, a medication that she took at bedtime for several months. We saw a slight improvement in Allison, but our anxiety about our daughter continued. We knew we could not bring Elke back nor could we help her to understand the situation.

Derek had been thinking about it too and he came up with an idea. If Allison was missing her friend, then what she needed was new friends. He approached Allison's teacher and was given permission to initiate what he called a "Between Friends Club" in the school. Interested normal students were invited to join the pupils in the Junior Pre-Employment class for lunch once a week. The intent was to help the other students understand and appreciate those students with handicaps and to help bridge the gap between them. Derek knew that once his friends had met and knew how to be with Allison, they would be comfortable with her, so he suggested that the teachers could help by teaching the members of this club what to expect and what to do when they were with these children. He had come up with a very creative idea – we were very proud of our son. There were about twelve school children interested and the club was formed and Derek helped the teachers orientate the members. After a few weeks the teachers believed they were ready to be left on their own and they left the room, although they could be reached if needed. Joan thought that the kids would be more spontaneous without the presence of teachers and she was correct. One day they returned to find the group in hysterics. They had been playing a game and it had deteriorated into a throwing match and pieces of tiddly-winks were flying around the room and the kids were climbing all over each other, roaring with laughter. The teachers recognized that this horseplay was entirely normal behavior for young teen-agers. This club was highly successful and all of the children benefited. Allison had some new friends and was beginning to respond to them and one girl in particular, Vickie, took a liking to Allison and this friendship blossomed. Allison's depression was lifting and we all felt relieved and thankful to Derek, who had demonstrated his sensitivity and was instrumental in solving this problem. He remained in the club the first year, but did not participate the following one and although we were disappointed about that, we knew he had his own interests to attend to and understood his need to break from the club. Derek continued to be friendly with Allison's classmates and often dropped into the classroom to visit them.

Speech therapy was very much part of Allison's program in her younger years, but the results had been disappointing. We used behavioral techniques, rewarding her efforts at making sounds with the hope

of shaping these into words. I knew that children who have not developed speech and language skills by the age of eight are not likely to do so and I had already faced the reality that Allison was not going to learn to talk. Although accepting that fact was not easy, I realized that we were wasting our time and energy on speech therapy. Verbal communication is not the only way people are able to make their needs known, so we shifted our focus to finding other methods of communication that we could assist Allison in developing. I read that some non-verbal, autistic children were able to learn sign language. Allison did not have the fine motor skills needed to actually sign letters, so I concentrated on concepts. One sign that she learned quickly was the one for music. We chose to work on this sign first because, not unlike many autistic children, Allison had a passion for music and it was a powerful motivator. In teaching her, I would take her hand, move it in a circle, prompting her physically and I immediately played a favorite record. The music was the reinforcer, her reward. Allison never mastered the skill of actually signing for music herself, but she learned that she could take my hand and move it in a circular pattern. She was prompting me. She had been paying attention to my behavior and imitated my actions, although she could not develop the concept that she herself could produce the sign and this worked for her. In addition she learned and utilized some other signs, including touching her chin as the sign for drink, patting her stomach for food and brushing her hand diagonally across her chest, a gesture meaning please. Using a modified form of sign language was a good start and a breakthrough in my opinion, but her repertoire of signs was very limited.

In school Alli was encouraged to use her limited number of signs. Joan read an article about the use of a symbol system to help such children develop a means of communicating and to learn to anticipate events to come. One of the characteristics of autism is a strong resistance to change. Once engaged in an activity, they often find it difficult to stop and resisted attempts to direct their attention to something else. Alli could concentrate intensely on one thing or task for an extended period of time, but found it difficult to shift her interest to another. A factor could be her inability to anticipate what was coming next and verbal explanations were ineffective. Alli did not like it when an activity she had been enjoying came to an end and each time they attempted to introduce a new one, she would become resistant, even if they knew she would enjoy it once she got started. We decided we would develop a symbol system for Allison and began by gathering up objects that clearly represented the activities in her school day. For example, we had a small toy trumpet to represent music class, a piece of paper in an envelope to represent her job of delivering message to teachers in their classrooms, a jar of peanut butter to indicate food and lunch time, a glass for drink, a toy car to indicate going for a ride in a car and going home, a book to mean she would be read to, a cassette tape to represent playing music, some doll clothes to mean they would be working on dressing skills, a dish cloth for cleaning up after snack and lunch and so on. We stapled a number of empty two-liter milk boxes together and put the representative toys and objects into the boxes in the sequence that things were to occur over the day. When she was to begin an activity, she was taken to the symbol boxes and prompted to pick the object that represented the activity out of the box. She took it with her and kept it in sight throughout the activity. When it was time to finish what she was doing, she was be taken back to the symbol boxes and asked to place the object, the symbol, it in the "out box," signaling the end of the activity. With prompting she picked up the next object in the sequence and the process was repeated. This was very effective and Allison soon learned to anticipate what was to happen next and became more tolerant of a change in activities. She even tried to manipulate the system by picking an object out of the boxes that represented something she enjoyed doing, skipping those she liked less. After several months of using the symbols they gradually replaced the object or symbol with a picture of it and eventually having the boxes in sequence was no longer necessary. Using pictures was more portable and there was no need to return to the symbol boxes in the classroom between activities. Some symbols, such as the glass or peanut butter jar continued to be available for her to use in communicating her needs.

We had a series of symbol boxes at home and encouraged Alli to use her symbols there too. Using her symbols she was interacting with others in a very basic way, make her requests known. She brought a glass when she was thirsty or the peanut butter jar when she was hungry. Although she was not able to pour the juice herself, she had a symbol that she could use to communicate her need for a drink. Alli even discovered some of her own symbols and taught us. When she first brought me her shoes it wasn't hard for me to understand her message, she want-

ed to go for a walk. When she wanted the tape changed in her tape recorder, she would find a new tape and present it to one of us. Although she did not have the fine motor skills and cognitive abilities to meet all her own needs she certainly was able to comprehend the power of using symbols to communicate her need and desires to others. Non-verbal communication can be very effective and one only needs to be imaginative in discovering techniques that can be useful and meaningful. Using symbols and modifying this system reduced some of Alli's frustration. This was all about giving Allison some control, empowering her.

Along with utilizing the symbol system at school they continued to work on helping Allison with self-help skills. We had been trying to teach Allison to dress and feed herself for a number of years and we eventually had to accept the fact that she needed help with these things. Some of her muscle groups did not seem to work appropriately and her problems with dexterity were likely related to her motor and perceptual problems. However, she was cooperative and compliant and when we handed her a shirt she could slip it on over her head. If we helped her to get her legs into her pants, she could pull them up. We encouraged her to do as much as she could herself and stepped in to help when she needed it. Allison could be manipulative and if we were not careful, she would feign complete incompetence and let us do everything for her, so we had to continually assess her abilities and figure out how much she could actually do. We tried to help her to understand that we expected her to participate and do what she was capable of doing. We had to apply the same principles in helping Allison with meals. We had a soft rubber handle that could be attached to a spoon, making it easier for her to hold and she could take food on the spoon from the plate to her mouth. Manipulating the spoon and moving it across the plate to fill it with food was something she was unable to do, even when we put a ridge on the plate to help her. So we put the food on the spoon or the fork, put it on the edge of the plate and she took it from there, returning the utensil to the plate for us to repeat the procedure. She could manage to feed herself if she was given a sandwich or finger foods. She could drink from a glass or cup on her own, although needed to have someone fill it for her first. In terms of toileting, Alli needed assistance in wiping her bottom and flushing the toilet after going to the bathroom.

Grooming and personal appearance had always been an issue for me. I believed that disabled persons already had enough going against them and they deserved to look their best. Therefore I made sure Allison was always well dressed in clean, stylish clothes and her hair was clean, brushed and cut in a style that suited her. In buying her clothes, I searched for elasticized waistbands so she could manage her pants on her own and avoided blouses or tops with buttons that she could not handle. We put a loose-leaf ring on the zipper of her coat so she could pull it up herself. Sometimes I had to hunt to find appropriate clothing, but always managed to find outfits that were fashionable and flattering to her. Allison was not overly enthusiastic about shopping and although I took her on occasion, I was usually able to select her clothes without having her there to try them on. We could do that at home where she was more comfortable. I believed that it was my responsibility to ensure that Allison always looked nice.

Music was very much part of our lives with Alli and I believed music was not only entertaining to her, but was therapeutic as well. Playing music for her when she was upset had a dramatic calming effect. If she seemed unusually sad or withdrawn, we could cheer her up by singing to her or playing happy sounding music. We also used music to help keep her up at night when she wanted to go to bed. It's not that we

*Allison playing
a keyboard.*

wanted to deprive her of sleep, but if she was allowed to go to bed too early she would get up in the middle of the night, full of energy. If we could keep her up until after ten, she was more likely to sleep through the night, everyone benefited and none of us became sleep deprived. Music was helpful in other situations as well. Allison loved to ride in a car and playing music added to her pleasure. Music gave us something we could share with Allison in a very normal way. Sometimes we would dance with her, although her dance skills were limited given her problems with balance. Alli responded to almost all kinds of music including children's songs, country and western, pop, classical and easy listening. Even as a young teenager she would sit in front of the television and watch an opera, completely attentive, not moving for more than an hour at a time. She appreciated singing, instrumentals and any combination, with the exception of the pan flute, which seemed to be irritating to her. Unfortunately we couldn't take her to many live concerts as she was noisy and disrupted both the artists and the audience because she simply could not contain her joy and would make all kinds of noises in her delight. We solved that by getting her videos that she could watch at home, making all the noise she liked. When she was a toddler she would sit and listen to my sister, Shelley, practice on her flute. Shelley is a professional musician, playing a golden flute in the Edmonton Symphony Orchestra. If Shelley took a break during a practice session that Allison was listening to, Allison would reach over and take her hand, direct it to the flute, asking for more. Small children normally have a short attention span, but not Allison when it came to music. She could listen to the flute for long periods of time. As Shelley played Alli would sway and rock, completely absorbed in the music. Other times she would dance around Shelley and as Allison got taller Shelley had raise her flute to allow Alli to get around her.

When Allison was about six we went to an evening Christmas Concert at church and because we were late, ended up sitting in the front row. The man sitting beside me was a friend and he pointed out that his fourteen-year old daughter was going to play the flute that night. I proceeded to tell him of Allison's love of the flute, how she could listen to it for hours, bragging somewhat. The concert started and Alli was delighted with the choir, clapping her hands and making her usual happy sounds. When the young girl started to play the flute Allison turned to me, looked me right in the eye in obvious distress and started to cry out loud. In fact she howled and tears streamed down her cheeks and I immediately knew what was wrong. The girl was just learning to play this instrument and her flute squeaked at times, as it does when not well played. This was not music of the caliber that Allison appreciated and knew and to her ears it was quite painful. I was embarrassed, couldn't calm her down, and because of my previous comments, couldn't really make excuses to her father. We couldn't leave because the church was very crowded, we were blocked in and escape was impossible. The girl's father recognized the real problem and he simply took my hand telling me he understood. Allison quit crying abruptly when the girl finished playing and to my relief, enjoyed the organ music and singing, happy once again. Unfortunately the whole scenario was played out a second time when the girl came forward again and she couldn't help but hear Allison's reaction. I have no idea what her father told her later. My bragging certainly backfired. The lesson here was that Allison did have an ear for good music and was indeed selective. The one exception to that was that she liked me to sing to her and my singing voice had always been less than perfect, to say the least. My sister must have inherited all the music genes. But my limited musical talent didn't matter to Allison. I guess her love for me was unconditional.

The teachers at school were well aware of Allison's love of music and integrating disabled students in classes with "normal" peers was one of the goals in special education at the time. It was not appropriate for Allison to attend the usual academic classes because of the severity of her disability, but she could share her love of music with other students. Plans were made to integrate her into the grade seven band class and the music teacher was enthusiastic and even provided Allison with a tambourine to play and found her a seat among the group at the back. He wasn't at all concerned about the possibility that she could be disruptive. The first class was a disaster. This was at the beginning of the year and some of the students were learning to play musical instruments for the first time. Needless to say, Allison howled and had to be removed from the classroom. When her teacher told me about this incident later, I was not surprised, given our recent experience with the flute. I suggested that perhaps Allison could participate in the grade nine band program. Students in this orchestra were much more experienced and their music might be more acceptable to Allison. We did not have to abandon the integration concept after all and Allison went on to participate with this

higher-level band. She might not have been able to read or write, but she certainly had a sophisticated appreciation of music. Allison never learned to play an instrument in the school band, but the benefits for her came from being able to listen to the music, participating and socializing with the students in a very normal activity. Her classmates accepted her into the class and were able to appreciate her ability to distinguish between good and not-so-good music.

Allison had several "jobs" to do at school in the Junior Pre-Employment Program and one of them was to deliver daily attendance sheets to the teachers in their classrooms each morning. She, Quality and her teacher aide made their rounds daily, entered the classrooms and put the papers on the teacher's desk. She had some problem delivering these to her dad's classroom, because she always wanted to stay and visit, but she learned that this was not part of the job. All of Allison's teachers were creative in finding things for her to do. Some ideas failed, though, and one was watering the plants at the school. She received no satisfaction or pleasure from this task, so it was abandoned.

In the second and third year that Allison, Derek and Gord were all in the same school, we had some other interesting situations to deal with. In his early teens, Derek had put some distance between himself and Allison. When he was younger he had such a wonderful attitude about his disabled sister and was so much more involved with her. At first we were somewhat troubled by the fact that he spent less time with Allison and even seemed to ignore her at school. Considering his age and the stage of development that he was in, we realized that it wasn't necessarily "cool" to have a sister in the same school, let alone one that was handicapped. Derek needed his own space and we began to decrease the expectations we put on him regarding helping with Allison. He needed to be allowed to be a normal teenager without these added responsibilities. Gord was in charge of international travel in the school and in 1988 made arrangements to take a group of grade nine students to Russia for ten days over the Easter holidays. One other teacher agreed to go, but because they needed another chaperone, I willingly volunteered for this role. We made the decision to include Derek, although he was in grade eight, and he along with another boy in grade eight were allowed to join the travel group. Going on this trip was something we could do with Derek and we made arrangements for Allison to stay with neighbors. Eighteen students and the three chaperones embarked on a

unique educational travel experience. We visited Leningrad, now Saint Petersburg, Minsk and Moscow and at that time Russia was still under the communist regime. Life in this communist country was difficult and very different from ours and the students learned to appreciate Canada and our culture. All of them came home changed. Allison and Quality were well looked after and this trip was a much-needed break for all of us. Derek felt special and appreciated that we were able to leave Allison and include him in our travels.

In 1989 when Derek was in grade nine and Allison was in her last year at the Okotoks Junior High School, I came home from work one day and Gord told me that there had been an "incident" at school that day and Derek had been suspended. I couldn't believe it and was anxious to hear the details. Apparently at noon hour he was walking down the corridor on the second floor of the school. Allison and Quality were ahead, near the stairs about to go down. A grade nine student suddenly shoved Allison, causing her to fall down. This young fellow had done it on purpose, but he didn't know that Derek had witnessed his action. Fortunately Allison did not fall down the stairs but it was it was close and she and Quality could have had a serious accident. The teacher with Allison reprimanded this boy and told him to report to the Principal's office because his behavior was unacceptable and this had not been the first time he had behaved inappropriately around the disabled students. In the past he had been known to mimic them and tease them, calling them names. This child was not well liked by the teachers and he had been an ongoing annoyance. Derek was furious, but knew that the teacher had handled the situation. For the rest of the day he thought about it though, fuming, and after school hours he lost his temper. He met this boy in the hall and they ended up in a fight. Derek was very tall and even at the age of fourteen, he was six feet three inches tall and because he was athletic he was very strong. The offender was small and was just over five feet tall. Derek grabbed him, picked him up and banged him up against the lockers. As he proceeded to bang him on the lockers all the way down the hall he yelled at this frightened fellow, "Don't–you–ever–touch–my–sister–again–or–I–will–beat–the–#*!#*#– out–of–you!" With each word this boy was hammered against another locker. A crowd had gathered and the kids were cheering and egging Derek on. Some of the teachers were silently cheering too, but that could not be known. Eventually the physical education teacher was able

to break up the fight. Gord was the Vice Principal and the Principal was out of the school at the time. Gord asked another teacher to handle the situation because of the obvious conflict of interest. Both boys were suspended and scheduled to meet with the Principal the following morning. As I listened to this story my reaction changed. Upon hearing that Derek was in trouble, I was angry with him, but this changed to pride once I heard the facts. And we had been concerned that Derek didn't seem to care as much for his sister as he did in the past! Now we had very clear evidence that he did care after all, but was being macho and couldn't display his love of his sister publicly, except if she were threatened in any way. Gord and I had to be careful how we handled the situation with Derek, because we did not condone violence. He had been big and tall for his age all his life and we had talked about his need to be gentle around others because he could hurt them. We told him that we were proud that he stood up for his sister, but we did not approve of him beating this boy up and left further discipline measures up to the Principal.

The next day when he saw the Principal, Derek told him that he had been taking verbal abuse and teasing for years and had walked away when other kids had called his sister a "retard" or other such demeaning names. "My mom and dad taught me to ignore these comments and I know that words cannot hurt me or Allison." He then told the Principal that he would not walk away if anyone touched Allison or tried to hurt her and would fight again if the situation arose. He stated that "Allison cannot protect herself and anyone that even tried to hurt her would have to deal with me!" He would not say he was sorry because he was not, so he had to face the consequences of being suspended for three days. He was allowed to go to school, but had to stay in the time-out room and work on homework. This was fair and Derek accepted his punishment without question. The Principal told Gord of his conversation with Derek and he, along with many the other teachers, believed that the boy that had pushed Allison really got what he deserved, although they could not tell Derek this nor condone his fighting. The young fellow that caused all the trouble in the first place was suspended for a week and during this time he was not allowed back into the school. He also had to apologize to the students and teachers in the special education class and promise to stop harassing them. Needless to say, that was the last time anyone tried to abuse Allison to our knowledge

and the word was out, Derek would always be there to protect his sister. We no longer questioned his devotion to his sister.

The time came for both of our children to leave Okotoks Junior High School and move to the Foothills Composite High School. In June they had a graduation ceremony and dance and these were very moving. Allison's friend, Vickie, from the Between Friends Club offered to sit with Allison and Quality during the ceremony and Gord and I sat in the audience, watching both our children receive their Junior High School Diplomas. Allison was given a Service Award for her contributions in delivering attendance sheets to the classrooms each day and Derek was given a Citizenship Award for his contributions in initiating the Between Friends Club and his relationship with the students in the Junior Pre-Employment Class. Dealing with the school bully was not part of this award, of course.

We all went to the dance for a while. The students were all dressed up and Allison and her classmates were included. It was touching to watch how well the other students completely accepted those with disabilities. Many of them had known the handicapped students since they were in elementary school and considered them to be part of their graduating class. Kyle danced with great enthusiasm, weaving his way through the crowd, and some of the graduates would talk to him and all of them were comfortable with his presence and that of the others with disabilities. Allison sat up right beside the speakers and sometimes she too danced to the rhythm of the music. I think Derek was relieved when Allison and I left and he was free to participate in the festivities without his mother watching.

During the time Allison and Derek were in the Junior High School, I continued to work and did several presentations about Canine Companions for Independence. Through the Continuing Education faculty at Mount Royal College where I was employed, I arranged to conduct two one-day workshops. I donated the proceeds from these to CCI to support the organization. The people that registered for these included nurses, parents of disabled and autistic children, rehabilitation specialists, caregivers, a veterinarian and a dog trainer. In the presentation I outlined the program at CCI, explained the various specialty dogs and what they did for disabled clients and took Quality to demonstrate. This was a great deal of fun for me and I was fulfilling an obligation to inform the public about these special dogs. A mother of an autistic boy

who was about eleven years old attended one of my presentations and we talked at length after. She went on to apply and received a Canine Companion for her son several months later. Allison, Quality, Allison's first teacher and I met them at the airport upon their return and we kept in contact with them for some time later.

Having a daughter with autism has provided me with information and experiences that I have been able to share with others, including nursing students. For a number of years in my teaching career I spoke to students studying pediatrics about autism and disabilities in general. After Allison got Quality I also provided information about Canine Companions. I would take Quality and Allison to class so the students could meet them and see a little of what Quality could do for Allison. In the coming years I was to teach a class in the baccalaureate Nursing program at the University of Calgary to first year students. The topic was "Living in a Different Reality" and although the focus was on autism, many of the principles of care are the same for people with other disabilities. I was sharing the lived experience of raising a daughter with autism. Over the years, many nursing student in Calgary have learned about autism, the programs we had initiated and Canine Companions for Independence.

Further to these presentations, I was asked to be a guest speaker at the annual PALS meeting. This organization, Pet Access League Society, arranges for people to take their dogs and other pets into nursing homes and other institutions as a form of pet therapy and they were interested in learning about Canine Companions. I took Quality with me and she stole the show, impressing everyone with her skills. I also spoke at a conference for parents of deaf children and they were most interested in signal dogs. Quality remembered enough of the commands in sign language, although I needed help from the audience myself in delivering the commands by signing. For me it has always been fulfilling to give lectures and teach others about our lives with Allison and autism. In a way, this was a healing experience for me. It was a way I could contribute to helping others learns about autism and I believed that sharing how we have tried to enhance the quality of Allison's life provided some valuable lessons.

At one point I had been involved with various parents support groups. In the late seventies I had joined Foothills Association to Aid the Handicapped and was still a member years later. This was a parents'

group based in High River, Alberta, that took action and made things happen in the community. We planned activities for families and our children and the membership included families with children with various disabilities, physical and mental. It has gone on to become Foothills AIM Society. AIM stands for Advocacy in Motion and this society has established a day and residential program for adults with disabilities in High River, Alberta. Allison was to become a client later in 1992.

Other parent support groups were not as valuable. I attended one at the school for autistic children in Calgary in the late seventies. We were to read and discuss a book written by a father of an autistic child. He had written another book when his son was very young and I had read and enjoyed that one, but the second book was depressing. The author focused too much on the negative aspects of being a parent for my liking. At one point he talked about feeling so miserable that he wished his child would die and I could not relate to this kind of thinking. I did not find the discussions around this book at the meetings helpful at all. The leader believed that parents needed to deal with the negative aspects of having a child with autism and we needed to discuss all the negative feelings associated with that and I objected to this. In my belief, it was far more helpful to focus on the positive aspects of parenting than to spend time lamenting about our losses and anticipating future problems. Concentrating on negativity was not healthy; at least it wasn't for me. I had found that taking one day at a time allowed me to recognize daily accomplishments and decreased my anxiety about potential future problems. Worrying about negative possibilities was not something I was prepared to do anymore. I am sure some of the participants and leaders thought that I was in denial, but I knew otherwise. I was being critical and had to come to terms with the fact that the needs of each parent are unique and different. Other parents may have found this to be supportive and helpful and I respected that, but I had no need to revisit my negative feelings and this group was not meeting my needs. Perhaps I was in a different phase of the adjustment process and had already worked through many of my feelings. Time had already healed many of my wounds.

Gord and I had attended a similar parents' group at Children's Hospital, and although it had a different focus from the other group, we both felt that it was not something we needed. In my opinion, parent

support groups are not necessarily supportive. They can sometimes perpetuate negativity and problems and I learned to be very selective in choosing groups to belong to. Perhaps my stand was seen as arrogant, but it wasn't because I hadn't needed help along the way; I had. Adjusting to the realities of life with Allison was an ongoing process and although it was difficult and painful at times, I had sought out and received professional help on occasions that I needed counseling and additional support. I had one resource in particular, a psychologist who had run a women's group in Okotoks when Allison was a toddler, who was always available if I needed some counseling or just someone to talk to. I was often most comfortable receiving support on a one-to-one basis and not in a group setting, with people that I didn't know. The psychology student who worked with Allison earlier had been supportive to both Gord and I and he helped us gain many insights. We also had a strong support system in place. Caring, compassionate people had surrounded me in my nursing career and my medical friends had impacted and facilitated my adjustment process. The members of both Gord's and my families had always been there for us, offering their support, as had our circle of friends. I also benefited from personal growth programs that included many different people, not just parents with autistic children. That helped me to keep my problems in perspective. Making emotional adjustments was also a very personal journey and sometimes I needed to do this on my own, independently, as did Gord. It was a spiritual process for me and I felt I needed to develop and draw on my own inner personal strengths and faith. I could share my insights later, but the process of gaining them was often private. Certainly I had memberships in various societies associated with autism and found these to be helpful, but groups with a focus on simply discussing problems and airing negative feelings were not appealing to me, unless the intent was to solve problems in a positive way and create strategies to assist families in coping. It was also far more therapeutic for me to teach others, to explain what I knew about this disability and to concentrate on healthy adjustments and positive actions parents can take.

As a family with a disabled member, we had to make an effort to "normalize" our lives, build in breaks and ensure that all of us were healthy and had our needs met. We had to find ways to create a balance in our lives. Relationships need nurturing and Gord and I tried to ensure that we had some time for us alone, as a couple without our chil-

dren. In Allison's earlier years we didn't get out a great deal and this had been a strain on our marriage at times. Finding suitable sitters for Allison and Derek was always an ongoing problem, but we had to persevere in our search. As our children got older, we were able to take occasional trips and get-away-weekends. Neighbors, a family mentioned earlier, welcomed Allison into their home in spite of the fact they had a large family and they looked after Allison for two or three of our trips. Gord coached the University of Calgary Dinosaur Hockey Team in 1983 and had the opportunity to take the team to Anchorage, Alaska, over the Christmas break for a tournament. I was able to go just because of the willingness of this family to take our children. This same family also looked after Allison when we went to Russia in 1988 and again the following year when Gord and I chaperoned a school trip to Portugal and Spain. Some may have thought that traveling with a group of four-teen- year-old students was not necessarily a break for us, but in fact it was. These were educational tours and both Gord and I loved to travel and learn about different countries, the history and the culture. Taking students provided us with the opportunity to travel to various parts of the world we wouldn't have been able to afford otherwise. The tour company provided excellent tour guides and our role was to chaperone the group members. These trips also provided the students with an opportunity to get to know Gord in a different light, away from the school atmosphere.

Over the years we had a few weekends away on our own or with friends. One destination we enjoyed was Las Vegas. The atmosphere there was completely different from our usual lives, and although we were not big-time gamblers, the glitz and various shows provided great entertainment and a chance for us to have some fun together, without responsibilities and worries. We were able to put these on hold for a few days and we developed the practice of not phoning home to constantly check on the children. We could always be reached and had to trust that if problems arose, we would be contacted. At first this was difficult for me as a mother, but in the long run, it allowed me a true break and although I would wonder how things were going at home, I learned to relax and enjoy our special time together. As a nursing instructor I had access to nursing students and on a couple of occasions I hired a senior student to look after our children. Having a young adult with a medical background staying with the children made me feel comfortable. The year Elke was with us we had a weekend in Vegas, knowing that she was capable and reliable in caring for Allison and Derek.

When we had social events to attend at home we were usually able to find a suitable sitter. We preferred to hire adults because of Allison's disability and we had one woman who was in her sixties who became a regular sitter. As well as caring for our children when we went out in the evening, she would come to our home when the kids had a day off school and Gord and I had to work. As Derek got older and capable of staying with Allison, we were careful not to expect him to look after Allison very often. If he did, we paid him just like any other sitter to be fair to him and as a teenager, he appreciated the extra cash. The first time we left Derek alone with Allison for a few hours, he was about fourteen. We left specific instructions and reviewed many safety precautions with him. He was not to use the stove but he could use the microwave. Our neighbors were home and had agreed to be a back up if Derek needed help with Allison and he just had to call them. When we got home we found out that there had been an incident. In his diligence, Derek had made frequent "rounds" of the house and had even checked the basement and found a "fire" burning in the furnace. He immediately got the fire extinguisher and put out the flame, emptying the extinguisher. In actuality he had put out the pilot light on the furnace and because the furnace fan was still on, our house was filled with white dust from the contents of the fire extinguisher. After the "fire" was out he called the neighbors and they had to relight the pilot light and call the people from the gas company to check the furnace. Derek and I had quite a lot of cleaning up to do, but the important thing was that Derek and Alli were fine and we certainly knew Derek took his babysitting responsibilities seriously.

We continued to take Allison with us on many outings, but we did have some limitations. She still did not tolerate crowds well and taking her to restaurants was often disastrous so we avoided eating out with her. We were able to take her to a number of different concerts and events if we knew her noises would not disturb the other spectators. I took her to a Sharon, Lois and Bram concert when she was about fourteen. Allison's junior high teacher took her to a Beach Boys Concert when they were in Calgary and Allison was absolutely delighted. This group was one of her favorites and she loved their music. We took her to the Ice Capades several years running, again because she loved the

music, lights and the action. Derek and Gord would often attend hockey games and other sports events for their entertainment and male bonding.

Allison, Gord and I continued to support Derek in his participation in sports and went to most of his hockey games. One time Derek asked me why I didn't go to his dad's games anymore, except for tournaments when we all went as a family. Gord was still involved in hockey, coaching and playing old-timers hockey in the late eighties. I liked to watch my son's team, but there was a limit to my interest in hockey. I told Derek I didn't go to Gord's games because it was like going to the same movie every Friday night for twenty-five years; I had seen it, been there and done it! The males in the family did not especially appreciate this response.

Allison and I continued to go swimming and walking together to help her with her fitness and stamina. It was important that we all cultivated our own individual interests as well. I found it therapeutic to continue with my swimming, on my own without Allison. Not only was it good exercise for me, but swimming also provided me with an emotional release. When I was frustrated or upset, swimming hard would help dispel my negative feelings. When I was swimming I was totally absorbed in what I was doing. I couldn't hear anyone, I couldn't see well without my glasses, so it was a total escape for me. This was something I could do without interruption and it was almost a meditative experience for me. I made it part of my routine for years to swim three or four times a week in the evenings and because I was a strong distance swimmer, I often swam up to a hundred lengths which was two and a half kilometers or about a mile and a half. Along with hockey, Gord got his exercise through jogging. In fact, we both enjoyed running, so we would take turns going out for a run while the other one stayed with Allison. Our whole family went in a five-kilometer Terry Fox Run when Allison was six years old. I was able to borrow a wheel chair from the college so Allison could ride. She could walk that far, but we wanted to run and this was not something she could do. We ran together taking turns pushing Allison and even Derek was able to keep up and take his turn pushing the wheel chair. Gord and I were both athletic and valued exercise and a healthy life style. It was important for us that we all had the opportunity to participate in activities that helped us maintain our physical fitness and we managed to ensure this happened

over the years.

We also tried to keep in close contact with our relatives and families and frequently went to visit my mother and Gord's family. When Gord was at hockey school during the summer with Derek, often Allison and I would go to visit the relatives at the same time. Allison's cousins were all very accepting of her and found unique ways to entertain her. My sister, Shelley, had twin girls when Allison was thirteen years old and we went to Edmonton to meet her new cousins when they were about eight weeks old. It was quite a weekend because Allison did not like it one bit when the babies cried. Every time one of them cried, Allison would get a distressed look on her face and start to cry herself. Newborn babies cry to make their needs known and with two babies there was often one crying, so Allison shed a few tears that weekend. We weren't sure if it was the noise of the crying that upset her or if she was feeling sorry for the babies when they cried. We knew Allison was sound sensitive and found uncontrolled noises or the sounds of upset children disturbing.

In her early teens Allison was doing well and we seemed to have things under control generally. I had worried about Allison's adolescence and how she would be once her hormones were racing and she would undergo the physical, emotional and chemical changes of puberty. At about thirteen she began to have more and more problems with sleep and often woke up in the night and was up for a few hours. If one of us didn't get up with her, she would get into all kinds of trouble. One night after being up alone for a few minutes she arrived in our bedroom covered with blood. I was alarmed and immediately jumped out of bed to come to her rescue. Once I cleaned her up I found out that it wasn't serious, she just had a number of small cuts on her fingers. Upon investigating further I discovered that she had been into the china cabinet and had broken a number of my crystal glasses. My sister had given me a couple of brass liqueur glasses for a gift at Christmas and Allison discovered that if she banged them together it made a lovely musical sound that she enjoyed. That night she had been trying to duplicate that sound using crystal glasses and of course they broke. She had tried this with several glasses and as a result many were broken and she had cut herself. After that we had to get locks on our china cabinet and when she got up in the night we tried to be more diligent in getting up with her right away. We did sometimes fail to respond immediately because this prob-

lem was causing us all to be somewhat sleep deprived.

On another occasion she got up at about four in the morning and we could hear her downstairs playing and making all kinds of happy noises. Neither Gord nor I were in a rush to leave our warm bed to supervise her. I always heard her get up, but sometimes needed a few minutes to wake up and work up the energy to get out of bed. Allison had a fixation on light switches and had the habit of turning on all the lights in the house, so we knew she wasn't in the dark. She had a toy box in the family room and we assumed she was playing with her favorite toys. When I finally made my way downstairs to check on her I found her sitting on the floor, holding a bottle of Kahlua liqueur. She was spilling it out and was merrily licking it up off her fingers and her night-clothes. Somehow she had gotten the cap off and was enjoying her first indulgence in alcohol. Fortunately it was a small bottle and she didn't get a great deal of alcohol, but she was quite "happy" and wired-up for several hours and I was not able to get her back to bed until the effects of the alcohol had worn off later that morning. By then she didn't feel well at all, likely had a headache and was quite willing to lie down. She was experiencing a hangover and fortunately it was the weekend, so none of us had to go to school or to work. I would have had trouble explaining that one. There were consequences when we delayed getting up with Allison, so most often one of us made the effort to crawl out of bed to supervise her as soon as we heard her get up. We also made a few changes to "Allison proof" our house and any alcohol we had was put high up in a cupboard that she couldn't reach.

Our home had always been childproofed and we had to continue to be vigilant long after Allison was a young child. She would open cupboards and get into things. We had tried to teach her not to touch some things, ornaments for example, but we had not been completely successful. She learned what "no" or "don't touch" meant and would respond to these, but we had to be present in the room for this to have meaning for her. When we weren't around, to her the rules changed. I believed it wasn't because she was being difficult or obstinate, but she simply was unable to transfer or generalize her knowing not to touch things to other circumstances. This inability to generalize something learned in one situation to another is common in autism. To solve the problem and to make our lives easier, we simplified things by not having articles around within Allison's reach that she could not have or

things that were valuable or breakable. We may have been in error in our decision, but repeated scolding and attempts to help her understand did not seem to have any effect. She liked to carry things around with her, but once she tired of them, she would drop them, so there was a risk of these getting broken. Most of our home decorations were made of wood, were unbreakable and were things Allison could carry around on occasion. Once we let her have a new ornament or object for a few minutes, often that was enough and she would not touch it again. I had brought a particular wall plaque, a sailing ship, home from our trip to Portugal that Allison very much wanted to hold. I let her, but because it was ceramic and I knew it would break if she dropped it, I supervised her when she had it. This one she did not want to give up. I had to put it up high on a wall, out of her reach and she would lead us to it, asking to have it. We did not give in to her requests and she eventually learned that she could look at it, but could not have it. For a while she would take houseguests over to the wall and reach for it, hoping they would give it to her. As the years went by we were able to leave more and more of our possessions out, but for the most part it made sense to keep our home environment "Allison proofed."

Another ongoing issue was Allison's resistance to change and need for routines. We moved a few times over the years and I made an attempt to help ease our first move for Allison by decorating her new room with the same wall paper she had in her old one. This worked well and I was pleased with how easy this was, because she didn't seem to be affected at all by the move. However, I took her back to the old house the day I returned to clean it and prepare it for the new owners and she went wild. She became very upset, running from room to room looking for our possessions and the things that belonged there. She could not handle seeing her previous home empty and I had to remove her from the situation. I wasn't too disappointed that I had to have a cleaning lady do the final clean up; I didn't like the job much myself anyway. It taught me a lesson too. Allison was comfortable in the new environment once all our belongings and furniture were in place and our new home quickly became familiar to her. Of course she would check out all the rooms but surprisingly she was becoming more adaptable. Change is a fact of life and although difficult for Allison, it was something that she had to learn to cope with. The symbol system helped her at school and at home to deal with the change in events once she was able to

anticipate the next activity. She did not like it if we went into a building in a different door than usual, and would get upset, but sometimes we did this on purpose so she could accept that there was more than one entrance. Although we respected her need for routines, we also tried to vary her routine at times, again, so she could learn to be more flexible.

We always believed Allison understood much more than many people thought she did, so we were always careful in explaining things to her. Being non-verbal didn't necessarily mean that Allison didn't understand the words spoken by others. People often made the assumption that a person who cannot speak cannot understand and this was not true. We frequently reminded people of that, particularly if they started talking about Allison in her presence. I would stop them, remind them that Allison could hear and suggested that she be included in the conversation. Anything they had to say about Allison should be something they wanted her to hear. This was bought home to me one day when I was talking on the telephone to another mother of an autistic child. Someone had referred her to me and she had questions about one of the programs we had used with Allison. I was telling her of the problems we had when Allison was very young, when she would twirl for long periods of time, and was explaining how we had extinguished that behavior, years ago. Allison was in the background playing and I wasn't even aware that she might be listening. After I got off the phone she started to twirl. She laughed and did this a few times, telling me in her own way that she had heard and understood what I had said on the phone.

Allison continued to teach us and many other people valuable lessons and by the time she and Derek were scheduled to begin school in the Foothills Composite High School, we were ready to take on the challenges and lessons that this would bring. We had confidence in the school system and because Allison's junior high teacher, Joan Burke, had made the decision to move to the high school the same fall, we knew and trusted that Allison's transition would not be too difficult.

Chapter 9

Allison's First Year in High School

I was enjoying my position at Mount Royal College in Calgary as a nursing instructor. We were moving into a new phase in nursing education and many different initiatives were being planned and developed in the late eighties to change the nature of nursing education throughout the country. The three existing schools of nursing in Calgary were planning to combine resources, including faculty, and form one collaborative baccalaureate nursing degree program. Our program at Mount Royal College was a two-year diploma course and many of our faculty members were in the process of upgrading their educational credentials. I certainly agreed with the concept of nurses having a degree on entry to practice, so I decided to start working towards attaining a Master's degree and had been accepted into graduate school at the University of Calgary in 1988 and had started taking graduate courses in the Faculty of Education in the Teaching and Learning Program. I chose this faculty for several reasons, but most importantly I was interested in studying more about how people learn and methods of increasing teaching effectiveness. I started by taking courses in the evening, one each semester, and another course in the spring session. I had made a commitment to my family that I would not go to summer school. It was my intent to take courses for two years on a part-time basis and then apply for a sabbatical to finish my degree. It was difficult and demanding to attend night school, work full time and look after my family, but I was able to juggle all my responsibilities. By the summer of 1989 I had successfully completed three courses at university and was ready to attend one more year on a part time basis before I took my final year towards my Master's degree. Our family life was going smoothly, Allison and Derek were about to start attending high school and my timing in returning to university seemed appropriate.

Although we all enjoyed having a break from school and work over the summer, it did pose some problems for us. When Allison was at school her time and her program were structured and she was involved in many different activities throughout the day. Allison needed routines and structure, so we had to find things for her to do and ways to entertain her over the summer break. She was unable to initiate play or activities on her own, as is common in autism, and if we did not provide her with activities she would simply sit and do very little except watch television or listen to music. My challenge was to prevent Allison from doing that and keeping her occupied, so I continued to take her swimming on a regular basis. Having Quality gave Allison some responsibilities and taking Quality for walks was something we enjoyed doing together. Going on holidays gave us time together as a family and many interesting things to do and see. For the first ten days in July, 1989, we went camping in British Columbia. By then Gord's hockey camp had expanded to becoming a four week school in Ponoka, so Gord was away from mid-July until the third week in August. Therefore I was on my own with Derek and Alli a good part of the summer, although Derek joined his dad at hockey camp for a couple of weeks and Allison and I went to Ponoka to visit Gord, his family and my mother for a few days.

Over that summer of 1989, when Allison was seventeen, I was having increasing difficulties with her behaviors and she began to get more and more irritable. Her sleep disturbances were escalating and she was going on four or five hours of sleep a night, which was likely contributing to her irritability. She frequently made unhappy sounds, almost like crying but without any tears. She was restless and I had difficulty getting her to sit at the table for meals and she was becoming less compliant with many of her self-help skills. She kept pushing me away. I wondered if these problems were perhaps a sign of the troubles in adolescence that often happen in autism. Although Allison was seventeen, she had been delayed in all of her developmental stages and I thought some of the negative behaviors and her increasing non-compliance was just a phase of puberty.

One night in August when Gord and Derek were away, I woke up to a sudden loud noise at about two in the morning. For a few seconds I lie there in my bed half awake, wondering what had caused me to wake up. I listened and heard a banging sound but it went away after a minute or so. Generally I was not nervous about being at home alone with Allison, but I was feeling some anxiety that night. After the noises stopped I got up to check Allison and I found her lying on the floor in her room. She was very drowsy and seemed disoriented, so I assisted her back to bed, crawled in with her and she went back to sleep. As I lie there beside her I had a disturbing feeling that she had had a seizure. In the morning she seemed her usual self and I wondered if she had just

gotten up out of bed and had fallen. I couldn't explain the repeated banging or thumping sounds I heard and deep down I suspected it was from the part of her body banging against her bed during a convulsion and she did have some bruising on one leg. Because of my concern I called the nurse in Allison's neurologist's office. The last time Allison had been assessed by this doctor was when she was about four years old. She had had an EEG, or electroencephalogram, a test that assesses the electrical activity of the brain and the results of the test showed that she did have some abnormal electrical patterns coming from parts of her brain. In spite of this the doctor suggested we discontinue the Phenobarb she was on at the time and if she did not have further seizures, she would not have to be on further medications. She had been seizure free and we had not seen the neurologist since. In fact, Allison's health in general had improved considerably and she had been quite well for a number of years. After the mysterious incident during the night and my nagging feelings of concern, I needed to talk to someone about it. I knew Allison's neurologist's nurse personally and thought she might be able to help shed some light on the situation. I explained what I thought had happened and she told me that they didn't get concerned if a child had only one seizure. She suggested that I watch Alli carefully and if she had any seizures to call her and she would make an appointment for Allison to see the neurologist. I agreed to this although I was still worried about Allison and glad that Derek and Gord would be home in a few days.

A week after the first possible seizure Gord called me one morning just after we had gotten up because Allison was lying on the floor out in the hallway outside her room and was having another seizure. She was unconscious and her body was convulsing rhythmically. Her foot was banging against the door, so we moved her out of harm's way and I maintained her airway throughout the course of the convulsion. This lasted about a minute and then she became quiet and was semi-conscious. Then she got up, became very restless and agitated and paced around the house for close to an hour, after which she settled down and went to sleep. As soon as the seizure was over, I called the neurologist's office and talked to my nursing friend. An appointment was made for us to see the neurologist in a couple of days and she called me back a few minutes later with a prescription for Mogadon, a medication that was an anticonvulsant and a sedative. Allison was to be given 2.5 mil-

lograms of this medication at bedtime each night until we saw the doctor. The nurse had spoken to the doctor and Allison was to have another electroencephalogram just prior to seeing him. On the day of Allison's appointments, she was not very cooperative during the EEG. She resisted touch and did not like having someone put a series of electrodes on her head and she would not lie still for the tracing once they were on. I tried to help the technician and we did the best we could although in the end we had to allow Allison to sit up. In any event, the doctor was able to get a reading although it was not accurate because of her resistance. He confirmed that her EEG was abnormal and in all likelihood Allison had epilepsy with the risk of having further problems with seizures. The doctor was trying to be encouraging and he also said that some teenagers only have one or two seizures and we could hope that would be the case. She had been doing well up to this point in time and he suggested that Allison should continue taking the medication Mogadon at bedtime and we would wait and see what transpired.

Approximately twenty to twenty-five percent of children with autism develop epilepsy in adolescence and I should not have been surprised. Because she had a history of seizures as a small child, the risk for Allison to develop them again in puberty was even higher. I had worried about this possibility, but because it had not happened in her earlier teen years I had hoped that we were beyond the time that it might happen. Because it had occurred, although later than expected, I was distressed and knew I would have to once again deal with my fears and negative feelings about seizures, to say nothing about how it might affect Allison and her life.

The doctor expected that Allison had likely been having headaches earlier in the summer and possibly even subliminal seizures that were causing her sleep disturbances and irritability. Following the doctor's directions, over the next few weeks we increased the dosage of her Mogadon to five milligrams each evening at bedtime and soon she was sleeping better again and feeling much better. She became more compliant and we seemed to be getting her epilepsy under control, so my level of anxiety was slowly diminishing.

Derek, Allison and her dog Quality started school in the Foothills Composite High School about a week after Allison's second seizure and after the medication had been started. Allison was registered in the Senior Pre-Employment class with other disabled students and once

again we were blessed with the good fortune having Allison's teacher from Junior High, Joan, teaching this group of students. She had moved wanting to be more involved in teaching young people with disabilities during their transition from school to the work setting. Another woman had been hired to work directly with Allison. Over the summer I had talked to one of the lifeguards at the pool, Jan Smart, who was good with Allison and disabled people in general. I suggested that she apply for the position, as I would love to have her working with Allison. She decided it was time for a career change, applied for the position and was hired as Allison's classroom aid. Jan was an enthusiastic woman with lots of patience, high energy and she loved to be outdoors and walking. Allison, Quality and Jan would be together for the next two years. At the beginning of the school year I informed the teachers of Allison's epilepsy and the fact she was on medication. They knew the appropriate first aid and agreed to call me immediately if Allison had any seizures. Fortunately, the medication was working and her epilepsy was under control and Alli did not have any more seizures during her first year in high school, much to my relief.

Because I was working and the kids were not in the same school as their dad anymore, we had to make arrangements for Allison. The school was on the other side of town about two kilometers from our home and a school bus was available for students in our neighborhood. I arranged to have a neighbor girl ride the bus to and from school with Allison. I couldn't rely on Derek because he had made the high school football team and often had practices before and after school hours and besides, we had decided that we would not expect him to take his sister to school. We had moved into a new house earlier that year and our new neighbors had already become our friends and all of them, including their teenaged son and daughter, had taken an interest in Allison. They had a trampoline in their back yard and they invited Allison over to jump on it with them on many occasions, which she thoroughly enjoyed. One of them would bounce with her holding her hands and she would laugh and squeal with delight as she was hurled up into the air. She also loved to "hang out" with them in their basement and listen to their rock music. Allison had two new friends and the girl, Crystal, had already done some evening babysitting for us. After the episodes with the seizures, I had explained what to do in the event of one happening and Crystal seemed confident. She was not intimidated by the

possibility of a seizure and she agreed to accompany Allison and Quality to school on the bus.

In the High School, the focus for Allison shifted somewhat and the teachers began to look for things she could do both inside and outside of the school in preparation for her adult life. They continued working on those social and self-help skills that were so important. Joan was very creative in planning activities for each of her disabled students and she always took the strengths and likes of the student into consideration. Her goal was to find each one of them volunteer work in the community that could translate into future jobs once they left the school system. She knew Allison and Quality loved to be outside walking and she knew Allison had been successful in distributing messages to teachers in the junior high school and based on that she and her classroom aide, Jan, came up with a courier route for Allison. Okotoks had a post office where business people had to pick up their mail each day. Some of these businesses were small and had few staff and getting the mail might mean that their store or office had to be closed for a few minutes while someone went to the post office. Joan did a survey and found that many business people were interested in having a form of mail service. Allison would stop by the business each morning, pick up their mailbox key and anything they had to be mailed and go to the post office for them to retrieve their mail. In doing this she would be providing a service in the community and her needs were being met as well. Allison and her dog were already well accepted and known in Okotoks and the town had been very good about supporting those people with disabilities. The arrangements were finalized and Allison and Quality began their courier route assisted and accompanied by Jan, Allison's teaching aid, now job-coach.

A system was devised in which Allison wore a backpack and each business had a different color-coded envelope for their mail. Each morning beginning at about nine-thirty, Allison would walk into the store or business, pick up the key and items to be mailed, put them into the designated envelope and return the envelope to her backpack. At first she required prompting and assistance from Jan and the business people were asked to have one particular place for their key and outgoing mail. This helped accommodate Allison's need for structure and sameness and allowed her to always know where she could find these items. There was one main street in Okotoks at the time and Allison,

Quality and Jan would make their way to the post office starting at the opposite end of the street from it, stopping at the ten or twelve businesses that had requested this service along the way. Once they got to the post office, Jan assisted Allison in first taking out each envelope and placing the outgoing mail into the main mailbox. Then Allison would be prompted to take out the appropriate key, unlock the mailbox and extract the mail. Of course Jan had to identify and direct Allison to the correct box because she could not read the numbers. Allison needed hand-over-hand assistance in turning the key but soon learned to empty the boxes on her own. Alli then would place the mail in the appropriate envelope and return it to her backpack. Once all the mail had been retrieved and all the envelopes were back in the backpack, they were ready to deliver the mail. They followed a similar routine on the way back up the street. Sometimes if the owners of the businesses were right there and available, Allison would walk up to them, turn around and let them take their own envelope out and remove their key and mail. If not, she would remove the colored envelope from her pack, take the key and the mail out of the envelope and put it in the designated place. She then returned the envelopes in her pack, ready for the next day. Making their rounds on this courier route took most of the morning and Allison, Quality and Jan returned to the school to join the rest of her class for lunch.

In my estimation this was the perfect job for Allison and Quality. Not only were they helping small-staffed businesses but they were outside, walking and were visible working in the community. The people of this town got used to and expected to see Jan, Allison and her wonderful dog out on the street each morning delivering mail. The community was learning that even severely disabled people, if given the right support, were capable of contributing to society and being productive. Alli was developing many friends in Okotoks, some of them I didn't even know. They stopped for a juice break on the way back and met the regular customers having coffee each morning in a local restaurant along with the proprietors. The people Alli worked for looked forward to her coming to their establishment each morning and certainly appreciated what she did for them. It prevented them from having to lock up the shop and may have even prevented them from losing customers that might have come when they were away getting the mail. Not all were single-staffed places, but all of them no longer had the has-

sle of finding someone to leave to get the mail. A beauty salon was one such place, as was a grocery store that volunteered for this service mainly because they knew Allison well and were very good friends of ours. There was another benefit as well. It was a known fact that epileptics are less likely to have seizures when they are active and occupied and this might have had some preventative effects for Allison. She certainly was focused when she was on her courier route. The only time the courier route was cancelled was if there was a blizzard or the outside temperature dropped below minus twenty-five in the winter, because it was too cold for them to be walking outside. Otherwise they were prepared for all kinds of weather and rain or shine the business people in Okotoks could count on Allison and Quality to be there for them to pick up and deliver their mail.

Alli had other activities to occupy her afternoons. Jan believed in physical fitness and she taught Allison to ride an exercise bike that they had in the classroom and Alli put some kilometers on it most afternoons. Because Allison did not like getting her hair washed and cut in a beauty salon, they decided to help her learn to tolerate this by arranging for her to have her hair done in the school's Beauty Culture program once a week. One young schoolgirl was willing to work with Allison. She had a model, so to speak, and had Allison to practice on and learn the skills of hairdressing. This was a challenge, but they gradually worked up to the point where Allison enjoyed this experience. She had lovely, thick hair that was easy to work with, but Alli's behavior and resistance posed some problems. Jan went with Allison at first and helped the girl and together they solved problems as they arose. They started with simply brushing and combing Alli's hair. After she could tolerate sitting while this was being done, they convinced Allison that she could sit in the shampoo chair, put her head back and allow her hair to be washed. They even blow-dried and were eventually able to cut and style her hair. Sometimes the "do" was not one I would have chosen, but at least they didn't try to dye her hair purple. The girls, Allison and her student hairstylist, were developing a unique friendship and were having fun together and that was all that mattered.

Previous to this I had always washed Allison's hair in the bathtub and going for haircuts had always been problematic. She would not sit for very long and the hairdresser had to be fast. Alli also did not sit still and this created problems for the stylist having scissors in her hand.

Whether or not Allison got a nice haircut depended on her mood and willingness to cooperate and this was never predictable. Therefore, for the most part, I had cut Allison's hair myself at home. I could take my time, give her lots of breaks and did not have to have her sitting in a chair. I was not a skilled hair stylist by any means, but was able to give Allison an acceptable haircut. A hairdresser had shown me the basics of cutting hair when Allison was a young child. On occasion we had braved the beauty salon, but I was not always sure Allison would cooperate; nor could I be sure of the results. One time when Alli was about twelve, I even got up the nerve to give Allison a perm. This was hilarious, because I knew there was no way I could get her to sit still and tolerate me putting in those the necessary perm rollers and papers. I came up with a scheme and was ready for battle. I put Allison in the bathtub for the procedure. She loved her bath, would stay in the water for some time and besides, she could not get away on me. Once she caught on to the fact that this was more than her usual bath, Allison was not at all pleased and resisted me throughout the procedure, but once I got started I had to continue. Many times I had to reapply the curlers that she pulled out. I finally managed to complete the process and we survived this ordeal, but because of the hassle, that was the first and last perm I ever gave Allison. As a matter of fact, after Allison's experience in the high school Beauty Culture program, much to my relief I was off the hook for being responsible for cutting and styling her hair. The next year we were to discover and appreciate another benefit to the hairdressing venture when Alli had to have another EEG at Children's Hospital for her check-up with the neurologist. That time Allison was most cooperative in having the leads applied to her head and she even lay down when the tracing was being done. The doctor was able to obtain a much more accurate result from this test and I had the school to thank for that.

In the spring of Allison's first year in the high school we had an opportunity to do something different with Allison. My mom had an adult three-wheeled tricycle that she rode after she had a below-the-knee leg amputation, but because her health was failing, she was no longer able to ride it. She gave it to Allison and I was determined to find a way to allow her to ride this five-speed tricycle. Allison was already able to ride the stationary bike, so she knew the mechanics of pedaling. The teachers at school and I discussed different possibilities. We took the bike to the staff and students in the Industrial Arts program in the high school and asked for their assistance in designing some kind of device that would allow Allison to ride, but also allowed someone else to be in charge of steering and controlling the brakes. Allison's new bike underwent some creative modifications. They welded a long curved metal bar to the end of the handle bar on one side. This bar extended around the seat, far enough out so that it would not touch the person riding, and ended at the back of the trike, almost encircling the rider. The hand control for the brakes was re-attached to the rear handle bar, but the control for the gears was left where it was on the front because Allison could not manage these anyway. Allison would sit up on the seat of her bike holding the handlebars and pedalling. Foot guards were added to keep her feet in place and Allison had a helmet that she always wore for safety reasons. A second person would be behind her, holding this extended handle bar and had control of the actual steering and the brakes. This was one ingenious invention!

My mom had put a tall orange flag on the bike so people could see her coming and we left it there to serve the same purpose. We were quite the sight riding/running down the street. There was also a wire basket carrier on the back that was the perfect size for Quality, so we put a mat in it and this was to become the dog's passenger seat. Steering took some getting used to and we had to make a wide sweep in making turns. The person behind had somewhat limited vision and had to look around Allison to make sure they didn't run into things and to watch for traffic. This bike gave Allison the illusion of freedom and riding on her own, even though she actually had little control of the direction taken. She sat up front, pedaling and generating the forward motion and her co-pilot walked behind, providing the necessary steering and manning the brakes. Allison also had access to a bell up front and she would often gleefully ring it. We had to teach her to keep hanging on but even if she lifted her hands off the handle bar for a short period of time she was able to maintain her position.

Initially Allison would not pedal and we had to push her along and a third person provided hand-over-foot prompting. We were not going at breath-taking speeds at this point. Although Allison could pedal the stationary bike, she did not transfer this skill to her mobile bike and she needed help in applying what she knew in one situation to another. To her it was a different circumstance and she had to relearn the skill of

pedaling. For weeks she would move her feet back and forth, but one day her feet began going in the circular motion needed in pedaling and we were off. Gord, Derek and I all could maneuver this bike and it was a good thing we were quite fit, because once Allison got the knack of pedaling, she wanted to go fast. We could set the gear on a low speed and she could pedal quickly, but we did not have to run too fast. If we did happen to get going too quickly, we could apply some pressure to the brakes to slow us down. We had to go on the road, so we were careful in taking Allison out on her bike and kept to residential areas and avoided times when we expected an increase in traffic. People in cars could certainly see us and were able to pass when necessary, but we tended to distract the drivers because they had never seen anything quite like this before. We were quite a spectacle, flag flying, Allison sitting up front pedaling, me running behind and Quality peeking out from her seat in the basket. The three of us went into another Terry Fox Run with this bike and we also went in an Okotoks Sport's Day parade in 1992. We decorated Allison's bike and we followed a car that was representing Gord's hockey camp, that had been expanded to Okotoks.

Allison's first year of high school was coming to an end in June, 1990, and she was about to turn eighteen in July. We were delighted with the program at the high school and Allison's achievements over the year. Her courier route was a great success, she now had a bike and this gave us one more exciting thing to do with Allison and Quality. Her epilepsy seemed to be under control and we were looking forward to having a pleasant summer off. I had applied for a sabbatical in the spring and this had been granted, so I was looking forward to having a year away from teaching and was getting excited about attending university on a full time basis beginning in the fall. If all went as planned, I would have completed all my courses towards my Master's degree the following spring.

Chapter 10
The Return of Epilepsy

By late spring of 1990, when Allison was almost eighteen years old, she was doing very well and there was no evidence of further seizures. Her first year in high school had been a success and we were looking forward to our summer. Gord and I decided to fly to Las Vegas for three days in the first week of July after school was out for a little holiday. We hired a young woman that we knew to come and stay with Derek and Allison. Upon returning to our room on our last evening in Vegas, we had a message to call home and I was immediately anxious. There had been a problem with Allison. They had been at a family picnic and she had a seizure. Gord and I flew home the next morning after a very long night of worrying. When we got home Allison was still lethargic and I phoned her neurologist. He increased her Mogadon dosage up to 10 milligrams and for the next few days she was drowsy from the increased dosage of anticonvulsant, but had no further seizures. Gord and Derek had to go away to hockey camp in Ponoka in the middle of July. I was still anxious about Allison and not very happy about them leaving us alone for four weeks. However, Gord had a commitment and there was nothing I could do about it and I did have neighbors and friends I could call on if needed.

Our problems were just beginning. Allison had a seizure just a few days after Gord and Derek left, which was fifteen days after the last one. I was upstairs making the beds in the morning and suddenly I heard Quality running up the stairs and then a loud crash. I almost tripped over the dog as I ran down the stairs. I found Allison convulsing on the floor in the family room. She must have been on her feet when it came over her and she had fallen backwards. This was a generalized tonic-clonic, or grand mal seizure, and it lasted what I estimated to be about seventy seconds. Following the seizure Allison became very restless, began pacing and wandering all over the house, with Quality and me following closely behind. I believed that the little dog had sensed that something was wrong with Allison and she had been on her way upstairs earlier to find and alert me. She rarely left Allison's side following this seizure. Once Allison quit pacing she went to bed and slept for three hours. I called her neurologist as soon as I could and he increased

her Mogadon to 15 milligrams at bedtime in an attempt to prevent more seizures. I was upset about Alli having another seizure and he tried to be reassuring and believed that we would get a handle on this once we had Allison on the right dosage of the anticonvulsant.

Coincidentally, I received a phone call from Foothills Advocacy in Motion Society a couple of days after this second seizure asking if I would like to have some relief over the rest of the summer. Part of their mandate was to provide support to parents and family members of disabled children in our area. They were unaware of our recent problems with Alli, but the timing of this call was so fitting given my anxiety about being home alone with her. They had a young woman, Erin, who was available to provide me with some respite. Arrangements were made to have Erin come to our home three mornings a week. Erin arrived the next day to be oriented and I was pleased to note that she was only a couple of years older than Allison. Erin had a certain quiet air of confidence about her and I liked her right from the beginning. She loved dogs and was eager to learn Quality's commands so she could take Allison and her dog out for walks. She had experience with disabled people, was comfortable with Allison and quickly developed a rapport with her. When I told her that Allison had epilepsy and had two recent seizures, she was not at all intimidated and wanted to know more about epilepsy, Allison's seizures specifically and what she should do if one occurred.

In orientating Erin I explained the syndrome of autism and how it was manifested in Allison. We discussed the use of Canine Companions and Quality's role in Alli's life. I told Erin about Allison's seizures and tried to be very straightforward in my explanations. I wanted her to feel confident and at the same time to know exactly what to do during and after a seizure. Seizures are frightening to witness and having some understanding of the physiology and what should be done during a seizure helps dispel some of mystery. As a nursing instructor I taught neurology so I was certainly familiar with epilepsy and seizure management. I had cared for patients having seizures on several occasions, but it was very different when the person in convulsions was my daughter and it was much more difficult for me to be objective because of my emotional attachment to Allison. I had a dread and even fear of Allison's seizures, but I did not want to transfer this to Erin. Teaching Erin helped me to put things into perspective and telling her what to do rein-

forced my own competencies. In discussing Allison's seizures with Erin I included instructions about what she should do if Alli had a seizure in her presence. Throughout these teaching sessions and discussions Erin asked many questions and seemed to genuinely want to understand epilepsy, seizures and her responsibilities in the event that Allison had one. Because we were just getting to know Erin and I was not confident that we had Allison's seizures under control with her medications I would not be leaving her alone with Allison for a while anyway.

After the second seizure that summer I was very worried and did not let Allison out of my sight. We had moved into a new home earlier in the spring and it was a split-level with many stairs and that concerned me. She was in danger of injuring herself if she fell down the stairs during a seizure. We were in the den less than a week later and Allison had another seizure. She had been sitting on the floor and suddenly tried to stand up, but the seizure was already starting. It looked to me like Allison might have had an aura and was trying to stand up and get away from the sensation. Her eyes rolled back and off to the right, she arched back and fell to the floor. I timed this one to be more than eighty seconds and although this does not sound like a long time, when observing Allison having a seizure it seemed like an eternity. Once the seizure had stopped I was unable to reach her neurologist, so I called our family doctor and he came right over to our house. By the time he arrived, Allison was in her usual agitated state of pacing. The doctor assessed her and was concerned about the fact that she had three seizures in such a short period of time, so he stayed with us until we were able to put her to bed. The next morning he notified the neurologist and in consultation they decided that we needed to increase and split the dosage of her Mogadon to ten milligrams each morning and another ten milligrams at bedtime. They also prescribed a second anticonvulsant. I was concerned about the high drug dosages considering that Allison was not very big, but was reassured that it was obvious that she needed these drugs.

After the changes in her medications Allison was drowsy most of the time, which was expected until her body adapted to the increased dosages. In spite of that she did not sleep well at night and as a result she was often irritable and unhappy. It is important for people with epilepsy to keep active, because this seems to reduce the incidence of seizures, so Erin and I took Allison and Quality for walks and even tried

to take her for rides on her bike, but she had little interest in this activity, in fact she had little interest in doing anything. We even went swimming and I showed Erin the things we did to encourage Allison in the pool. In hindsight this was probably not the best activity for Allison given her recent seizures and we were fortunate that she did not have any problems at the pool. We read to Allison, played her favorite music and encouraged her to be involved in the care of her dog. She was not happy with anything we tried to do with her and obviously was not feeling well. It was important to carry on with our usual activities, although deep inside I had a nagging feeling of anxiety and feared further problems.

Sure enough, things were to get worse and six days after the third seizure Allison had another, the fourth one in less than a month. This time the dosage of Mogadon was increased further to 15 milligrams twice a day. I was exhausted and an emotional wreck and had been sleeping with Alli at night waiting for something to happen. I was angry, angry with everyone! Each evening I talked to Gord on the phone and I was angry with him for not coming home. I realized that he had his job to do and he couldn't do anything more than I was for Allison, but I just wanted him to be there. I was mad at his whole family for running the hockey school that was keeping Gord away from home. I was angry with the doctor for not being able to prevent these seizures. I was angry with God for allowing these seizures to happen and for not making them go away. The only people I was not angry with were Allison and Erin. Erin was like a breath of fresh air and I felt better when she was around. I felt badly for Allison and I just wanted to hold her and protect her from these horrible seizures. This was one time that she did not resist cuddling and she allowed me to hold her and rock her. She was too drowsy and ill to resist.

By the middle of August I was completely absorbed with my fears, anxiety and concern for Allison. I certainly was not thinking clearly, but I wanted to see Gord and Derek. I did not want to be alone with Allison another day, so I called the neurologist and asked him if I could safely take Allison to Ponoka for the weekend. Hockey camp was ending on Friday, the second week of August, and they had the traditional family slo-pitch tournament planned for the weekend. I was surprised when the doctor suggested that going away was a good idea. He seemed confident that the new drug combination and dosage was going to work

and thought that both Allison and I would benefit from a few days away. He gave me a telephone number where he could be reached on the weekend if problems arose

I really should have had my head examined, but just days after Allison's last seizure, we got in the car and drove to Ponoka, which was a three-hour drive. We arrived safely and met Gord at my mother's home, where we decided to stay. Gord had been staying with her during hockey camp because she lived in a seniors' condominium across the street from the arena. Although she only had two bedrooms, hers and Gord's, which had a single bed, I was prepared to sleep in the living room with Allison and Quality. Derek was staying with his cousins at the farm and although there was room for us, I wanted to stay in town and knew we could manage. Mom's place was also across the street from the ball diamonds, so the location was perfect for the weekend's events and tournament. My mom was a retired nurse and I felt relieved to be staying with her that weekend and I definitely needed her support. She was well aware of our recent problems and she had always been supportive of me and admired all the things we had been able to do for her granddaughter. In the past she had to come to terms with Allison's disability along with the rest of us and she now accepted and loved Allison dearly. Once we settled in I was no longer angry and I was relieved to be surrounded by my family.

The next morning we were to go to the first ball game, but I was concerned because Allison would not go to the bathroom and she had not voided since the night before at bedtime. I finally decided to take her to the game anyway, knowing we were only a few minutes away and could return after the game to try again. Allison seemed to enjoy going to the ball game, something she loved to do, and all her cousins, aunts and uncles were glad to see us. Gord's sister and her husband had brought their motor home to the ball diamond and the family had set up a gathering site around it. We had a lawn chairs, a picnic table and everyone had brought enough food to feed a crew of people. Gord's brothers and sister and their spouses were there along with all the nieces and nephews, so we totaled about twenty immediate family members along with a number of other friends and relatives who joined us for the festivities of the day.

After the first game I took Allison back to my mom's place because I was still concerned about her inability to void and she would not go

in a public washroom. She still would not go to the bathroom and I wondered if her drowsiness and the medications were contributing to the problem. We were sitting in mom's living room visiting and Allison suddenly was incontinent of urine, wetting her pants and soaking mom's couch. To my relief she did not have a seizure, although it was unusual for Allison to have such an accident. After I got things cleaned up Allison went to bed for a little nap. After she woke up she seemed fine, so Quality, Alli and I walked back to the ball diamond. The whole gang was there and Allison, Quality, Gord and I staked out a place on a blanket on the ground and visited with our relatives. Allison perked up and seemed happy to see everyone. Her cousins were even able to make her laugh and I relaxed a little, enjoying being outside and visiting with family and friends. I could not get her to eat anything. but this was not unusual because Allison often would not eat when we were out and in a crowd. Suddenly Allison's eyes rolled back, she arched back over her right shoulder and her whole body went rigid. I knew she was going into a seizure, called out to Gord and we lay her flat on the blanket. Fortunately we were right there and were able to protect her from injury. I held her head in my lap throughout the seizure and we both talked to her, assuring her we were right there with her. Many relatives tried to help, but Gord asked them to stand back to give us some space. Of course I was in tears. Once Allison's convulsing stopped and she was beginning to regain consciousness, she was incontinent of urine. The whole family witnessed this seizure and it frightened the cousins and some of the other children there. Thankfully Gord's sister, Marion, took them aside and tried to explain what had just happened to Allison. Derek was upset because although he knew about Allison's epilepsy, this was the first seizure he had witnessed. We tried to comfort him and at the same time try and decide what we should do. By this time it was late in the afternoon and we were reluctant to drive home to Okotoks, although that is exactly what we wanted to do. Allison was getting agitated and needed to walk, so Derek, Quality and I headed back to my mom's while Gord got the car. I knew I needed to call the doctor and we decided to wait until I had talked to him before making any decisions. Once we got to mom's and Gord joined us, I was able to contact the neurologist right away. He was alarmed too and instructed me to give Allison 15 milligrams Mogadon immediately and another dosage in five hours at bedtime. I was horrified at the dosage because that would mean she would receive 45 milligrams in twenty-four hours and

to me that was an overdose, but he warned me that in all likelihood she could have another seizure in a few hours so he wanted her to have this amount. He suggested that we stay in Ponoka that night because he did not want us on the highway with Allison in this condition and it would be safer in the morning after she had a couple more doses of the Mogadon. I was instructed to call him as soon as we got home or if Alli had another seizure.

In the meantime, Gord had talked to his brother and made arrangements for us to stay at their place where there was room for our whole family. The disadvantage was that Gord's family all lived in the country about twenty kilometers out of town, but we felt we had no other choice so we gathered up our belongings and headed to the farm. We had just turned into the driveway and Allison had another seizure in the car. This was the second one in just a few hours. We stopped long enough for the seizure to run its course and then drove directly to the hospital back in town. Once the doctor in Emergency heard our story he agreed to admit Allison for the night. While I was admitting Allison, Gord took Derek back to the family campsite and explained what had happened. Arrangements were made for Derek and Quality to stay there and Gord and his sister Marion returned to the hospital. I had difficulty convincing the doctor in Ponoka hospital to give Allison the dosage of Mogadon that had been recommended, and in fact had to ask him to call the neurologist, which he did. Once the doctors had discussed the situation he agreed to order the drug, although he was still reluctant to do so as he had never seen this amount given in such a short period of time. Allison slowly regained consciousness and after this seizure she went wild. This time she didn't pace, she ran. Well, she couldn't really run, but she was going at a fast clip. We went up and down the corridors of the hospital for more than two and a half hours. Fortunately she was not noisy, so I don't think we disturbed the other patients as we followed her back and forth down the halls, hoping that she would soon get tired. Gord, Marion and I were all there, so we could take turns going with her. The doctor and nurses were amazed and couldn't believe what they were seeing, especially after giving Allison enough Mogadon to knock out a very large man three times her weight. It was two o'clock in the morning before she finally settled down and went to sleep and then she only slept for four hours. In the morning she received another large dose of Mogadon and we made preparations to return home.

We had to work out a system for the drive to Okotoks because we had two cars in Ponoka to bring home. We decided to drive in tandem. Gord would take Allison, Quality and Derek with him in the lead car and I would follow. If Allison got into trouble, Gord would put on his signal light, pull over and stop on the shoulder where I could join them to help out. We were all extremely nervous as we set out, but Allison did not have a seizure for the three-hour trip home and we arrived safely. My hands shook on the steering wheel all the way and I followed closely behind Gord's car. I took some comfort in seeing Allison sitting next to Gord in the front seat and I could see her head bobbing to the music on the tape recorder. It was Sunday and once we were home I called the neurologist and was disappointed when he said that he was off duty the next day. He suggested that Allison had been seizure free for several hours now and the increased medication was preventing seizures, so he felt it was safe to wait until Tuesday morning to see her when we could bring her to his office. In hindsight, we should have taken Allison directly to the hospital once we reached Calgary, but once again I wasn't thinking clearly and didn't even think about it.

Our nightmare continued and the very next evening Allison had another major seizure. This time we called our family doctor and he immediately came to our home. After assessing Allison, he recognized that she was in serious trouble and recommended that we take her immediately to the Emergency Department in Children's Hospital in Calgary, the hospital where our neurologist had admitting privileges. He provided me with a syringe of Valium, a sedative and anticonvulsant used to abort seizures, and instructed me to give it to Allison intravenously en route if she had another seizure. We thought about calling an ambulance, but the doctor felt we must hurry and the ambulance would have to come from High River, twenty kilometers away, and we would lose valuable time. We all knew Allison's condition was critical; she needed immediate medical attention and time was of the essence. As we were leaving, our doctor told us that he would call the RCMP in Calgary to arrange for a police escort and sure enough a police car met us on the outskirts of Calgary to escort us to the hospital. I sat in the back seat holding my semiconscious daughter and we prayed that we would make it to the hospital in time. Normally this trip would have taken us forty-five minutes, but we made it in record time, thanks to our escort.

Gord and I carried Allison into the Emergency department and just as we got through the doors she had another seizure. Nurses and the doctor immediately surrounded us in emergency and they took over. Allison was carried into a room and the doctor administered intravenous Valium. One of the nurses was a former student of mine and I was relieved that someone I knew was assigned to care for Alli. Once the seizure stopped, I provided the doctor with Allison's history, explaining the events of the past few weeks. When I asked him to call our neurologist, he indicated that he was required to call the neurologist on call first. This neurologist did not come to see Allison and refused to call our own doctor, but sent a resident in neurology to assess Allison. I could not call our doctor myself because his number was unlisted and I did not have it and I felt so trapped by the system. The neuro resident came right away and after assessing Allison, he established that the diagnosis was status epilepticus. This is a serious complication of epilepsy in that there is prolonged seizure activity or a series of generalized seizures occurring without full recovery of consciousness between attacks. This constitutes a medical emergency and requires immediate treatment because the cumulative effects of the series of seizures put great metabolic demands on the brain. The repeated seizures also interfere with respiration, which compromises the brain further because of decreased oxygen supply. As a result the brain can swell and this can cause irreversible brain damage and can even be fatal. I certainly was aware of the risks of seizures in rapid succession and both Gord and I were numb with fear.

To make matters worse, after the resident talked to the neurologist on the phone he came back with more bad news and another issue to discuss with us. The neurologist not only didn't come himself to see Allison, but he wanted her to be transferred by ambulance to the Foothills Hospital across town. There she would be admitted to the neurology unit and be seen by a neurologist that cared for adults. Allison had turned eighteen a month earlier, on July 14, and because this was a children's hospital they could not admit her. The resident was actually upset with these plans too and was very supportive. He told us that although Allison could not be admitted to the hospital, no emergency department could refuse to treat a patient in crisis, no matter what kind of hospital it was or what age the patient was. By law they could treat the patient for up to twelve hours. He knew he could be in trouble for telling us this, but he recognized the seriousness of Allison's condition and he was willing to continue to care for her. He did not agree with the neurologist and was being a patient advocate, much to our relief, in spite of the repercussions he would have to face with this other doctor later. I told him that I would not consent to a transfer to another hospital at this hour and had no intention of changing physicians during this crisis. Allison's doctor was a pediatric neurologist and he did not have admitting privileges at Foothills. We all agreed that we would wait in Emergency until Allison's own neurologist arrived in the morning and in the mean time the resident would provide the necessary emergency care.

The nightmare and horror of status epilepticus was to continue throughout the night. Allison did not even wake up between seizures and the Valium was not effective in stopping them. The neuro resident and the nurse I knew were in constant attendance, giving Allison repeated doses of intravenous Valium. After three more seizures, he asked for our permission to administer intravenous Ativan. This drug is another anticonvulsant used in such seizures, but is considered dangerous for children as it can cause serious cardiac complications, including cardiac arrest. Hospital policy dictated that if it is given the child must be on a cardiac monitor and a doctor must be in attendance. We agreed, not having a great deal of choice, so Allison was moved into one of the surgical suites where she could be monitored and suction and other emergency equipment was available. The drug was administered and fortunately Allison did not have any cardiac complications. As a result of the effects of this medication the seizure activity gradually decreased and Allison fell into a deep sleep at about five in the morning. Actually she was in a coma due to the drug, but we were all watching her carefully and this was better than repeated, potentially harmful seizures. Her body twitched at times and her eyelids fluttered, indicating that abnormal electrical activity continued in her brain, but the convulsions were arrested. She even rocked herself, something she often did to comfort herself, and Gord and I wept silently as we sat at her side, holding her hand.

Just before eight in the morning I called Allison's neurologist's office and told his nurse that we were in Emergency with Allison and briefly explained the events of the past twelve hours. Upon hearing the details, she was most upset and assured me that she would send our doctor

down to Emergency just as soon as he arrived. The neurologist came roaring into Allison's room a few minutes later, his white coat flapping in the wind he was creating. He was an imposing figure with an aura of authority. He was a large man with a head of dark curly, unruly hair, and much of his face was covered with a beard and mustache. I could have sworn smoke was coming out his ears and his eyes were dark, flashing with anger. He was a leading specialist in the management of childhood epilepsy and seizures and we had a great deal of confidence in his abilities. Because we knew him we were not taken back by his appearance, although we had never seen him in this state before and needless to say we were quite relieved to see him. Once he assessed Allison and learned about our nightmarish experiences, he was not pleased with the situation and became increasingly irritated. The resident was still there with us and the neurologist asked him to step outside because he wanted to talk to him privately. It wasn't too private because they stood just outside the door and we couldn't help but hear almost every word. The resident explained his dealings with the neurologist on call that had refused to call our doctor and directed the resident to transfer Allison in the middle of the night. The resident told him that he had ignored that directive and in consultation with us, her parents, decided to keep Allison in Emergency until her neurologist arrived. Our doctor muttered some things we couldn't hear clearly, but he did not sound happy with what he was hearing. He grunted his approval about the decision to keep Allison in Emergency for the night. The resident went on to describe Allison's recurring seizures and stated that he finally had to give her the Ativan because "her mother was so upset." Our neurologist suddenly raised his voice and was almost yelling at this poor fellow. "What? Because her mother was so upset? Of course she was upset. Her daughter was in critical condition and she had every right to be upset. I should think you gave this medication to abort the obvious status epilepticus!" The conversation continued on for a few more minutes and then the doctor returned to talk to us further. First he apologized to us for the ordeal we had been through and said we had done the right thing in refusing to consent to this "ridiculous" transfer. He was obviously irritated and stated that "nobody transfers a patient of mine in the middle of a crisis and I don't care what the rules are in this institution. Your daughter has been a patient of mine for years and I should have been notified before anyone entertained any such idea of transfer, especially in the middle of the night." He had some rather vivid descriptors of the

neurologist on call and indicated that he would deal with his colleague later. Because of Allison's age he admitted that he would have to arrange for her care to be transferred, but this was certainly not the time. Once he had Allison's epilepsy under control he would make the appropriate arrangements to have her care transferred over and he would recommend a suitable neurologist who specialized in treating adults with epilepsy. In the meantime he said he was going directly to the Hospital Administrator and assured us that he would see that Allison was admitted to this hospital as soon as possible. "I will raise the roof off this place if I have to! Your daughter is handicapped for goodness sake; she is merely a child really. I don't care how old she is, she belongs right here in Children's Hospital." After this he checked Allison again and then turned on his heels and left, shaking his head, telling us he would be right back.

The neurologist was gone for about a half an hour and when he returned he calmly told us that he had everything under control. Allison was to be admitted as soon as the arrangements could be made. He told us he wanted to read her chart and review his records of the past few weeks, but he would be back shortly. Allison was still sleeping and was somewhat stable for the time being and the neuro resident was readily available. Our neurologist returned later to talk to us further. He told us that Allison was presently in status epilepticus and based on my descriptions of her seizures these past few weeks, he concluded that she had mixed seizures, or a combination of different types of seizures that were difficult to treat. We were all well aware of the fact that the medications she had been taking were not effective. The doctor was very blunt and direct when he told us that there were few drug choices left. He said, "I want to try a relatively new drug called Valproic Acid. It can either cure her or kill her. There have been some cases of fulminating liver failure and by the time it is diagnosed it is fatal." He spoke very quickly and I had to ask him to repeat his statements because I wasn't sure I understood what I had just heard him say, and I had a medical background. Gord missed most of the statement and was sitting there in a state of shock, hearing only that it could kill her. Not only were we exhausted, but now we were almost paralyzed with fear. The doctor realized that he was being rather harsh in his explanations, but he told us that he wanted to be sure that we understood the risks. He did soften his comments somewhat in explaining that the recorded deaths had

been in young children and it was considered much safer for adults. In his opinion there really was no other choice but to try this drug in spite of the risks and we had no option but to agree. After gaining our consent, he stated that he wanted to get this medication started as soon as possible because the Ativan would soon start wearing off and Allison was at risk of having further uncontrollable seizures. Then he told us that normally Valproic Acid is started with a low dosage and gradually increased to the optimal level over several weeks. This helps reduce the risk of liver complications, but in Allison's case he believed we had to start her on a high dosage right away because of the status epilepticus she was experiencing. We realized that we would have to take the added risk given Alli's present circumstances. Then we were told that for the next few months, Allison would have to have weekly blood tests done to assess for liver complications and to ensure her blood levels of Valproic Acid were in the optimal range. In passing he mentioned a couple of other side effects related to this medication. Most people on Valproic Acid gain weight, maybe up to fifty pounds in the first year. The drug not only slows the metabolism, but it stimulates the appetite control center making the person feel constantly hungry. Hair loss was another side effect, so we were told to expect that her hair would thin as well. Gord and I were almost beyond thought by this time and our main concern was to stop the seizures and nothing else he could say could surprise us at this point. We knew we could handle the side effects as they occurred and our only real concern at that moment was whether or not this drug would be effective in alleviating Allison's present seizures. We hoped it would also be effective in preventing more seizures in the future and we were anxious about the potential for liver failure.

Prior to initiating this drug he wanted to conduct a few tests to rule out the possibility of a brain tumor or other lesions that might be causing the seizures and he had ordered a CAT scan, an EEG and blood tests. Just as our conversation with the doctor was drawing to an end, the porter arrived to take Allison for these tests. Gord and I accompanied Allison when she went for the tests and because she was still only semi-conscious, they were completed without difficulty. Once the tests were completed Allison's room was ready and she was taken directly to the adolescent unit and admitted. Shortly after a nurse arrived with five jellybean-sized pills that she expected Allison to take. I had to ask her to crush them and mix them with some yogurt because Allison could not

handle swallowing pills at the best of times and I knew she would choke on them. We did manage to get Allison to take the crushed pills, but she vomited them all up in about twenty minutes, so the valproic acid had to be given rectally, which I administered. The absorption of drugs given rectally is not as reliable as orally, so the dosage was doubled to compensate for that. The doctor visited us several times and informed us that Allison did not have any tumors or lesions in her brain and that her EEG was abnormal, as expected.

For the rest of that day Allison remained in a state of semi-consciousness and barely responded when the nurses checked her vital signs or did their assessments. Her vital signs, blood pressure and pulse fluctuated throughout the day, but were gradually improving. They left the intravenous running to help maintain her fluid balance because she was unable to eat or drink. One of the nurses and I took her to the bathroom in a wheel chair and this was difficult because she could barely even sit up in the chair, but expecting Allison to use a bed pan was out of the question. By early evening Allison had not had any more seizures and she was stabilizing, so Gord went home to be with Derek. Although I was exhausted, having not slept for several nights, I was not about to leave Allison, so I stayed at her bedside throughout the night. She looked so small, thin, pale, weak and so very vulnerable. It was another long night, but I took comfort in the fact that she had no further seizure activity. I remained with her throughout her hospitalization, but after the second night I went to the parent's room to sleep for a few hours each night. If Allison woke up during the night, the nurses always came and got me, so Allison knew I was close by.

Allison's recovery was slow, but the new medication was working and it appeared as though her epilepsy was finally going to be controlled. She had lost a great deal of weight through this ordeal over the summer and weighed eighty-eight pounds, down from her usual weight of one hundred and five pounds. She wasn't able to walk on her own for a couple more days and for the first time in her life was content to lie in bed. She started to drink some fluids and began eating small amounts. We asked about bringing Quality into the hospital, but because there was a teenager in the same unit with asthma and an allergy to dogs she was not allowed in the room, but we were allowed to bring her to the waiting room and Allison could see her dog there once she was strong enough to walk. On the third day Erin and Gord

brought Quality in and I took Alli down to the waiting room for a visit. Quality had been moping around at home, missing Allison a great deal, no doubt, and she immediately perked up when she saw Allison. She jumped up on her lap immediately after Allison sat down and Allison sat there for a while, stroking her dog. They both were glad to be reunited. When it was time to return to her room, Allison automatically took Quality's leash in her hand and expected that Quality would remain with her. Both had long faces when they realized that this was only a visit.

Allison was in the hospital for six days and finally the doctor thought it was safe to take her home. So far her blood tests were normal and there were no signs of serious complications, but we realized that the dangerous period was not over yet. As time goes by the risk of liver failure diminishes, but we knew it would be several weeks before we could feel confident that Allison could tolerate this medication. Allison was happy to be home, back in her familiar surroundings with her dog, and she continued to improve and gain her strength back. She was very drowsy, as expected, because of the medication, but she was still not sleeping well at night. I called the neurologist and he realized that we had abruptly stopped the Mogadon when she was in the hospital. This drug is a sedative as well as an anticonvulsant and she likely needed to continue taking it. I was not at all happy with this information because I did not like this drug one bit. However, he ordered ten milligrams at bedtime and suggested that over the next couple of weeks I could gradually reduce the dosage to between 2.5 and 5 milligrams depending upon how she slept and I agreed to this plan.

A few days after we got home, I really needed to get away for a while, so I left Gord with Allison one afternoon. Although I was thankful the crisis was over, my energy was spent and I was still in a state of constant anxiety and stress. Sometimes when I felt this way it was important for me to have some time alone and Gord realized and appreciated that fact. I literally ran away from home for a few hours that afternoon. I went to the park and schoolyard down the street from our house. As I walked around the park, I became more and more angry and silently cried out to God. I had a multitude of questions and I asked them all. Why was this horrible thing happening to Allison? Hadn't she had enough? This was not fair and I did not understand the meaning of all this. If this was a test, I had had enough. I didn't need any more!

Didn't we have enough to deal with? What did he want from me anyway? What was I to learn from this? How much more did I have to learn? I was distraught and about to burst and suddenly I felt the need to run, so I ran around and around the track, running several laps. I ran until the tears started to flow and I collapsed on the grass and wept. Fortunately nobody was around to witness my outburst. After a while I stopped sobbing and regained some composure. A sense of calm and peace gradually overcame me and I became enveloped with a sense of serenity. I sat there in the silence for a while and the words, "and this too shall pass" came into my mind.

Once I had regained control of my emotions, I walked down the street, wanting to see my psychologist friend who lived nearby and fortunately he was home. This man had been a tremendous support to me in Allison's early years when I was first dealing with the fact that she was autistic and I knew I could always count on him to be there for me. We sat and talked a while and I explained our recent troubles with Allison and as usual, he seemed to know what to say and how to be supportive. He listened while I talked and his wife made us some tea. After our discussion I felt much better and was able to return home and once again resume my responsibilities as a mother and wife.

Upon my return home I told Gord a little about my afternoon and we talked about it for a while. I knew he was hurting too, but he dealt with his emotional pain in a way that was very different from mine. He didn't seem to need the same emotional release that I required, nor did he need to talk things out in the same way that I did. He was a strong, quiet, stoic man who kept his feelings to himself and dealt with issues and his emotions in a very private way. It bothered Gord when I became emotionally upset, so I had always tried to be strong and in control but sometimes I needed to let all my feelings out as I had done that afternoon. Our relationship was built on a sense of trust and respect for each other and our individual needs and we both honored each other's personal space. However, we had to be sure that we continued to communicate with each other and our lines of communication were kept open so we could be sensitive to each other's feelings and needs. I assured Gord that I was feeling better after escaping for the afternoon and I had renewed my abilities to cope. Having a good cry was very therapeutic for me, but I knew Gord worried about me when I was upset. I also tried to assure him that I would always be there for him and I under-

stood that he was concerned about Allison and upset too and told him that his emotional pain was my pain.

By this time it was near the end of August and school was about to start again. In consultation with Allison's doctor we decided that although Allison was still rather weak and drowsy, it would be best if she returned to school. If it turned out to be too much for her, we could keep her at home or just send her half days until she was better. I had talked to her teachers earlier and Jan, the teacher's aide who worked with Alli, had been to our house on several occasions to visit Allison and take her out for walks and she was prepared to begin school with Allison again. I was not working because I was on sabbatical and planned to attend university full time that fall. My classes were in the evenings and I was home during the day; if we had to keep Allison at home, I would be there for her.

The horror of Allison's frequent seizures was coming to an end and it looked like we were finally gaining control of her epilepsy with the new medication regime. We were not completely confident and relaxed, but we were taking one day at a time, holding on to hope for more stable times ahead.

Chapter 11
Allison's Last Year In High School

In September of 1990 Allison was still recovering from her ordeal with epilepsy, although she started school on schedule. Her teachers were aware of the circumstances and knew what to do if she had a seizure. Allison needed structure in her day and returning to school helped in many ways. The teachers did not push her to do new things and allowed her rest periods and free time throughout the day until she was fully recovered. Allison and Quality resumed the mail delivery for local businesses and her clients were very happy to have this service back.

Allison was beginning to gain weight and her appetite increased, as the doctor had warned us it would. In fact, she was ravenous and constantly looking for food. She would steal food off our plates at mealtime and almost immediately after finishing a meal, she wanted more. The anticonvulsant was stimulating the appetite control center in her brain, causing her to feel hungry all the time. Because of her serious weight loss over the summer we wanted her to put on some pounds, but Alli was obsessed with food. It got to the point that we had to tie the door of our refrigerator shut to keep her out because she was continually taking things out of it or taking one of us to the fridge for more food. Our cupboard doors were constantly open as Allison searched the shelves for snacks. It helped somewhat to keep her occupied, but every chance she got she looked for food. I started giving her frequent small meals to help quell her appetite and for the first time in her life, Allison would eat anything so we gave her snacks of raw vegetables and fruit and tried to ensure that what she ate was healthy.

She resorted to eating non-food items as well and she would go into the bathroom, take the end of the toilet paper roll and put this in her mouth to chew on. As she walked away the paper would unroll so we often found a long string of toilet tissue that stretched from the bathroom out into the other rooms of our house. We had to hide the toilet paper in drawers so she couldn't find it. Allison would eat paper of any kind, so we had to be vigilant in keeping the mail and pieces of paper out of sight. One day she ate a cheque for a rather substantial amount of money Gord had just received for his work at hockey school and I caught her just as she put it into her mouth. I couldn't salvage the cheque, so Gord had to have another one issued by his sister, who handled the finances for hockey camp. She stopped payment on the cheque, but of course this was not entirely necessary; once Allison digested it what remained was not likely to be cashable. I told someone that Allison really loved getting greeting cards and she not only enjoyed having them read to her, but she would digest them completely if she got them to her mouth and we didn't stop her from eating them. She tore pages from books, so we had to supervise her and put the books away after reading her stories. I had to remove my plants or put them out of Allison's reach because eating the leaves was a temptation she could not resist. Her voracious appetite was driving us all mad, but the medication was preventing seizures, so we could not really complain too much.

Another side effect of the medication was becoming evident as well. Allison had lovely, thick hair like her dad's and I noticed that each time I washed it there would be a handful of her hair left behind in the bathtub. I knew some hair loss was expected and when I was disturbed about the possibility of this becoming excessive, I just had to remember the horror of our summer and somehow it didn't seem to be such a big issue. I hoped that she wasn't going to become bald, but I could even accept that if need be.

Once Allison was back in school, they had similar problems with her taking food from her classmates at lunchtime, which was not appreciated by her peers. The teachers had to find ways to discourage her inappropriate behavior. I sent many snacks to give her between meals. It was best to keep her occupied because being busy diverted her attention away from this obsession with food. Jan was very much into fitness and exercise, so she found ways to help Alli wear off some of the excess calories she was consuming. Besides walking the four kilometers on the courier route each morning, Allison rode the stationary bike and they often went outside for another walk in the afternoon. We took Alli and Quality for walks in the evenings and on weekends and Allison and I usually went swimming a couple of times a week. In addition to keeping her away from food, all this exercise helped Alli to regain her strength and endurance and she enjoyed being on the move.

Allison's neurologist continued to monitor her epilepsy and medication regime until we were certain she was well controlled. The dosage of her medication was based on her body weight and the blood levels of

Valproic Acid, which we had to have checked frequently along with the liver function tests. After a few months, Allison seemed to stabilize and there was no evidence of liver complications, her blood levels remained in an optimal range, her weight gain leveled off and although her hair was thinning, she had not gone bald. By mid-November her care was transferred and Allison was assessed by a woman neurologist at Foothills Hospital in Calgary who was a leading physician in the management of epilepsy in adults. Although she conducted further diagnostic tests and repeated the EEG for her records, Allison's drug regimen remained the same with only minor adjustments. Allison had one more seizure shortly after seeing this new doctor, but it was short in duration and nothing like the ones she had in the summer. Alli had been up in the night and I had gone back to bed with her and during the night she arched back in her sleep and had some jerking movements in her legs lasting about thirty seconds but she did not even wake up. The level of Valproic Acid in her blood was low, so the situation was remedied with an increase in dosage. By November Allison's weight had gone from the eighty-eight pounds she was in August to one hundred eighteen, so she had gained thirty pounds. By Christmas her weight had stabilized at about one hundred and fifteen pounds. At five feet four inches she was certainly not overweight, but I didn't want her to get much heavier. Allison's arms and legs remained very thin; she carried most of her weight around her middle and it was beginning to be difficult to find clothes that fit her properly. I also had some concern about my ability to handle her if she got much bigger and although I didn't have to carry her, I did have to help her out of the bathtub and sometimes physically direct her.

In the late fall her school teachers were in the process of finding her another appropriate job to do in the community and they found one at the post office. One of the tasks the staff had to do was to put each letter through a cancellation machine to verify the date and that there was appropriate postage on the document before it could be sent on. It was a repetitive, rather boring job, but Allison liked repetition and the machine made noises, which Allison seemed to actually enjoy. We had an occupational therapist assess whether or not Alli could handle this responsibility and to make the task easier for Alli, she devised a sort of metal attachment that Allison could put each letter into first, which then guided it through the machine. This compensated for Allison's problems with fine motor skills, making this something she could do

without difficulty. Jan taught Alli to pick up each letter that needed to be cancelled from a pile, put it through this device that fed it through the machine and then Allison manually pulled the crank to complete the process. Each time she pulled the crank it made the noise she liked, which reinforced the activity for Allison. Often she would smile or even laugh as the letter was cancelled. The staff at the post office were willing to have Allison work there and appreciated her contributions, especially because she was performing a task they did not like doing and Allison was engaged in something she did enjoy. After a few weeks Jan also taught her to sort mail and put letters into individual boxes, so the repertoire of things she could do at the post office was expanding. Allison now had two jobs in the community, her courier route, which she did in the mornings, and the sorting and canceling of mail, which she did most afternoons. As it got close to Christmas the post office was very busy with the burden of the extra mail and Allison was asked if she could come and work for longer periods of time and more often to help with the cancellation of letters. This request was accommodated and her services were valued and appreciated.

Gord and I were involved in any decisions regarding Allison's program and were consulted before Allison and Quality took on a new venture and were always asked for our opinions and ideas. We agreed with the plan to have Alli in the new job at the post office. Allison could not do either of her jobs unsupervised, so Jan accompanied her and provided the necessary coaching and encouragement to keep Alli on task. Allison became increasingly independent and proficient with many components of her jobs and often only required gentle prompting and minimal help with those tasks that required fine motor skills and she had become accepting of hand-over-hand assistance.

In the winter of 1991, Allison's teacher Joan called Gord and I to the school for a meeting. We had always been involved the planning of Allison's programs, so we assumed it was a meeting to discuss Allison's progress and to perhaps discuss plans for new activities for her. However, Joan informed us at the meeting that the school board had just changed their policy and disabled students were to leave the school or "graduate" at the age of nineteen. We were shocked and disappointed, because up until that point in time it was our understanding that there would be a school program available to Allison until she was twenty-one years old. We had expected her to be in school another two and

a half years. We knew her school program would eventually come to an end, but we were not prepared for this to be happening so soon. Our lives were just beginning to be settled again now that Allison's epilepsy was being controlled and now we had another issue to deal with. We had to begin to make plans for her future, because she would be finished school in June of that year, just before she turned nineteen. The policy change affected all of the students in the Senior Pre-Employment Class and although some would have another year or two in the school system the teacher arranged to have people come from various agencies to speak to the parents and inform us about alternative programs and services for young adults with disabilities once they leave the school system. Fortunately we did have some time to explore different options and we were drawn to a Calgary-based agency called Progressive Alternatives. The mandate and mission of this agency was based on the belief that disabled persons could and should work and be actively involved in the community. That appealed to us and was consistent with our goals for Alli. Because we lived outside of Calgary, they were a little reluctant to take Allison's case, but decided that they could manage her program even though she would be working in Okotoks, her hometown. Allison qualified for individual funding, so we were going to be able to hire an individual to work directly with her as a job coach. We were given the opportunity to find a suitable person if we so chose, although they would help if we needed assistance.

The person who came to mind was Erin, the young woman who had been involved as a volunteer with Allison the previous summer, so I contacted her. She was delighted and accepted the position as Allison's job coach and we made arrangements for her to begin officially in July. She was willing to spend some time at the school in the spring and be oriented to Allison's school program. Allison was going to be able to maintain those jobs that she had been doing once she finished school and we were grateful for that. After all, the program was designed to aid in the transition from school into the community and it made sense that those jobs would continue to be available to Allison. Her jobs would not change except that starting in July her program would be run out of our home and would be monitored and managed by Progressive Alternatives. We believed that Allison's transition from being a student to becoming an adult working in the community would not be too difficult for her, given that there would not be major changes in the activ-

ities of her day. She would not be going to school and would likely miss the contact with her peers and the teachers, but her new job coach was someone she already knew and was very comfortable with.

Throughout Allison's last year in the public school system I was able to attend university and complete my master's degree. Given all the plans we had to make that year and Allison's health problems early in the fall of 1990 year, my timing for going to university couldn't have been better. I did not have to take time off work in late August because I was on sabbatical, although at the beginning of the fall semester at university I still felt rather fragile emotionally. I was not confident that I would be able to continue because of Allison's problems, but as the months went by I knew I would reach my goal. My schedule was such that Gord could be with Allison and Derek while I was at university, because my classes were in the evening. During the day the rest of my family was at school, so I had time to complete my assignments and readings and I enjoyed the luxury of having sufficient time to do all the work involved with out the added stress of having to work as well. It was much easier to meet the demands of academia and I appreciated the fact that I had been granted a professional leave from Mount Royal College. I chose to complete extra course work rather than write a thesis. I did have many major papers to write and presentations to deliver in class, but for the most part I enjoyed completing the assignments. It was also healthy for me to have a break from teaching nursing and I had more time for my family. I admit that up until my leave going to school had often been a burden but the circumstances were different this year. Because I had already completed several courses, my course load was quite manageable. My academic advisor and supervisor was a wonderful, supportive woman and I was allowed to do most of my projects and papers with a focus on nursing and nursing education, so most of the courses were meaningful to me in my personal and professional career.

By spring of 1991 I had successfully finished all the course work and was about to embark on my final project. Gord was still organizing international travel in the junior high school and that year a two week trip with stops at Tahiti, Sydney, Australia, and Auckland, New Zealand, was planned. Because Allison had stabilized and I felt somewhat confident that I could leave her once again, I was considering going on this educational trip with Gord and the twelve fourteen-year-ld students as a chaperone. I had to discuss this with my advisor and

request a delay in being assigned my final project and the written and oral exams and she was most accommodating in granting me an extension.

We had some concerns about leaving Allison, but were able to hire Erin to stay with her and Derek for the two weeks we would be away. By this time I knew Erin well and trusted her and she welcomed the opportunity to spend more time with Allison. Because we would be away for two weeks, she could go with Allison to school and become oriented to Allison's jobs during the first week we were away. The second week was over the Easter holidays, so she and Allison would be at home, giving them time together. Derek was seventeen and very responsible in regards to helping out with Allison; he and Erin had become friends and we believed that together they could manage. We also had some back-up contacts arranged if they had medical problems with Allison. Leaving her and going away was taking a risk, but because Allison had been seizure free for several months I believed she would be safe. Over the years I had learned that although it was tempting at times to put my life on hold and simply stay at home and protect Allison, it was wise for me to continue to pursue my personal interests in order to maintain my own health and well being. Finding a balance in life was critical and in so doing I was better equipped to handle the added responsibilities of caring for Allison. Gord and I both had a passion for travel and I had been given a wonderful opportunity in going on this trip. It was a worthwhile venture not only allowing me to get away for a while, but also to have some time with Gord and his students. I wondered if I was doing the right thing. As parents of a child with a disability, we have many dilemmas to deal with and getting away once in a while was a difficult thing to do and often caused some anxiety. However, I did not think we needed to feel guilty when we attended to our own needs and desires and sometimes indulged in activities that involved leaving our children behind. Taking breaks and occasional relief from our responsibilities at home was a healthy thing for us to do and often would inject more energy into our relationships as a family. I would not have even entertained the idea if Allison were not stable. Having Erin stay with Allison ensured that she would be well cared for by a competent person. Perhaps I was trying to justify my actions, but this exemplifies and underscores how even trying to get away once in a while creates tension for parents. Somehow we were conditioned to feel selfish and guilty when we engaged in anything that took us away from our parental responsibilities. As it turned out, Allison was fine, she and Erin brought their friendship to a deeper level and we had a wonderful time on the trip, so all was well in the final analysis.

Once we returned home, I resumed my studies at university and wrote my final paper. In May I completed the written tests as well and was successful in my oral exam and defending my paper, so was scheduled for convocation in the fall. Given the stress of the past year I was proud of my accomplishment and at the same time pleased to be finished with my university courses. I looked forward to returning to my position as a nursing instructor in August and being in the more comfortable role of the teacher, giving and marking assignments rather than writing them.

Near the end of Allison's last year in school we heard about a revolutionary new technique being used with non-verbal autistic persons as a means of assisting them to communicate using words. Jan, Allison's teacher's aide at the school, and I attended a three-day workshop in Edmonton that was being sponsored by two reputable associations related to autism. In the workshop the use of a technique, Facilitative Communication, referred to as FC, was introduced. In the eighties a teacher in Australia, Rosemary Crossley, had been using this method with children with cerebral palsy and other severe motor difficulties that made speech difficult if not impossible for them. She found that with physical assistance and prompting, these children were able to type words on a keyboard, making it possible for them to communicate. An American sociologist and professor of special education at Syracuse University, Dr. Douglas Biklen, had gone to Australia to observe this woman and her work. Upon his return he introduced FC to speech pathologists and special educators working with autistic students. These students had been thought to have severe cognitive impairments and were considered mentally retarded. With facilitative communication, they were typing words, phrases and some were even able to type complex sentences. Autistic students were typing and using words that were appropriate for their age, showing normal or even superior abilities, although it had been thought they were illiterate. The results had been remarkable and we were told that this would change the understanding of the syndrome of autism.

At this workshop we were given information that was contrary to

what we had known and believed about autism. Proponents of FC were saying that autistic persons were of normal intelligence and not retarded as previously believed. One of the main neurologic impairments in autism was being described as apraxia, or a motor disorder characterized by difficulties in initiating, maintaining or terminating actions. To me this was the same as perseverance, something I was already aware of. We were told that speaking was a highly complex motor skill and therefore was difficult if not impossible for autistic people. Using facilitative communication, the motor problems were compensated for by providing physical support. The inability to stop a behavior once it was started prevented them from typing independently because once they hit a letter on the keyboard, they tended to get "stuck" on the letter and hit the same key over and over. The facilitator in FC was apparently able to interrupt this perseverance.

Facilitative communication was described as a method for providing assistance in typing using a keyboard or a specially designed communicator, which was a small, portable keyboard that provided a read out in the form of ticker tape. Facilitating involved a manual prompting procedure with the intent of supporting the hand and finger of the person with autism. Anyone could be taught to facilitate and the participants at this conference were taught this technique. For example, if I were to facilitate for Allison, I would hold and support her right hand in mine with her thumb and fingers curled under and only her pointer finger was to be extended. This was to help her isolate this finger and I held it in an extended position. I was to actually pull back, away from the communicator, creating a slight tension to slow the pace of her pointing. Once she struck a letter, I pulled her hand back and this backwards resistance was exerted to overcome her impulsiveness and perseverance. As the facilitator I was in no way to guide Alli to any of the keys. The role was to provide physical and emotional support and encouragement, but not direction. The question arose as to whether or not the words typed could be in fact coming from the facilitator and not the autistic person. It was a possibility that this was a "ouigi board effect" and the facilitator was unconsciously selecting the letters but we were assured that if the facilitator did not guide the autistic person's finger to the letter and applied traction away from the keyboard, the autistic person was making the choices. This issue was to be raised by many professionals in the years to follow.

Jan and I were fascinated by what we were hearing, although we both found this whole concept hard to believe and accept. To our knowledge Allison could not read and had limited knowledge of the alphabet, much less how to spell. We were told not to underestimate autistic people. Through FC it had been discovered that most were able to read, even without formal teaching, and if we had read to our children and exposed them to books, we were to assume they could already read. If they had watched Sesame Street and educational-type shows on television, we could assume that they had learned a great deal, unknown to us. We had been reading to Alli for years and she watched children's programs regularly and loved them. She turned the pages of her books when we read to her and it was suggested at this conference that if this had been the case, the child was probably reading the words and likely at a much faster pace than the person reading out loud. Over and over we were told to expect competence and believe that our children were intelligent, could read and with facilitation could be taught to communicate with us.

As a parent I was hearing things I wanted to believe and if true, this was wonderful news to me. Although I was skeptical, I was also anxious to try this technique and was enthusiastic about the possibilities. There were varied emotional responses from the parents and teachers in attendance. We were all in a state of shock and feeling overwhelmed by all this new information that was challenging the traditional views and so much of what we had assumed for years about autism and our children. Emotions were high and some mothers were having difficulty with the feelings of guilt that surfaced. The source of the guilt came from knowing we had believed and accepted the fact that our children were mentally retarded and if that was not true, the children had been served a great injustice and were perhaps even damaged by the way they had been treated. How could we ever face our children? Guilt was something I had to temper many times and once again, although I felt some regret for Allison, as the feeling of guilt seeped into my awareness I dismissed it, giving it no value or place inside my repertoire of feelings. I would not surrender to guilt. I believed that I had always operated in good faith in regards to Allison, following my heart and doing the best I could for her with the knowledge and information I had at the time. Nothing could change or threaten my unconditional love and devotion to her and I believed she was secure in knowing that too. If indeed she was not mentally retarded, this would be a blessing. I believed that Allison had the innate ability to be non-judgmental and would be forgiving if we had treated her in any way that had not been appropriate.

Those people presenting the workshop had been using FC with autistic children for several months and they cited many examples of what they had learned from their clients through facilitation. They suggested that the non-compliance and learning difficulties seen in autism were not due to mental retardation, but to motor impairment along with an inability to articulate words. Autistic people had been labeled as resistive, stubborn and not wanting to learn, but their students were telling them otherwise. In many situations it was not a question of them not wanting to comply, it was because they couldn't. Not only did they say they wanted to learn, but these children had been expressing feelings and many had indicated that they did not want to be isolated and withdrawn. They were proving to be sensitive to and aware of their environment. Expressing loneliness and wanting to have friends was common. Some autistic children had asked their facilitators to help them stop inappropriate and stereotyped behaviors, stating that they could not stop themselves and did not enjoy doing them. Facilitative communication was apparently allowing these autistic children to have a voice and the information they had been communicating challenged traditional assumptions about autism.

At one point in the workshop, autism was described as an extreme form of obsessive-compulsive behavior. Many of the bizarre and stereotype behaviors were now believed to be examples of how the environment controlled these children, rather than them controlling the environment. An example cited was a five-year-old boy who would spend hours playing with blocks at kindergarten. He lined them up, built towers and constructed complex structures, seemingly content to do this for hours. It was the assumption that he enjoyed playing with the blocks, so they were always made available to him. When he started to use facilitative communication, one of the first statements he typed was, "I hate blocks!" We were told that when this little boy saw the blocks, he was compelled to build with them. The presence of the blocks was the environmental stimuli and the blocks were controlling him. Once they moved the blocks out of sight, he was able to join the children in his class in other activities.

I had already questioned and challenged many of the assumptions

made about autistic children. Although I had been told Allison was mentally challenged and severely retarded, I knew she understood more than she could show or tell. Her level of intelligence was impossible to test with any degree of accuracy. I had accepted the fact that she likely had severe learning problems, but had quit worrying about whether or not she was mentally retarded; it simply didn't matter. She might always need assistance with many things and that was entirely acceptable to me. Perseverance was an issue for Allison and she was resistant to change, preferring routines. In my mind many of her problems related to motor and perceptual difficulties, but in all my dreams I had not imagined that we would be able to teach her to "talk" using a keyboard. I found it hard to believe that all the problems of autism could be distilled to being the result of a motor disability alone and still believed it was more than just a disconnection between what the brain wanted and the muscles could do or respond to. This might have applied to children with cerebral palsy, but I believed autism was much more complex than just being a motor dysfunction.

In any event Jan and I left the workshop with a sense of optimism and we were both most anxious to try facilitating with Allison. The technique was non-invasive and it certainly would not hurt her to try it. In deciding whether or not to become involved in any new methods of treatment and management with Allison, I always took this into consideration. I was trying to keep an open mind about facilitative communication and put my skepticism on hold for a while. Erin had been staying with Allison while I was away with Jan and as soon as I got home I began telling her and Allison all about the workshop. I sat down with Allison and opened a book, held her hand in the position I had learned for facilitating, isolating her pointer finger, and asked her to point to the bird on a particular page. Much to my amazement, Allison did just that. I believed that I did not direct her and was in fact pulling away, putting some traction on her hand. She repeated this kind of response as I asked her to point to other objects in the book and she consistently gave the correct response. Erin was enthusiastic and she tried facilitating with Allison with the same positive results. Allison seemed to enjoy pointing out the various objects we asked her to. We were not using a keyboard and did not even attempt to facilitate typing words at this point. However, up until that time Alli had never pointed at anything and with facilitation she was now pointing. I sat beside

Allison and apologized for the fact that I might have been treating her like she was retarded and explained some of the things I learned at the workshop, although I had no way of knowing if she understood what I had just said. She sat with me a while and did not resist my cuddles or try to leave.

I had ordered a communicator that was small and portable when I was in Edmonton, but we had to wait a couple of weeks before it arrived. In the meantime I tried facilitating with Allison on my computer keyboard. She did not particularly like sitting up to the computer, but I was able to develop the skill of facilitating and she was able to type out letters and a few words. One day I asked what she wanted to be called, Alli or Allison and she typed "Alli," hesitated and finished the "son." I was thrilled that she was able to let me know her preference in what we called her. Once the facilitator arrived, Allison took it with her to school and Jan started working on facilitating as well. Allison did not suddenly start typing phrases and complex sentences, but she did learn to type some words and we used the letter "Y " for yes and the letter "N" for no. Allison could make choices and indicate preferences, giving her some control over things in her life. We would ask her a question, take her hand in support and facilitate as she typed her responses. She did not ever initiate using the communicator independently, but cooperated once we started facilitating. Facilitating Allison as she typed was a slow process, but she was responding well and we were all quite amazed at her progress. The ultimate goal of facilitating was to have the person eventually learn to type independently, but we had been told that most autistic people would require facilitation forever and only a very few were actually able to type without this assistance. That was of no consequence to us, we were happy that she had a means of communicating using words. After Allison finished school in June, we continued to use this technique. We hoped that with additional experience with this means of communicating, Allison's use of words and phrases would expand and become even more sophisticated.

In the same year that Allison finished high school, my mother, who was an elderly widow living alone, was no longer able to take care of herself because of multiple health problems and we had to move her to a nursing home. Our whole family would visit her and it was quite the experience to take Allison's dog Quality into this facility. Many of the residents were elderly and often when we entered the building, a group

of them would be lined up in their wheelchairs along the corridor. I often wondered about that and why it was so characteristic to see this done in institutions. It looked like they were sitting and waiting for a parade or chorus line to go by. They didn't seem to acknowledge each other; they just sat there, often staring into space. I was thankful that my mother was not like that – she remained bright mentally and could wheel herself around. In any event, once we came through the doors, these seemingly out-of-it people would perk up, begin talking to us and often would reach down to pet this little dog wearing a backpack. Quality had a way of capturing their attention and even our short visits seemed to bring the patrons great joy. Having a social dog in nursing homes would indeed be useful and during our visits we witnessed some very positive responses to Quality.

Allison's last year in the public school system was drawing to a close and in June she participated in the graduation ceremonies at the Foothills Composite High School, along with the rest of the students graduating that year. She sat up on the stage accompanied by Jan, her teacher's aide, and of course Quality, her Canine Companion, was also right there beside her. She had gone to school with many of the students in the graduating class since play school and kindergarten and most of them knew her well. When her name was called out and she walked across the stage, the whole class rose to their feet and Allison and Quality got a standing ovation. Those in the audience stood and clapped for her as well and this was a touching, emotional moment for Gord, Derek and I. Allison did her own little dance of joy and she too clapped her hands as she was handed her parchment. Of course she had not earned an official high school diploma, but was given a special diploma for her unique efforts at school and this was as meaningful to us as was my Master's degree.

Nineteen ninety-one was to be a year of completions for Allison and I. Our family was preparing for the transition into the next phase of our lives. I had successfully completed my degree and was prepared to begin teaching in our new nursing baccalaureate program. It was called CCNP, or Calgary Conjoint Nursing Program, and it was being launched as a joint venture by the three existing nursing programs in the city of Calgary. Although we were saddened by the fact that Allison's formal school years were coming to an end, Gord and I were appreciative of the Foothills School Division and the programs and facilities that

had been provided for our daughter. We realized how fortunate Allison was to have had such marvelous, creative and patient teachers and classroom aides throughout her school years. Her individual needs had always been taken into consideration and she was privileged to have the one-to-one instruction that was so valuable given her disabilities. It was hard to imagine what our lives would be like without the support of the public school system, but Allison was now an adult and it was time for her to move on. These were the times when we believed we were truly blessed to be living in a province and country where people with disabilities like Allison are valued, cared for and supported. The residents of the town of Okotoks were to be commended as well for embracing their differently-abled citizens like Allison. She was accepted by the people of this community and treated with respect and dignity and we knew there would always be a place for her as an adult in Okotoks and the surrounding communities. Our challenge and responsibility was to ensure that positive, caring people would continue to surround her and work with her. It was our desire and mission to ensure that her life as a disabled adult would be one that would not only be fulfilling for her personally and respectful of her unique needs, but that somehow in her own way she would be able to contribute to the community in which she lived.

Part III:
Allison's Life as an Adult

Chapter 12
Letting Go and
Finding a Place for Allison

As soon as school was out in June of 1991 Erin was on board and ready to start working with Allison as her new support person. Until then Allison had not had school or a program over the summer, so it was nice to have Erin to help out in providing structure to Allison's day. Erin was already well oriented and she and Allison resumed the courier route and Allison's job at the post office. These businesses were pleased that Allison was available over the summer and her services were not going to be interrupted. The transition from school to a home-based program was relatively easy and Allison and Erin were developing a close relationship. Although Erin, Allison and Quality were out much of the day, they used our home as their base, returning there for lunch and for breaks between activities.

Erin was already familiar with Facilitative Communication and she and Allison used the communicator regularly. Allison carried her communicator with her, as it had a case with a strap so she could carry it over her shoulder. They used it on breaks and Allison could indicate her preference for the kind of juice and snack she wanted. When they were in our home they had other practice sessions and I too used the com-

Erin, Allison and Quality in 1991.

municator in the evenings with Allison. Eventually Alli could type up to three words in response to a question, but she did not type unless we asked her something and her responses were always simple answers and she did not express complex or abstract concepts. This was a little disappointing after hearing of all the wonderful things other autistic people were able to type but I had learned a long time ago to be patient and Allison would do as much as she could.

For the first time since Allison was born, I had some time for myself during the summer because of Erin's presence and I reveled in my newfound freedom. I took up the sport of golf, something I had been interested in but had been reluctant to pursue until that summer. When Derek and Allison were younger I didn't think it was fair for me to golf on weekends, leaving them with sitters, because I worked during the week. In the past I needed to be home with Allison over the summer when we were all off, but the circumstances had changed this summer. My mother had been an avid golfer and she had encouraged me to play the game when I was in high school. People who do not golf wonder what the attraction is, but for me this sport was definitely challenging and actually a form of recreational therapy. I had enough trouble keeping track of my ball, trying to figure out what to do next or what club to use that I had no time to think about anything else, much less worry about anything. When I was golfing, I became totally absorbed in the moment and had the added benefit of being outdoors in the fresh air. It was good for my mind and my body. Golf provided me with some exercise because I chose to walk rather than take a cart. Golfing became an activity that Gord and I enjoyed playing together and he was my favorite partner, although I continued to play with friends after he left for hockey camp.

I returned to work in mid-August and that whole next year went well for all of us. In the spring of 1992, we transferred the management of Allison's program from Progressive Alternatives in Calgary to Foothills Advocacy In Motion (AIM) Society in High River. This was more appropriate because Okotoks was within the Foothills region, the geographical area they served. The philosophy of this association was also more appealing because they not only facilitated access to employment for persons with disabilities, but they had a broader basis of support. The clients and work partners were encouraged to take part in recreational and social activities during the day in addition to working and this more holistic mandate was in keeping with our values. The program provided Allison with a nice balance of work and recreation each day. Allison's program was funded by Social Services and AIM Society looked after the allocation of the funds, so I did not have to worry about that aspect. Allison was able to maintain her jobs in Okotoks, and she and Erin made visits to the AIM office in High River to attend various meetings and events.

In the spring of 1992 we heard about another new therapy for autistic persons called Auditory Integration Training. This treatment for autism had been recently introduced into the United States, although its origin was France. It was designed to normalize the hearing of autistic persons, who often are hypersensitive to sounds and noises in the environment, using a form of sound therapy. There were many reported benefits to this therapy, such as improved attention, language skills, sleep habits, and auditory processing abilities or ability to understand others. There was also a reported decrease in irritability and distraction caused by environmental sounds. There was a woman coming to Calgary from the United States who had received specialized training to conduct this therapy and Erin and I took Allison to the orientation and subsequently registered her for the ten-day program. On the first day Allison received a standard hearing test and I had some concerns about its accuracy and reliability. Allison wore earphones and was to listen to sounds being played. She was expected to tell us the precise moment when she heard the sounds, but given that Allison was nonverbal, we had to use the communicator and facilitative communication to gain that information. To me the possibility of errors in interpretation of the audiogram was high and we had no way of determining that. Allison's history of sound sensitivities and love of music were taken into consideration, along with the audiogram results, and she was selected as a candidate for the therapy.

Allison was scheduled for twenty half-hour sessions over the next ten-day period and each day she had two sessions with a few hours off between. Apparently the audiogram identified those sound frequencies that Allison was hypersensitive to and based on the results, music that had been computer modified to remove those frequencies was played for her as she listened using earphones. This was supposed to normalize her hearing and reduce her abnormal sensitivity to sounds. It was pleasurable for Allison and she was completely cooperative. As she listened intently, she rocked and swayed to the music, absorbed in the sounds she was hearing. I questioned the effectiveness of the therapy, wondering how this was to supposedly re-train her brain and normalize her hearing, but I tried to keep an open mind. The audiogram was repeated mid-way and at the end of the sessions and we were told that the results showed improvement in her hearing. It was suggested that we should see changes for the better in Allison over the next few weeks. We were also encouraged to schedule a repeat session in this Auditory Integration Retraining in about six months, but we did not do so at the time because I wanted to evaluate its effectiveness before committing to another session. Over the next few weeks we noticed some subtle changes in Alli's behavior, slight improvements in her sleep habits and she seemed somewhat less sensitive to sounds, but I was not convinced that this could be credited to the treatments. Once again, as a parent, I was faced with a dilemma as to whether or not this should be repeated. Over the next few months, Gord and I decided that although this treatment may have helped in some subtle ways, we were not prepared to pursue it further. It was always so hard to evaluate the effectiveness of treatments being used in autism and I simply had to go with my intuition, taking the risk of perhaps denying Allison something that might have helped and I had to live with knowing that. However, I had not seen enough scientific evidence proving its efficacy to satisfy my questioning mind. When all one has to go on is subtle indicators and behavioral changes, it is hard to discern the true effects, particularly when Allison was unable to tell us what she experienced. Even using the communicator did not help, because her responses changed from day to day when we asked her if this auditory training made a difference to her and she didn't even seem to know. We acknowledged that it may have made a difference and let it go at that, deciding that we had other important issues to deal with. Allison turned twenty in the summer of 1992 and we began to make plans for her future.

I believe that our children are not our possessions and we are not meant to hold on to them. In our culture children grow up and eventually leave home and this is part of the life cycle. As parents, our job is to teach our children, help shape the development of their values and beliefs, care for and protect them when they are young and prepare them for adult life. Once they become adults we must then send them on their way, with our blessings.

There was never any doubt that when our son grew up he would leave home. I cried on Derek's first day of school, at his graduation and on the day he left home to play hockey in British Columbia after he finished high school. My tears were an expression of my joy and sadness. I was proud of him and happy that he was well on his way to maturity and adulthood. At the same time I was sad that my son was growing up, leaving my nest. In his late teens his childhood was quickly slipping away and we had to step back and let him grow up and take on the challenges of adulthood. Of course, both Gord and I would always be available to him for support, encouragement and he would continue to ask for our opinions, but we had to let him make his own decisions, to take responsibility for his own adult life and we were happy to wait with anticipation to see what his future would bring.

It is very different when one is a parent of a disabled child. Even when I thought of the possibility of Allison leaving our home, my head was full of thoughts and questions. How could I ever let her go? Where would she go anyway? She needs me for her very existence. No one can take my place. Nobody can possibly love her as I do. Allison will be my little girl forever; she will always be a child, even if she is in an adult's body. At times I believed it was my destiny to look after her forever. But was it?

I tried to envision what our lives would be like when we were old. When we are eighty years old she will be fifty-three. As an old, old woman, would I be able to look after her? Maybe not. I may need to be looked after myself and where would that leave Allison? What happens when I die? In all likelihood she will outlive me, children usually do live longer than their parents unless there are extenuating circumstances. Persons with autism have a normal life span. How could she possibly cope with the loss of either Gord or I, or both? Would she die too? I was filled with anxiety about her future. I had seen situations in which parents tried to care for their disabled children well into their senior years and witnessed some of the results. The lives of both can become very narrow, very isolated. Marriages can fail because of the strain for the whole family. The person with the disability may be over-protected, become even more dependent. All parties involved often have limited contact with the outside world and their lives can become restricted. The aging parents may not have the energy to ensure that their adult child gets the kind of care and socialization that is needed. When the parents become very old or ill, unable to care for their "child" any longer, the individual they so very much wanted to help is left helpless. Many simply cannot survive the change, cannot adapt to the loss of their parents. I knew that this must not, would not happen to Allison. The time had come to make realistic plans for Allison's future. The day would come when we, or I, would no longer be able to look after all of Allison's needs and I had to find some way to prepare her for this.

We also had to consider our own needs as well. Over the years Gord and I had made sacrifices and had put our own lives on hold at times in order to provide the love and care Allison needed. We did this willingly and any sacrifices we made were out of our love and commitment to our daughter and neither of us had any regrets. Our relationship and love for one another has been enhanced and strengthened because of the presence of Allison and her brother, Derek, in our lives. Through sharing the responsibilities as well as the joys and sorrows of parenting, we had developed a very close connection, a special bond. Our relationship had weathered many storms, endured a great deal of stress, and had remained solid. Like most parents, we dared to dream of a time when we would be free to travel, to play golf, to hike, or do whatever we wanted to do together or even by ourselves if we so chose. Would there ever be a time when we would know that our children, including Allison, would be fine on their own? Should we be denied this experience because we have a child with a severe disability?

I had to wrestle with this question and once again deal with the many feelings that emerged. Was I being selfish? Have I done enough for her? What more was expected? What is right? What feels right? How could I possibly move on into this stage of life? In dealing with the dilemmas involved in planning our future, I had to consider the needs of each of us individually and as a family. Again, I did not go through this process alone; Gord certainly had input. We finally were in a place where we could find solutions that would be of benefit to each of us equally, Allison, Derek, Gord and I.

This was not the same "letting go" that parents normally face when their children grow up, but the principles are not so very different. Allison needed to have a place of her own and a life separate from ours. She needed to be exposed to as many opportunities as possible and we might not always be able to provide those for her. At the same time, she will always have my love and her dad's as long as we are alive. That will

not change. It was with great difficulty and sorrow that I realized that the very best way I could care for her was to not always "care" for her in the physical sense.

This was a difficult realization, to say the least. Gord and I discussed it often and began to make some plans. We started by making a commitment to her when she was in her early twenties, promising her that we would find her a home within the next few years. We explained all this to Allison one day, not really knowing how much she understood. We began to explore different possibilities and scenarios. We felt that we did not ever want her to be institutionalized, well maybe not ever, but certainly not now. Someday that may be the best choice, although I found that hard to believe. The idea of finding a group home for Alli was frightening. Allison was a beautiful young woman and so very vulnerable. If she were to be abused in any way, how would we know? She was unable to talk or tell us what was happening to her. I am not implying that people in group-homes are necessarily abused or taken advantage of, but in Allison's situation, the possibility did exist. Because Allison was nonverbal the idea of a group home was not one we were comfortable with, so we explored other possibilities. I visited a condominium that a small group of parents had purchased for their disabled adult children. It was a type of group home, but it was owned and operated by parents who had control over the hiring of staff, managing the funding, planning the activities and so on and this scenario seemed more acceptable to us. In talking to some of the parents, they shared some of the problems they had to deal with. For one thing, they didn't always agree on what was to be done and often had different goals for their children. There wasn't always equal participation on the part of the parents and there were other tensions as well, but over all the parents were satisfied with this arrangement.

Purchasing an apartment for Allison was an option we considered. This way we would eliminate the issues of trying to share the responsibilities and conflicts that might arise if we were involved with a group of parents. We could hire someone to look after Allison, to provide her with the care and support she required. We talked about our plans with Erin and she was most interested in the concept of an apartment for Allison and she wanted to be involved as her residential support partner. She and a friend had been planning a holiday and Erin asked for a leave of absence from September 1993 until Christmas, so we made

plans to find and purchase an apartment for Alison and Erin in January of 1994.

In the meantime, after I took up golf Gord and I dreamed of living on a golf course in our retirement, although this was a few years away. We started to explore this possibility and began the process of finding out if this was something we could afford and make happen. We looked at some existing golf course communities and found out that the homes were rather expensive. We decided if this was our dream, we should move a few years before we retired. We would have to have a mortgage and the intent was to have our home paid for by the time we retired. At that time our dream was to gradually make the transition to retirement by working full-time until we were fifty-five and then working part time for a few years until we were psychologically ready to retire completely. Our financial situation would impact all of this as well. Gord planned to continue with his hockey school as long as he was able to and there was a market for such summer programs. After visiting a few different golf course communities, we found a home and location that seemed to suit our needs and purchased a condominium in Priddis Greens. In the fall of 1993 we moved from Okotoks to this golf course community west of Calgary. Gord was still teaching school in Okotoks and I was teaching in Calgary, so we both would be commuting, but we looked forward to living in the country.

We had wonderful neighbors in Priddis Greens and one couple in particular, Syd and Em Miller, took a special interest in Allison. Em came to my door the third day we were there with a batch of freshly baked homemade buns as a gift, welcoming us to the neighborhood. They lived next door to us and although they were both in their mid-seventies, they were very young at heart. Not long after we moved in, I told them about Allison and they were very interested in hearing about her disability, but because they went south to Sun City West, a retirement community just north of Phoenix, Arizona, for the winter months, they didn't really get to know her until the following spring. Early in our marriage, before having children, Gord and I dared to dream of one day becoming "snow birds" like Syd and Em. This dream had been abandoned because of Allison's disability and we knew there was no way that we could leave her for long periods of time, regardless of her living arrangements.

Allison remained with us in our new home in Priddis for the fall.

The executive director at Foothills AIM Society was informed of our plans to move Alli and Erin into an apartment in January and because Erin was to change roles, we had to find and hire another woman to work with Allison during her day program. Keely was hired and she would continue helping Allison with her jobs in Okotoks, taking on the responsibilities Erin had had. Keely had to drive to Priddis to get Allison on the two mornings I had to go to work early, but otherwise Gord took Allison with him on his way to work and they met Keely in Okotoks. Gord was able to bring Allison home with him as well. This was rather confusing and we had to made alternate plans often, but we knew this was temporary.

In mid-December Erin returned and we found and purchased an apartment in Okotoks. After doing some painting and finding furniture for their new home, Allison and Erin moved in the first week of January 1994. We had an arrangement in which Erin was responsible for Allison's care before and after her day program and every other weekend Allison would come home to Priddis to be with us. We were finally going to have some weekends "off," which was something we highly valued. Derek had been doing well in hockey and had been in Cranbrook, British Columbia, playing junior hockey since graduating from high school. Gord, Allison and I traveled to B.C. to watch him play on many weekends. Foothills AIM Society was able to continue to monitor Allison's day program and we hired an independent broker to manage Allison's residential program. The provincial government also funded the new residential program, so this venture was not going to be a financial burden for us. After a few months we asked AIM Society to take on Allison's residential program as well, because it made more sense to have both her programs under the auspices of one society and it was less complicated. In February Keely resigned after finding a better job for her financially and this was a blow to us. Once again we had to find another support partner for Allison; Foothills AIM society came to the rescue and Stacey was hired. Erin and I were involved in the interview process to ensure the chemistry was right between Allison's work and residential support partners. Stacey was married and she and her husband lived in High River close to the Foothills AIM office. Although she didn't have a great deal of experience working with disabled people, she was enthusiastic and willing to learn. Having Erin as a resource was an advantage and she oriented Stacey to Allison and her program.

Allison now had two young women close to her own age in her life and it seemed like all three of them would get along well and we were pleased with the arrangement.

Syd and Em returned in the same spring after their winter in Arizona and they were eager to get to know Allison better. It was not long before they became comfortable with her and she was very welcome in their home. Syd would sit on the floor beside Alli, talk to her, sing to her and "play" with her. Often he would tease her, trying to take her chain away and she would pull it back and try to hide it from him. Syd was always able to make Allison smile. Allison grew to love both Syd and Em and would give them a hug if they asked for one. When they asked her for a kiss, Alli would lean forward and turn her head to the side, giving them her cheek to be kissed. They treasured Allison's displays of affection, knowing she did not like to be touched. One day Syd started to whistle and after several attempts Allison whistled back and I think it surprised her as much as it did the rest of us. She made the whistling sound when she inhaled, but nevertheless it was a whistle. Whistling became a game for Syd and Alli and once they got started, both of them would end up laughing. On another occasion Syd asked if he could take Allison for a ride in his electric golf cart. He had the Cadillac of golf carts, complete with windshield, roof and sides that he could bring down if it was cool outside. I crowded into the cart beside

Allison and her friend, Syd Miller.

Alli to hold on to her. She loved riding in this cart and laughed, sang and made all kinds of sounds of delight, loving the wind in her hair and the motion of the cart. After the first time, Syd started taking Allison out by himself and I was banned from this activity. Off they would go, both singing and laughing, and they would be gone for over a half hour, driving all around the Priddis Greens residential area. Once they came home Syd would tell us all about how much fun they had and he was thrilled that Allison liked to be with him. This became a weekend event for Allison. One day my doorbell rang and there was Old Syd, as we called him, standing on the front step. When I opened the door, he asked, "Can Allison come out to play? I have my golf cart all revved up ready to go." His question triggered tears of joy, because this was the first time anyone had come to our door asking to play with Allison. Syd and Allison had a unique, close friendship and I marveled at the fact that a man of his age would take such an interest in our daughter.

Both Syd and Em enjoyed Alli's dog Quality as well and she too was welcome in their home. Em was a marvelous cook, one of those old-fashioned cooks who made everything from scratch, and Quality loved to be with her in the kitchen because she could count on Em dropping her some tasty tidbits to eat. Em had to adjust to always having the dog under her feet in the kitchen, but they became fast friends. Gord and I appreciated Em's culinary skills too and without a doubt, Em made the best homemade cinnamon rolls I had ever tasted, and I was a connoisseur of cinnamon buns. We developed a very close friendship with them and they became like family to us. Syd was an excellent golfer and both Gord and I enjoyed playing golf with him, although we were not as skilled at the game as he was. Em often reminded us they were old enough to be our parents, but she and I developed a special friendship and became like sisters, able to share our most personal thoughts and beliefs. Knowing Allison loved suncatchers, Em bought Allison one with a beautiful little bluebird and colorful flowers. As well, Syd had a chain tucked away in a drawer in his den, to be sure Allison had one if she forgot hers at home when she visited. Not only did they make an effort to learn and understand as much as they could about autism, they accepted Allison completely, loving and appreciating her for who she was. They told their relatives and friends about their relationship with Allison, teaching them about her disability. Allison had a way of bringing sunshine into peoples lives and Syd and Em gave testimony to that.

She was about to experience many changes in her life and it was nice that she had these new friends in Priddis to visit when she was at home with us.

The next few years proved to be very stressful for all of us and there were many changes in Allison's life. In the spring of 1994, the new manager at the post office in Okotoks announced that Allison would no longer be allowed to work there because having her as a volunteer was contravening the labor laws and policies of the union. She was doing jobs someone else could be paid to do. They felt they could not hire her as paid staff on the grounds that Allison could not perform at the same level of competence and speed as the "normal" staff, nor could she do all the tasks required of a paid position. The other staff members at the post office were sorry to have to let Allison go and we felt sad that in this society, volunteering caused trouble with labor unions. There had not been an official complaint, but a new manager had been hired and she felt compelled to follow the official guidelines and believed she was avoiding possible conflicts with the union. The staff had a wonderful farewell party for Allison and gave her many parting gifts and we knew that Allison's contributions at the post office had been appreciated.

In the summer of 1994 Erin and I had some problems and she decided that it was not working as well as we had anticipated with her living with Allison in the apartment. She loved Allison, but for various reasons she wanted to end the living relationship that had been arranged for them. In hindsight I could appreciate Erin's concerns. Alli and Stacey were in and out and Gord and I often dropped in as well, sometimes without calling first. Erin really had very little privacyand she felt that I was interfering at times, which I condede I likely was. Perhaps it was a control issue for me. Up until that time I had been making most of the decisions regarding Allison and her care, and I had trouble relinquishing this to Erin. She was responsible for Allison in the evenings and every other weekend and that cut into her social life. It wasn't realistic to expect a young, single woman to be so tied down, and Allison required constant supervision. Erin had a boyfriend and although he accepted and appreciated Allison, I am sure it wasn't convenient having the responsibility of Allison as they were developing their relationship. In the final analysis, there were a number of factors involved and no doubt I was not being sensitive to Erin's needs. I felt badly that it wasn't wroking out for her. As a result, we were in the position of having to

find another residential support partner. Derek was engaged by this time and his fiancé, Angie, moved in with Allison for a few months while Derek was in Edmonton taking a course in preparation for a new job. In the meantime Stacey continued to work with Allison during the day and she and her husband decided they would like to provide residential support, but they did not want to move to Okotoks. We decided to sell the apartment, giving up this dream of Allison having her own home, and she moved to High River to live with Stacey and her husband. Once again we were in the position of having to hire another daytime support partner for Alli.

It seemed that every time we turned around we had to make major changes in Allison's program and this was causing a great deal of stress for all of us, particularly Allison. She was losing weight and had become very thin, but thankfully she did not have any more seizures. Her sleeping habits had become a problem again and at times she wet the bed and showed other signs of stress. I was almost prepared to abandon the whole idea of finding a home for Allison, but the staff at Foothills AIM Society were convinced we would be able to work things out and encouraged us to persist with our plans. We hired another day support person and thought things were going well until Stacey and her husband announced in June of 1995 that they were moving away from High River and would no longer be available as Allison's residential support. Meanwhile we had found a woman, Lori, to work with Allison during the day, and she and Allison were getting along well. Allison was living with us out in Priddis and Lori continued working as her support partner in her day program. In early August Vince, the executive director at Foothills AIM Society, called to say he had an application from a young woman who knew Allison and was interested in becoming her residential support partner. Before abandoning the residential program altogether, we decided to give it another try and we rented an apartment in Okotoks for Allison and hired Carmen. She was one of the girls who had taken Allison to school on the bus when they were in high school. She had volunteered in the classroom, knew what to do in the event of seizures and she and Allison knew each other. It seemed to be a good idea to continue with the residential program.

Derek had met Angie when he was playing junior hockey in British Columbia, they had become engaged and in the winter of 1995 were making plans for their upcoming wedding in August. Helping them

Derek and Angie's wedding, 1995.

plan their wedding was quite fun. Derek and Angie did something that was very moving and meaningful to both Gord and I. They asked Allison to be a bridesmaid at their wedding. Their thoughtfulness was overwhelming and we realized that they had made this request with absolute sincerity. Allison could not be a bridesmaid in the traditional sense, but Angie wanted her to have the same dress as the other attendants, to be in the wedding pictures and recognized as a member of the wedding party.

Derek and Angie asked my sister Shelly to play her flute at their wedding and at the rehearsal Shelley noticed that Allison was weeping silently. Shelley felt bad; she did not want to upset Allison. We talked about it and I suggested that Allison's crying was not necessarily a negative thing. Allison had been listening attentively to the sounds of the flute and didn't seem to be distressed or anxious, although her tears were flowing freely. Perhaps she was moved to tears with the beauty of the music or maybe hearing the music precipitated the release of some pent-up emotions for Allison. Allison was not able to express her emotions like the rest of us and maybe the music was allowing her to cry. We were guessing, trying to figure out what was happening for Allison, but because she couldn't tell us we were left with speculation, attempting to interpret her behavior. Although Shelley worried about the possibility that her music was upsetting Allison, she also appreciated the fact that often music moved people to tears, touching them with its beauty in a

very powerful, positive way. It wasn't long before Allison stopped crying and soon she was swaying happily in time with the music.

Allison did not cry the next day at the wedding, much to Shelley's relief, although I did. Angie and Derek's wedding was lovely and I felt a deep sense of pride in both my son and my daughter that day. Allison and her dog Quality came into the church with Gord and I and sat with us, but Allison was recognized as part of the wedding party. She wore a corsage that matched the bouquets of the other bridesmaids and looked beautiful in her bridesmaid's outfit. Angie was radiant, an absolutely stunning bride and we warmly welcomed her into our family. I knew in my heart that Derek and Angie would be very happy.

Allison was living in Okotoks with her new residential support partner, Carmen, but this did not work out for very long. Carmen resigned in October after she was offered a position as a stage manager for a theatre company in Calgary. Lori stepped in and offered to have Allison live with her and her husband in Blackie, a small town near High River. We had been pleased with the rapport Lori had with Allison, so agreed to move Alli to Blackie, but once again we were faced with finding another day support person for Allison. This time we hired Lorna, a nurse looking for a change in careers who had applied to work for Foothills AIM Society. She turned out to be a strong advocate for Allison and it looked like we finally had found a good match for Allison both in terms of her day and residential programs.

For the next several months Allison seemed happy and comfortable with her support partners. By this time much of Allison's day program had changed. Lorna drove Allison to Okotoks for the courier route for a while, but Allison seemed to be getting tired of this job after six years, so it was decided that they would find new jobs for her in High River. In the spring of 1996 Lorna moved into an administrative position at AIM and they were altering the structure and arrangements of the day program. We all recognized that Allison had been subjected to considerable stress because of the frequent changes in support partners and living arrangements. Most people that had been hired to work with Allison in her day program on a one-to-one basis with her became tired and "burned out" after a few months. Allison qualified for individual funding and the money was available to provide individual support, but the system itself was not necessarily the best arrangement for Allison. I could understand that because I knew it was difficult to be alone with

Allison or any non-verbal person for an eight-hour day. Allison needed and liked repetition and routine, but this did not appeal to everyone, so her partners easily became bored and needed more variety and association with more people. Each time one would leave, Allison had to adjust to a new partner and this was very taxing for her, given her need for stability. The restructuring was creative and solved many of Allison's problems. They developed a shared-pool-program, which meant that Allison would have one-to-one supervision throughout the day when this was required, but at other times she was integrated into a small group. For example, one of Allison's jobs was in recycling and she needed one-to-one direction when doing that task. Allison was in a group setting during lunchtime and when they were doing other activities, but someone was always responsible for her welfare. Some of the other clients did not need the same degree of supervision and one adult could manage having Allison join their group. At the same time, Allison was provided the opportunity to engage in social and other activities with her peers and she had much more contact with other people, which was good for her socially. Rather than hire one individual to work exclusively with Allison, the support staff went on a rotating schedule. Allison had three to five different people working with her during the week and each one had particular responsibilities. For example, one support person would do recycling with her three mornings a week and another would take over for the other two days. Someone else would take her swimming or to the fitness center and so on. This provided for a variety of people to be involved with Allison and at the same time provided consistency. Because Allison had several different people involved in her daily activities, if one resigned her whole world would not fall apart because she still had familiar people around her. This rotation provided the staff with a variety of clients to work with and it was healthy for them as well, preventing burn out. There was less staff turnover once this system was implemented. Another benefit was the re-allocation of funds, which made the whole society more efficient at no cost to the quality of the services they provided, and in fact, it enhanced their programs. Gord and I were pleased with the restructuring and agreed that Allison's needs were being met in a favorable way. Her life in her day program stabilized and she was much less stressed and happier.

The bubble burst in the fall of 1996 when Lori announced that she was pregnant and was going to have a baby in January. I was thrilled for

her and her husband, but had concerns about how she could handle the responsibilities of caring for Allison and a new baby. During her pregnancy Lori had hired a woman, Cheryl Holmes, who also lived in Blackie, to provide her with some relief in caring for Allison. Lori wanted to continue having Allison live with her and her family and believed that she and Cheryl could work out a suitable arrangement once the baby was born. By this time my anxiety was mounting in regards to Allison and what was best for her. I decided she had had enough changes and disruptions to deal with, so I informed Lori that Allison would not be staying with them after the baby was born. Lori was understandably disappointed but I had to keep Allison's best interests in the foreground. I was prepared to bring Allison home and re-think this whole residential support program. I also informed Cheryl and within a few days she called and indicated that she and her husband, Bill, had discussed the situation and they wanted to bring Allison into their home and their family. Cheryl and Bill, her husband, had two daughters, Jade who was eight and Keara who was almost three years old. Cheryl knew Allison well and already had developed a special relationship with her. She had worked at Foothills AIM Society herself as a support partner in the day program and was experienced in caring for persons with disabilities. Gord and I decided we would give this residential support idea one more try and consented to a three month trial period with the Holmes family. Plans were made to move Allison into their home in January, a couple of weeks before Lori's baby was due.

At one point between 1994 and '96, we had another issue emerge related to facilitative communication. Each new person working with Allison had to learn the technique and we were not all having the same results. One of the support partners in particular had experienced what she thought were amazing results with Allison, through facilitating. Allison began typing complex sentences, expressing all kinds of feelings, and I began to experience some anxiety about the authenticity of this. The young woman believed Allison was reading peoples' minds, and was communicating with a fetus to name a few of the bizarre things that were happening. No one else could duplicate this. The answers Allison typed to questions were not congruent either. I would ask her what her favorite television show was and she would type, "Muppets," and when this woman asked the same question, Allison typed, "Babar." To my knowledge Alli didn't like that show because she had not been interested in watching it at our home. There were many other examples of opposing answers and I began to question whose words were being typed, Allison's or those of the facilitator, including me. All of us believed we were not directing Allison in the process of facilitating, but perhaps we were subconsciously typing our thoughts and not Allison's at all.

I did some investigating and discovered that the validity of using facilitative communication in autism was under question. There was a great deal of controversy about the process and some experts were concerned about the lack of research and scientific evidence to support it, while others still believed it was a true representation of the autistic person's thoughts. Many were suspicious about whose "voice" was being heard and believed the "ouija" effect was occurring. I knew each person facilitating with Allison was convinced that Allison was expressing herself, but I was suspicious and realized that the facilitator could indeed be affecting the words being typed on an unconscious level. I felt like we were caught in the middle of all the controversy, but based on my observations and my concerns decided that we would limit the use of the communicator. We found other ways in which we could facilitate or assist Allison in communicating and making her needs known. She still used her symbols and we started to offer her choices. In selecting her clothes for the day, we would put out two or three outfits and have Alli pick the one she wanted to wear. We offered her choices in the kind of juice she wanted, what tape she wanted played and so on and she quickly learned to make personal choices using gestures. Because Allison was not at all upset when we reduced the use of the communicator, I had to believe she was not finding it useful and this supported my decision to abandon it. Here was yet another example of the dilemmas we as parents find ourselves faced with. It is hard to know what to believe, especially when the "experts" were in a raging storm of controversy and disagreement about something that directly affected our child. I believed I had made a wise decision based on my observations and growing concerns about the validity and authenticity of facilitative communication. By the time Allison moved in with the Holmes family, we had abandoned the communicator. Cheryl was comfortable with Allison's ability to communicate non-verbally and she was uncomfortable with the use of facilitative communication, so the communicator was put away. Although many autistic persons may have benefited from the use of facilitated communication, it just hadn't worked out the way we had hoped for Allison and I was not in any position to judge the usefulness of this technique for anyone except our daughter.

There was another unavoidable change for Allison. Quality was getting older and it was becoming harder and harder to keep her involved in Allison's program because she was not able to keep up with the active schedule. Canine Companions were normally "retired" when they reached this point, so with permission from the association in California, Quality was retired from active duty with Allison and moved home to be with Gord and I in the fall of 1996. Quality was thirteen years old, which is elderly in a dog's life, and needed to be relieved of all the walking and activity involved in being with Allison. Allison still had her dog on the weekends when she was home with us. The original arrangement of us having alternate weekends off had not been working well and as a consequence we had been bringing Allison at home on weekends for several months. Initially Allison missed Quality's companionship, but she had found that Quality had been slowing her down and this was frustrating for Allison. Quality's retirement was not a difficult transition for Allison after all and we were delighted to have Quality with us. She was not left alone for very long because our neighbors Syd and Em looked after her when Gord and I were at work. I had asked them to come over and take her out once during the day, but soon

Allison at 24 years old, with her new nephew, Justice, 1996.

I realized that they kept her at their house most days, not wanting her to be left alone.

Meanwhile Derek and Angie had moved to British Columbia and lived in a small town near Cranbrook. In early December of 1996 their first child was born, a son they named Justice Gordon. Gord and I were delighted to become grandparents. Gord, Allison, Quality and I went to Derek's to see the new babe when he was about a week old. I turned to mush as soon as I saw this darling baby and spent the whole day holding him, giving him to his mother only when he had to be fed. Allison paid little attention to her new nephew, but she liked all the toys that he had already acquired. She sat on the floor at my feet as I held Justice and occasionally stole a glance at him. When I finally gave him up and put him to bed in the evening, I sat down and was talking to Derek, raving about his new son. Allison abruptly stood up, walked over to me and sat down – right on my lap. She grabbed my head with her hand and pulled my face close to hers. We all laughed and realized that she had been patiently watching me cuddle the baby all day and now it was her turn for some attention from her mom and she made no bones about demanding it. She was jealous, of course, but we all admired her patience.

Our new grandson was a ray of sunshine in our lives and it was nice to be ending that year on a positive note. Our lives had been stressful for the first few years after Allison left the school system because of the constant changes in her residential and work programs. Gord and I experienced a constant undercurrent of anxiety, wondering what the next crisis would be, to say nothing about how this had affected Allison. She had experienced so many disruptions in her programs; many changes in her support partners and place of residence, her communicator had been abandoned and her dog had become too old for her to continue working. The only constants other than our presence in her life were her suncatchers and chains, and these had become very important to Allison. She clung to them and they continued to provide her with some security and somehow they helped her to endure the turmoil in her life. Our persistence and patience had been tested almost to the limit, but because we had such a positive feeling about the Holmes family we were optimistic that the residential support program might work out after all. We looked forward to Allison's next move with anticipation.

Chapter 13
Allison's New Home and My Healing Journey

We moved Allison into the Holmes residence in Blackie, Alberta, in the middle of January 1997 when Allison was twenty-four years old. She needed more stability in her life after all the unsettling experiences and frequent changes in her living and working arrangements. The Holmes family ended up providing her with that very thing. It was not long before they came to love and appreciate our daughter. Bill and Cheryl were in their early thirties and they had two daughters, Jade who was eight and Keara who was almost three. They also had a dog, Cruise, a toy poodle. Cheryl was a beautiful woman, inside and out. She was vivacious, had a great deal of energy and was very committed to her family and she was to become one of Allison's strongest advocates. Cheryl had been working at Foothills AIM Society as a consumer support person for another disabled client, but after becoming Allison's residential support partner she was able to stay at home. She really appreciated the opportunity not only to care for Allison, but also to be able to spend more time with her little girl Keara during the day. Cheryl and I were very much alike in many ways. Our children and family life were priorities and we were committed to creating a positive, supportive climate for our families. Our values and beliefs were congruent and I think this was of benefit to Allison because of the similarities in our home environments and she was equally comfortable in each home. Our families shared common interests as well, providing a certain consistency for Allison.

Allison seemed to adjust quite well to her new home-away-from-home. She soon discovered that Bill was very musical and he played the guitar, the piano and could sing, so he quickly became Alli's friend, especially when he serenaded her in the evenings. Bill was an elementary school teacher and had a wonderful way with children. He was not at all hesitant to make funny noises for Allison and he teased her often, causing her to laugh. Jade accepted Allison into her life as well and when someone asked her what was wrong with the girl living with them, she replied, "There is nothing WRONG with Allison, she's autis-

Cheryl and Bill Holmes with their dog Cruise,
Allison, and daughters Keara and Jade, 1997.

tic and doesn't talk, that's all." Keara was delighted to have another "older sister" and she would climb on Alli's back, sit on her lap and crawled all over her. It was interesting to watch Allison's response because she did not like to be touched, but for some reason she tolerated and even seemed to like all this physical contact with Keara. Allison always liked to sit on the floor, had done so for most of her life, and that made her fair game for Keara to crawl over. Keara was also quite interested in Allison's chain and because Allison did not share hers well, Cheryl got Keara one of her own. Keara was very motherly, was helpful in caring for Allison and liked to teach her things. Not long after Alli moved to their home, Keara came up to me, put her hands on her hips and told me that she had been working with Allison. She said that Alli was getting very good at going to the bathroom on her own, but she simply had to teach her to "wipe her bum and flush the toilet." The Holmes' dog, Cruise, was fascinated with Allison and if he wasn't lying on the floor beside her, he was watching her from across the room. At our home Allison had a small carpet on the floor in front of the fireplace, which was her favorite spot. She liked the warmth of the fire and enjoyed watching the flames dance. In every house we lived in we had a special fireplace screen installed for Allison's safety, so she could sit by the fire and we didn't have to worry about her burning herself. Alli also

preferred to sit on the floor in front of the television set if she was watching TV. Because of her height, she often obstructed the view for others, so we had our television positioned high up on a stand so everyone in the room could see it. In the Holmes residence Allison was provided with the same spot in front of the fire and eventually they too put their television up high. They made an effort to make Allison feel at home and wanted her to be comfortable living with them.

The Holmes' basement had a rumpus room that was set up as a playroom and filled with an abundance of toys. When Allison was down there she was in her glory, finding so many wonderful things to play with. She also discovered some real treasures. Allison's eyes lit up when she first spotted a bookshelf entirely filled with children's books, among them a complete set of Dr. Suess books that she recognized. Ever since her early childhood Alli had a preference for these stories, likely because of the cadence and rhythm of the words, and loved having them read to her. One time I had her with me in a bookstore and she took one of this author's books, *Green Eggs and Ham*, off a shelf and would not give it up, so I had to buy it for her in order to be able to leave the store. In the evenings the "girls" had story-time with Bill and Cheryl and frequently Allison commandeered Bill to read another of her favorites – *Fox In Socks*. This Seuss book is a real tongue twister, causing Alli to laugh uproariously when Bill stumbled over the rhymes and mixed-up words. Allison's adjustment to living in the Holmes' residence was facilitated by the love and kindness of each member of the family and the presence of such a wealth of special toys, books, videos, CDs and tapes to entertain her.

After a few weeks Cheryl and Bill offered to have Allison with them every other weekend and we appreciated this gesture very much. When we originally set up the residential program, the intent was for Allison to be at home with us on alternate weekends, giving Gord and I some time alone together. This had not worked out well for some of Alli's residential support partners, so more often than not she was with us on weekends. My position as a nursing instructor was becoming more demanding and I was putting in long hours at work as well as preparing lectures, marking papers and writing student evaluations at home in the evenings and often on weekends. I was coordinating a course and although I wasn't actually teaching more hours than in the past, our class sizes were much larger because of the amalgamation of the three former nursing programs. As well as teaching in the classroom, I had a group of eight students on two different units in the hospital two days a week. I enjoyed clinical teaching because of the contact with patients and a smaller number of students, but it was very demanding physically and mentally. On those clinical days I started with a pre-conference with students at six-thirty in the morning, so I had to get up at five o'clock in order to be there on time. Teaching and supervising nursing students was a demanding and high-energy job and I was beginning to feel my age. By the weekend I was very tired and although I really enjoyed having Allison at home, I felt like I had very little time off or to myself. If Allison did not sleep well, as was often the case, I was already sleep-deprived when I went back to work Monday morning. When Cheryl offered to have Allison alternate weekends I was very grateful and relieved, knowing that I needed more rest than I had been getting up until that time.

In planning our weekends we did not have a fixed schedule and both Cheryl and I were flexible, allowing for changes to accommodate special events or activities either family wanted to attend. One time Cheryl called to ask if they could have Allison on a weekend that she was scheduled to be with us. They were going to a family reunion and they wanted to take Allison in order to introduce her to members of their extended family who had not yet met her. It was a good feeling, knowing our daughter was being considered a valued member of their family.

During the week Cheryl was responsible for getting Allison up, bathed and ready for her day and we had arranged to have a driver take her back and forth from the AIM office in High River. As spring approached, the Holmes family decided that it would be more convenient for them if they lived in High River. There was talk of discontinuing the driving arrangements and Cheryl would have to start driving Alli each day. Along with her concern about the driving, Cheryl believed that High River would be a better place for Allison to live because there were more places for Alli to walk, more facilities and things for her to do. I was amazed that they were willing to move from their home for the sake of Allison, although Cheryl admitted that they were all quite happy with the idea of living in High River. This had been both Bill and Cheryl's hometown and many of their friends were living there. Bill's parents were there as well and they were looking forward to

having more contact with their grandchildren. Bill did not seem to mind the fact that he and Jade would be commuting to school each day. Cheryl was sensitive to Allison's needs and her difficulty adjusting to change, so they took her to see the new house a few times before they moved. Allison with us the weekend they actually moved, so when we took her back to High River and the new house, Allison's room was all organized and her possessions were in place, ready for her.

As the months went on Gord and I recognized that Allison's life was finally becoming stable and secure. We trusted the Holmes family completely and knew they cared a great deal about Allison. Bill and Cheryl often commented how she was contributing to their lives and those of their children. It wasn't the first time that someone had told us how much their children were learning from their association with Allison, lessons about tolerance, acceptance and the uniqueness and value of all human beings, disabled or otherwise. After a few months of living with the Holmes, Allison was happier and healthier than she had been for years.

Allison continued in her day program at Foothills AIM Society and the new arrangement with rotating support partners was working well and Alli enjoyed being with a variety of people throughout the week. Allison's jobs had changed over the years, but the staff at AIM always took Allison's strengths and likes into consideration in planning her activities. They started a program in High River, called AIM to Recycle, in which local residents could sign up for recycling service for a very reasonable fee. Recycling became one of Alli's jobs, something she could do which allowed her to be active and out in the community working with her peers. The customers were asked to put a bin with the material they wanted to recycle out on the step on the days they had the service. The people on Allison's "route" were asked to put their bins in the same place every day to accommodate Allison's need for sameness and make it easier for her. The bins were picked up and taken to the recycling depot, where the contents were sorted and put in the appropriate place. Allison understood her responsibilities and was supervised by her support partner. Eventually she required very little hands-on prompting and her job coach only had to direct her. On very cold days in the winter, when it was well below zero, Allison often would not get out of the car, she knew it was too cold. In that case, the support partner retrieved the bin and Allison did the sorting once they arrived at the depot, where it was warm. In addition to her job, daily walks and swimming were incorporated into her weekly schedule, so there was a balance between her work and recreation and she had a variety of things to do during the week.

I had debates about the issue of age-appropriateness with Allison's schoolteachers in the past and again with the staff at Foothills AIM Society. This was something that rehabilitation workers, teachers and care-providers promoted and rightly so. It was their goal to teach persons with disabilities the social skills, behaviors and activities that were appropriate for normal people of their age. All these things made people with disabilities less conspicuous, helping them to fit in better with the general population. This was in keeping with my beliefs and I had always supported this philosophy. However, there was one issue I had to address every time Allison moved into a new program and that was related to her chains, suncatchers and other toys. It could be argued that it was not appropriate for a young woman in her twenties to be carrying these things around, but as I pointed out, although chronologically Alli was the age of an adult, she was really ageless. Her disability precluded her from doing many things that normal adults could do, so if she was denied her pleasures, she really was left with very little to do. If having these toys brought her joy and comfort I did not want to take them away from her and I believed she had a right to making some choices in her life. Furthermore, when she had these symbols of security, she was much more compliant and able to handle change and the demands made of her. Of course she would not have access to these when she was working at her jobs, but I wanted her to have whatever she wanted during her free time. Adults engage in a variety of activities during breaks and many participate in behaviors that could be defined as self-stimulation when they smoke cigarettes, drink alcohol and the like. I was much happier having Allison flick her chain and look through her suncatchers than doing these so-called "adult" activities. After pointing this out, I was usually able to convince the staff that it was acceptable for Alli to have the freedom to choose to do whatever she wanted during her breaks. We provided Alli with the opportunity to engage in many age-appropriate activities and she participated in a variety of social and family events when she was with the Holmes family or us. Some of her time was structured, but she did have "down" time and then she was free to do as she wished. Cheryl was in complete agreement with my point of view and Allison had a toy box at each of her homes and toys, suncatchers and chains were available to her.

Allison had the habit of biting her hand when she was anxious or upset and although she had been doing this for many years, we had not tried to extinguish this negative behavior, although it was a form of self-mutilating behavior seen in autism. Because Allison was not able to communicate verbally, we realized that this hand biting was an indicator of her feelings and decided that it served as a sort of barometer, telling us she was feeling distressed and anxious. Cheryl appreciated that it was useful in knowing when something was upsetting Allison and understood our rationale for not trying to stop Allison from biting her hand.

Cheryl and Bill made an effort to involve Allison in many of their family activities. They took her to both Jade and Keara's soccer games, Jade's basketball games and even took her to a few professional baseball games in Calgary. Allison loved the action, the noise and being part of the crowd and she cheered along with the rest of them. She might be holding her toys, but she fit in with the rest of the noisy crowd of spectators. Allison also participated in the various programs planned for the disabled members of the community and Bill and Cheryl took turns taking her to these events. On Mondays Cheryl took her bowling and on Wednesdays Bill took her to the other sports activities planned. Allison had been bowling for years, but Cheryl took her to a whole new level. In the past we had been able to teach Allison to take the bowling ball up to the line, bend over, put it down and then push the ball forward. She didn't do this with great gusto and direction and if the ball managed to stay out of the gutter, it rolled ever-so-slowly down the lane. Sometimes the ball didn't even make it to the other end and if it did, it rarely had enough momentum to knock many of the pins down. Allison didn't even watch her ball because it moved so slowly. When Cheryl started bowling with Allison, her average score was about fifteen, which was not too impressive to anyone who knows anything about bowling. However, the score did not matter or mean anything to Allison and that was not the point. The important thing was that she was participating in a game with her peers. In consultation with the staff at the bowling alley, Cheryl came up with a creative idea. Because people in wheel chairs could not walk or bend over to deliver the ball, they had a ramp, which stood about four feet off the ground and looked like a small ski jump, and it allowed them to bowl. After aiming the ramp, one simply

had to place the ball on top of it, give it a gentle nudge and the ball rolled down the ramp, building up enough speed to get it to the other end. Cheryl tried this with Allison and sure enough it worked well for her. Allison began to take more interest in the sport and even watched her ball as it rolled down the ramp and out onto the lane. Cheryl taught Alli to go and get her own ball and bring it over to the ramp she had in place for her. After Alli had the use of the ramp, her scores went up dramatically and she occasionally scored over a hundred.

Aside from this, it was truly remarkable to witness the unique sportsmanship that people with disabilities had when they were bowling. If anyone had a good shot, got a spare or a strike, the whole bowling ally erupted and everyone cheered and clapped for that person. These disabled athletes loved to bowl, but were not particularly competitive in the sense "normal" people were. They loved to win, but that was not the focus. They were equally happy for anyone who did well, even if it meant they personally did not win the game. They honored each other and it didn't really matter who won. Bowling for them was not about winning or losing, it was about having fun, playing a game together. One day Alli's second ball knocked over three pins and she got a spare. When the cheering and clapping started, Allison didn't know what had happened. She turned, looked around and realized they were cheering for her, so she laughed, did her little dance on her tip-toes that she did when she was excited and reveled in her moment of fame. Nobody contested Allison's use of this ramp or thought that maybe Allison had an unfair advantage. It was simply something she needed and they accepted that without question.

In the winter and early spring of 1997 we had some losses to deal with. In February my mother died at the age of eighty-three. She had been living in a nursing home and although we were all saddened by her death, she had suffered many health problems in her last years. Even though it was a blessing, my mother was very special and I grieved her loss. In May we suffered another loss. One weekend Quality suddenly became very short of breath and after I assessed her lungs and heart with my stethoscope, I knew she was in heart failure. I called her vet and made an appointment to see him on Monday morning, knowing that in all likelihood it was time to put her down. Quality was almost fourteen years old and that was elderly for a small dog. Although she had slowed down in the past few months, she had been quite well and I was

relieved that she did not suffer for long. Allison was home for the weekend and we tried to explain to her that Quality was very sick and would likely die, so would not be there the next weekend when Alli came home. Allison held her dog gently for a while and seemed to understand the gravity of the situation although she did not show any obvious emotional response. I sat up all night with Quality, holding her and trying to comfort her. I called my immediate supervisor at work and told her I would be late on Monday because I had to take Quality to the vet, but little did I know it would be a couple of days before I could return to work. As I expected there was very little the vet could do for Quality and we agreed that it was time to be compassionate and euthanize her. The vet was very understanding and allowed me to hold Quality when he gave her the injection and suggested that I hold her head close to mine, so the last thing she saw was my face. After Quality was gone I requested that she be cremated and I left the building in tears. As I drove away I was overcome with emotion, and had to stop the car and weep for several minutes before I was able to drive home with any degree of safety. When Gord came home from work that afternoon, we went for a walk in the country and both of us mourned the loss of this very special canine companion. Losing Quality was not unlike losing a child and the grief we felt was profound. Allison actually handled it better than we expected. We knew Alison missed her special friend, but she did not feel abandoned because she had already adjusted to not having Quality with her during the week. Later that spring Gord, Allison and I went for a walk in the woods and scattered Quality's ashes together. We wanted Allison to be part of this ritual, so explained what we were doing and she was very quiet and seemed to sense something of what this meant. We considered getting another special dog for Allison, but because of all the training involved decided against it, partly because the Holmes had a dog. Allison had Quality at a time when this was very meaningful for her and Quality had been a wonderful addition to Allison's life. This little animal taught all of us about the true nature of unconditional love.

That same spring we came to the conclusion that it would be best if we sold our house in Priddis and moved back to Okotoks. This was particularly difficult for me because I loved living in the country and believed we would stay there well into our retirement. However, the location was not convenient, we were both commuting and Allison

lived a long way away. After making the decision things happened very quickly. Our house was sold less than twenty-four hours later and I conceded that this must be meant to be. We were able to negotiate a delay in the possession date until September, allowing us another summer at Priddis to enjoy the golf season as well as time to find a new home without a great deal of pressure. We finally decided to build a house in a new condominium complex being planned at Heritage Point. This was a golf course community just south of Calgary on the way to Okotoks and the location was perfect for us because Allison and the Holmes family were only twenty minutes away. Building of the villas was to start over the summer and we thought we would be able to move into our new home by the end of October. Things got complicated and did not work out as expected. We had to move out of our Priddis home on the first of September; we lived with friends on an acreage for a few weeks and then moved back to Priddis. Syd and Em were most gracious in offering their home to us and we ended up living in their house over the winter while they were in Arizona because the completion of our house was delayed several times.

That summer before we moved, Cheryl and Bill had a joint birthday party for Jade and Alli. Their birthdays were on the same day in July and it was Jade's ninth and Allison's twenty-fifth. This was Allison's first official birthday party to which people other than her immediate family were invited and many of the Holmes' friends and relatives attended this celebration. Gord and I were touched and very impressed when we found out that the guests had brought gifts not only for Jade, but for Allison too. The two girls sat on the floor opening their presents together and Jade was delightful. She read each of Allison's cards aloud to her and then helped her open each present, patiently waiting her turn to open one of her own. Each gift Allison received had been carefully selected for her and she received such things as CDs of her favorite music, several suncatchers, a music box and toys of the sort that she loved. Obviously these people knew Allison and what she liked. After dinner we had a birthday cake which had nine candles for Jade and a special candle with the number "25" for Allison and everyone sang Happy Birthday. Allison smiled and after we finished singing, to everyone's surprise and delight, she sang her own rendition of Happy Birthday by singing the first line of this song, clearly articulating the words and clapping her hands. Not only did Cheryl and Bill have this

birthday party, but they also took Allison on a week's holiday camping with them in August. Allison had been completely assimilated into the Holmes family and we were so thankful that they had come into our lives.

In September of that year, about eight months after Allison had moved in with the Holmes, she had a short seizure. It happened when Allison was in the bathroom one morning with Cheryl and Jade. I had explained epilepsy and Cheryl was well aware of what she should do in the event of seizures. Bill's mom, a nurse, lived only blocks away and she came over immediately and was supportive and helpful to Cheryl. It was of comfort to me knowing they had capable help nearby if Allison got into trouble – in any way, not just if she had a seizure. As it turned out the blood level of Alli's anticonvulsant was too low and she was seizure free again after we increased the dosage of her medication. Because Jade had witnessed this frightening experience, Cheryl asked me to talk to her about it, which I did later on that day. She wanted to know what she should do if Allison had another seizure and she was the first one to find her, so I explained as best I could, telling her that she should call for help and if she could, she should to try and move anything out of the way so Allison would not hurt herself. Jade seemed able to understand my explanation of Allison's seizure activity and I made sure I answered all her questions. Both Cheryl and I were thankful that Keara had not witnessed the seizure.

Our lives were in a state of chaos for several months and Gord and I felt we needed a special break at Christmas, so we planned a trip to California and booked a time-share in Palm Springs for a week. This time we took Allison, wanting her to have a holiday with us. It had been a few years since we had taken her to Disneyland and Sea World and we knew she loved these destinations. We had a wonderful time except that I had a fall. Early one morning I went out to buy the morning paper. Suddenly I slipped and fell backwards on the cement pool deck, hitting my back, neck and head. I saw stars and was unconscious momentarily. When I woke up I found myself lying on my back, my glasses had flown across the deck and I had a goose egg on the back of my head. Apparently there had been frost that morning, which was unusual for southern California, and one of the maintenance men had hosed down the deck, causing a thin film of ice to form which was not readily visible. He had tried to block off the area with chaise lounges, but I had not

noticed this in my rush to get the newspaper. I lay on the deck for a few moments until I could see straight and had just gotten into a sitting position when Gord arrived, looking for me. He couldn't figure out what was taking me so long. After he helped me back to our suite, I checked my own neurological status as best I could and my pupils were fine, so I wasn't too worried. I had a terrible headache and was dizzy and nauseated and this lasted for a few days. In hindsight, I probably should have gone to see a doctor, but I believed I could look after myself. Although I was a little shaky I did not let this spoil our holiday. On our way home we drove to Sun City West in Arizona and spent a couple of days with our friends Syd and Em. Allison was delighted to have the opportunity to ride in the golf cart again with her friend Syd. They had a neighbor who had been a commercial artist and although she was eighty years old, she still painted beautifully. I had sent a photo of Quality to Em and the artist had painted a portrait of the little dog from the photo; this picture was waiting for us when we arrived. This same artist painted a portrait of Allison a year later and these paintings still grace our home.

In March of 1998 I experienced a serious neurological illness that came on suddenly early one Sunday morning. I woke up and my right arm and hand were numb and within a few minutes the whole right side of my body was tingling and numb and I was finding it difficult to talk. I woke Gord up and managed to tell him I thought I was having a stroke and that he had to take me to Foothills Hospital immediately. Because I taught neurological nursing, I was familiar with the early intervention program for stroke victims and this was available only at Foothills to my knowledge. I knew that there was a clot-busting drug that could abort a stroke, preventing damage to the brain, but there was a very narrow window of time in which this had to be given after the onset of symptoms. Because we had Allison home with us, Gord ran to the neighbors for assistance. Our neighbor drove Gord and me to the hospital in Calgary and his wife looked after Allison until Bill and Cheryl were notified and came and got her. By the time we got to the hospital I was almost paralyzed on my right side, unable to speak and drifting in and out of consciousness. I had diarrhea, developed a severe pounding headache, nausea and vomiting, could not tolerate light (photophobia) and was overly sensitive to noise. A CAT scan was done immediately and it did not appear that I had a blood clot in my brain,

so the use of this medication was not warranted. After several hours in emergency, I was admitted to the critical care area of the neurological unit where I could be monitored. Gord called my sister and my brother Brian, a neuro-ophthalmologist practicing at the Mayo Clinic in Rochester, Minnesota, and he was in frequent contact with my neurologist over the next few days. Gord also notified Derek and he and his wife Angie arrived Sunday evening, as did my sister Shelley. It flashed through my mind that this must be serious, because my family was gathering around me. I recognized everyone but was quite confused, frightened and kept drifting off. I managed to ask one of the nurses on the unit, Dawn, a colleague and close friend, to come and stay with me all that night. Her specialty was neurological nursing and I was quite relieved to see her each time I opened my eyes.

I underwent several diagnostic tests, including an MRI, cerebral angiogram and several blood studies, although I was barely aware of what was going on. The neurologist ordered several other tests to rule out cardiac problems because of my family history and the fact that my father had died of a heart attack when he was forty-four. Based on the test results, the doctors concluded that I did not have a stroke after all, but had experienced the symptoms of one as a result of a severe migraine headache, a hemiplegic migraine as they called it. With migraine headaches there are intermittent spasms and dilation of blood vessels in the brain and this can cause severe headaches and the symptoms I was having. The MRI confirmed that I had a few patches of what looked like scar tissue, but the neurologist did not think that was significant given my age. I was within days of turning fifty-three at the time. Over the next three days, the sensation and strength returned to my limbs and I was able to talk, although I still had some minor difficulties articulating words and stuttered at times. I had no history of migraine headaches and in fact, up until that time, had been very healthy. In thirty years I had not been off work because of illness or used any sick days except for the few days I missed after the ectopic pregnancy in 1971. Of course Gord was very concerned about me and throughout my hospitalization we both experienced considerable anxiety. When I was aphasic, meaning unable to speak, I felt frustrated and helpless. I could hear and believed I understood what others were saying to me, but I could not respond. When the doctor asked me my husband's name I could not answer and the look on Gord's face was one of disappointment and grave concern. I knew what they wanted me to say; I just couldn't get the words out. When I overheard someone say I was disoriented and confused, I wanted to scream at him. I remember thinking that this must be what it is like for Alli, being unable to speak and misinterpreted by the people around her and it certainly gave me a better understanding of her problems and frustrations. My symptoms gradually subsided and by Thursday I was discharged.

Three days later all the symptoms returned and the whole scenario was repeated. Gord had to rush me back to the hospital and this time the neurologist did a lumbar puncture to obtain a specimen of cerebral spinal fluid for analysis. The results indicated that I had white blood cells and protein in my cerebral spinal fluid, or CSF, indicating the presence of an infection, although no organisms were identified. It appeared as though I was suffering from an infection in my brain and central nervous system. Once again I was discharged after five days and began the long road to recovery. I had four more of these attacks in which I experienced similar symptoms, but because they did not last as long I did not require hospitalization. For the next several weeks I saw the neurologist almost weekly, had numerous laboratory tests and was provided with a prescription to help control my severe headaches. My doctor had been discussing my case with another neurologist and they thought my diagnosis was Handl's. This was a gnomonic: "ha" for headache, "nd" for neurological deficits and "l" for lymphocytosis or white blood cells in the cerebral spinal fluid. This was a rare neurological illness and although the specific cause was unknown, it was believed to be the result of a viral infection. A neurologist at Mayo Clinic had first diagnosed this condition and after telling my brother this, arrangements were made for me to go to Rochester to see this specialist in consultation in July and the diagnosis was confirmed.

For the next several months I had constant severe headaches and was generally unwell. There are no specific drugs used to treat Handl's because it was believed to be viral in nature and "tincture of time" was the best medicine available. I was able to walk only short distances before becoming dizzy and lightheaded. My balance was poor and I had problems with right-sided numbness and tingling, chills in the evening and woke up frequently during the night with night sweats and numbness and tingling all down my right side. The doctor prescribed a medication that was used to prevent migraine headaches and I took it for

five weeks, but my headaches did not lessen and this drug had side effects I could not tolerate, so I asked that it be discontinued. It gave me heartburn and made me nauseated and hungry at the same time, so I ate frequently and gained about ten pounds in five weeks. Depression was another side effect and I would suddenly burst into tears and could not stop crying. I felt so out of control, so ill and so pathetic. I could not take other medications normally used to prevent or abort migraine headaches because I had a history of asthma and these drugs are con-traindicated. Of course I was unable to look after Allison, but I saw her at least weekly and either the Holmes came to Priddis to see us or we went to High River to visit her. We don't know what we would have done without the support and kindness of the Holmes family and I know the scenario would have been much worse if we didn't have them around. Allison's reaction was interesting in that she seemed to know I was unwell and when we visited with her she sat quietly beside me, made no demands and was content just to be with me. In fact, I put my feet up on her lap and she became my support. Our roles changed because usually she had her feet in my lap. Over the next few months she was unusually affectionate and gentle with me.

I was unable to return to work for several months and needed time to heal. We continued to live in Syd and Em's house and because the completion of our new house was delayed even further, we stayed with them after they returned from their winter in the south. I had been stay-ing alone during the day and was very anxious about that. I felt isolat-ed out in the country, because the residents of Priddis either worked or had not yet returned from their winter in the south. Each day I waited nervously for Gord to return home and worried about being alone. A friend living on an acreage nearby and I had a system in which I would phone her if my stroke-like symptoms returned. All I had to do was to hit the phone with a wooden spoon if I couldn't talk and she would know who was calling. I used this system once and she and her husband came over immediately to attend to me. The symptoms did not last for more than an hour or two, but when they occurred I was terrified until they started to abate. After Syd and Em came home I felt more secure, relaxed considerably and really appreciated the tender loving care they provided, although we felt badly that we had to impose on them. With the help of Derek and many friends, we moved into our new home at Heritage Point in the middle of June. We were the first occupants in this district and although we lived in a construction zone, I was happy to be in my own home.

I had many friends who were instrumental in my recovery. Years ago I heard the Canadian singer, author and song writer Ann Mortifee sing and particularly appreciated one of her songs, *Are You Lonely in There?* This had become a theme song for Allison and me. Although Ann did not know either one of us then, she could have written this song for Alli. In one stanza in particular, she seemed to speak to Allison:

> *Are you lonely in there, do you want to come out*
> *Do you feel you have nothing to say?*
> *Do you watch from the curb as the world passes by*
> *Afraid you might get in its way?*
> *Are you lonely in there?*
> *Are you lonely in there?*
> *Come out to play.*

In June I attended the annual spring retreat planned for the nursing faculty at Mount Royal College, although I was not yet well enough to return to work. I had been involved in the planning process for this and had arranged to have the workshop led by Ann. She was involved in working with and helping women and presented workshops called The Healing Journey. I had met her earlier at one of her workshops and thought that this would be a good topic for our nursing faculty. After all, we were in a healing profession. Little did I know how meaningful this workshop was going to be for me and this retreat was exactly what I needed at that time. The program was a success and my colleagues appreciated Ann's leadership. In addition, she was very sensitive to my needs and took special care of me. She was very aware of the healing process and she invited me to come to a woman's retreat called "Women's Mysteries" held in British Columbia in July in which she was a leader and facilitator. Because I was unable to drive that far or go by myself, my close friend and colleague, Dawn, agreed to take me.

The six days we were at the retreat were wonderful and I received a great deal of support and guidance from the other leader and Ann in particular. Our friendship grew and we had many conversations in which she helped me sort out my feelings and clarify the meaning of this illness. The focus of the retreat was on helping women consider their own health, self-care, spirituality and awakening to our interconnection with the universe. Among other things we studied the concept

of living in a holistic way. We examined four central themes or aspects of our selves that should be in harmony and balance. These include our mental, spiritual, emotional and physical selves. Characteristically I made decisions and led my life from my head, and this was hurting. I had been living my life from an intellectual level and I needed to pay more attention to the development of the other three areas, integrating all four, honoring all my needs and aspects of my life. The concepts of energy, balance and increasing consciousness were topics of discussions. We were involved in meditations and many interesting activities in which we were to awaken to a more holistic way of life. I realized that I had been ignoring and neglecting my spiritual needs, suppressing my emotions and as a result my physical body had collapsed, making me ill. I had not been listening to my body or my soul. The lyrics of the following song, written by Ann, resonated with me at a time when I felt fragile, vulnerable and weak emotionally and physically. I was trying to move from just surviving to living once again and her words were inspirational to me. When Ann sang this song I wept, knowing this song held true for me.

Born to Live

We were born to live, not just survive
Though the road be long and the river wide
Though the seasons change and the willows bend
Though some dreams break, some others mend.

We were born to give and born to take
To win and lose and to celebrate
We were born to know and born to muse
To unfold our hearts, take a chance and choose.

We were born to love though we feel the thorn
When a ship sets sail to return no more
Though a door be closed and we feel the pain
To chance it all and to love again.

We were born to reach, to seek what's true
To surrender all to make each day do
We were born to laugh and born to cry
To rejoice and grieve, just to be alive.

We were born to hope and to know despair
And to stand alone when there's no one there

> *We were born to trust and to understand*
> *That in every heart there's an outstretched hand.*
> *We were born to live, to be right and wrong*
> *To be false and true, to be weak and strong*
> *We were born to live, to break down the walls*
> *And to know that life is to taste it all.*

After this retreat I felt renewed faith and began to feel more positive about my recovery. Bill and Cheryl had planned a family holiday for a week in August and by that time I believed I would be able to handle looking after Allison, so agreed to have her home with me. By then I had managed a couple of weekends with her and things had gone quite well, but by this time Gord was at hockey school so I was on my own with Allison. In consenting to look after Allison I wasn't being very realistic and was in denial of sorts, but I soon realized that this might be too much for me. I still experienced considerable fatigue, poor balance and coordination and dizzy spells. I had headaches almost constantly, did not sleep well and had the spells of numbness and tingling in my right arm, hand and leg. The first night we were alone together I felt a sense of panic. I realized that if something happened to me and I had a return of the stroke-like symptoms, we would be in serious trouble. Allison was not able to help and she would have no idea what to do and there we would be locked up inside our house and nobody would even know we were there. Gord telephoned each evening, but he might assume we were out for a walk and might not become alarmed for several hours. My imagination was on overdrive and I did not sleep at all that night. I had become friends with the man who sold us the house and his wife and they knew of my illness. I called them first thing in the morning, explaining my concerns and they agreed to check on Allison and me every morning and evening. All they had to do was call and if I didn't answer the telephone, they were to come over and check further, and I gave them a key so they could let themselves in if necessary. By that time there was one other couple living on our street and I talked to them as well and they too agreed to keep an eye on us. I was much more relaxed after I had this safety-net arrangement in place and as it turned out, Allison and I were fine. I noticed that both couples kept a sharp eye on the two of us, checking on us much more often than I had requested. They always had some excuse when they dropped in, but I knew their true motives and appreciated their diligence.

I tried going back to work in August of 1998 and although I knew deep down that I was not well enough, I suppose I thought I would get better just by resuming my normal activities. I was still denying my limitations. Because of the ongoing symptoms and fatigue, I was unable to handle working, so had to take more time off. For the rest of the fall semester I stayed home and worked very hard at trying to rehabilitate myself. Alli came home most weekends and I was able to care for her with Gord's help. During the week I took frequent rest periods throughout the day, went for walks and began swimming once again, although at first I could only swim a few lengths. My doctor sent me to another neurologist specializing in infectious disorders of the nervous system and multiple sclerosis. He repeated the lumbar puncture and there were no organisms identified, but he found that the cells in my spinal fluid had half the normal life span. He concluded that my lingering symptoms were likely caused by scar tissue in my brain and might be something I would have to learn to live with.

Although my illness was likely due to a viral infection, I believed that my resistance to organisms had been compromised because of the cumulative effect of all the stress I had been under in the past few years. Although the doctors did not think my fall and head injury in Palm Springs was related to this illness, Gord and I were convinced it could have been a contributing factor. Certainly all the unsettling events associated with Allison's life up until the time she moved in with the Holmes family were stressful for me. I was also finding it increasingly difficult to keep up with the escalating demands of my position as a nursing instructor. I had been working long hours and my working environment had become stressful. The delays in being able to move into our house, the death of my mom and the loss of Quality were other factors contributing to my stress level. There were other factors too, but the important thing for me to realize was that I had let the stress build up and had not found an effective way to diffuse this. We all have stress in our lives and it is not so much the stress that causes the problems, but how we deal with it. This illness was a wake-up call and I recognized that I needed to pay attention to my own needs, rest more and find ways to manage stress more effectively.

I knew it was in my nature to be a fighter. Adjusting to Allison's disabilities was already testimony to that, but now I felt so humble and weak. I also realized how hard I was on myself. I measured my self worth

in terms of my accomplishments and I had fallen into some of the traps I had been teaching others to avoid. Interesting how some of the things we teach others are really lessons we ourselves need to embrace and learn. Just days after I was discharged from the hospital, I had what I considered to be a near-death experience. I awoke with a jolt one night and realized that I had not been breathing. I reached down and touched my body and I was ice cold and I felt like a corpse. I had the physical sensation that all my energy was leaving my body, pouring out from my feet. I was extremely frightened and knew I was close to death, so I hung on. I hung on physically to the bed and forced myself to stay awake, to stay alive. I drifted off once and the experience was repeated, but this time after I woke up I was able to stop the sensation of the energy loss. I refused to surrender to death. Once morning came I knew the worst was over, although I was shaken and I didn't understand what had transpired other than I knew I would survive.

Having a serious illness provided me with many valuable lessons and I went through a great deal of soul-searching and emotional upheaval. I was on a healing journey and this illness precipitated what some have called a "dark night of the soul" experience.

In this process I had to confront many of my fears along with the other negative feelings. I feared death, I feared Allison's seizures and I feared failure. I was afraid I might have an irreversible stroke and I would be dependent on others, becoming a burden to my family and unable to take care of Allison. What would happen to Allison if I too became disabled? Being unable to talk was another fear. I learned that fear was the underlying source of many of my negative feelings. Fear was crippling me and blocking the flow of my energy and if I gave it too much power, I knew I would lose my energy, my life force. I feared losing control as well, and in fact I felt so out of control, which in turn perpetuated my fear. My task was to replace my fears with faith. I had to let these fears surface, confront them and finally let them go. I had to call on my own strength and reawaken my faith, the spiritual part of who I was. My personal goal became one of not trying to outwit death or become immune to disease, but to be able to handle all the challenges in my life and my body without fear. I had to develop the faith that no matter what happened to my physical body I would be all right. I could not master the physical, but I could master my spirit. I also realized that I had the tendency to give my energy away, particularly when I had neg-

ative feelings or felt that I was not in control. Control issues were a main contributor to my "dis-ease." I felt so out of control in terms of my illness, Allison's seizures and the recent problems related to her life and this was reinforcing my negative feelings. I had to let my need to always be in control go, to trust others, the Creator and myself. I realized the powerful nature of thought and I needed to nurture my ability to focus on the positive, which had always been one of my strengths. I learned to recognize negativity, to acknowledge it but not be trapped in it. I could detach from negativity but I needed to build in psychological boundaries, enabling me to interact with the external world without giving my energy away.

The process I was going through took many months and after consulting with my neurologist it was decided that it would be best if I did not return to full time employment. Arrangements were made for me to return to work on a half-time basis in mid-December of 1998, giving me a little time to make the final preparations for the course I was coordinating starting in January. I had been doing some planning for the course at home before I officially returned to work, but had to pace myself and ensure I took my needed rest periods. I was assigned a workload that allowed me to coordinate a medical-surgical nursing course and teach in the classroom, but I was exempt from teaching in the hospital. I was grateful that I could do that much and welcomed the opportunity to return to my profession.

Gord, Allison and I went to Cranbrook for Christmas that year to be with our son Derek, his wife Angie and their children for a few days. They had an addition to their family, a baby girl they named Mikayla Avery, born the day before her brother's second birthday in early December and we were anxious to see her. Mikayla was beautiful, had red hair and was already bringing joy into our lives. When we visited this new grandchild I was somewhat more sensitive to Allison's needs, but she showed no signs of jealousy this time, having so many toys to play with and her nephew Justice to entertain her. This was a special Christmas for our whole family and we had a great deal to be thankful for. We were near the end of a very difficult year and the arrival of our granddaughter was such a blessing, giving us hope for better things to come.

Nineteen ninety-eight had indeed been a challenging year for me. In no way was I blaming Allison for my health problems, this was not

her doing. In fact, since she had been living with the Holmes family her life had stabilized and I did not have nearly as much anxiety about her or her future. I realized that Bill and Cheryl had come into our lives at a most opportune time and this was part of our destiny. Throughout my healing journey I was not concerned about Allison, I knew she was happy and well cared for. Because of the trust and complete faith I had in Bill and Cheryl and their abilities to care for Allison, I was given the opportunity to concentrate on re-gaining my strength and creating balance in my life. Furthermore, through my experiences I had an even better understanding of Allison's disability and could appreciate a little of which she had to deal with every day of her life. I knew a little more about Alli's chains of autism, her challenges and frustrations. Allison continued to be a source of my personal growth, my process of finding meaning in this life. Somehow my difficulties paled when I thought of her and I realized and appreciated what personal strength she had, what tenacity. She had such an amazing, strong, sweet soul and continued to teach me so much.

Chapter 14
More Suncatchers and Chains

I was able to handle the responsibilities of returning to work part time in January 1999, although I still had headaches and other lingering symptoms and needed extra rest. Gord was completely supportive, helping with the household chores and most evenings we went out for a walk. Allison came home alternate weekends and Friday nights. The program at Foothills AIM Society continued to go well and Cheryl kept an eye on what was happening. Allison got along well with her support partners and her peers in the program, but she did have an ongoing conflict with another disabled client. This young woman was very sensitive to noise and she did not like the fact that Allison had music playing at lunchtime and during breaks. She asked that it be turned off because she found it so irritating. Of course, Allison loved her music and could not understand why she could not have her tape recorder on when this woman was present and this upset her. Furthermore, the other young woman did not like the noises Alli made; she complained about the racket and would often put her hands over her ears showing her disgust when Allison was vocalizing. One day Allison looked directly at her and began to whistle. Alli knew she could not tolerate this noise and it appeared as though Allison was aggravating her on purpose, getting her back for having the lunch hour music stopped. Her intention was obvious. On another occasion Allison walked over to this woman and touched her, which she knew would not be met favorably because she was as sensitive to touch as Alli was. They almost came to blows and so the staff separated these two at the AIM office because neither one of them was very tolerant or accepting of the other. Allison ate her lunch in another room where she was able to enjoy her music, away from this woman.

Allison could be manipulative in other ways as well. If she wanted to get out of doing something, she would put her head on her support person's shoulder and give her a hug. She knew the staff were thrilled when Allison showed affection, something she didn't do very often because of her sensitivity to being touched, so when she did, they responded by hugging her back and making a big deal of this. Allison had figured out that she could use this to distract the person from the task at hand. She had some other tricks as well. One day she did not seem to be feeling well at work, had been lethargic and unwilling to participate in the day's activities. Lorna, one of the administrators, decided it would be best if she took Allison home to Cheryl at lunchtime, but just as they got to the house, Allison perked up, started to sing and make her happy noises and Lorna realized that she had been "had." After they visited with Cheryl for a few minutes, they decided it would be best if Allison returned to work, because letting her stay at home would only reinforce the behavior. Allison's admirable attempt to outwit the staff had failed.

Cheryl continued to be very thoughtful and asked if she could become more involved in looking after Allison's needs. I know she was trying to take some of the pressure off me, although she was sincere in wanting to get to know Allison's doctors, her dentist and the routines associated with her check-ups. Cheryl took Allison for her regular blood tests and the level of her anticonvulsant remained in the desired therapeutic range and we were confident that once again Allison's epilepsy was controlled. Brushing Allison's teeth had always been tricky, but we did the best we could, given her dislike of having anyone near her mouth and flossing was out of the question. We never knew if Alli had a toothache because she could not tell us, so we had to watch her for other clues, such as increased resistance with brushing or reluctance to chew her food. Because of this I made sure she had her dental check ups regularly. Allison's dentist specialized in treating people with disabilities and had taken an interest in her. He had been very accommodating in allowing Quality right into his office and in fact he had a newspaper picture of Allison and Quality displayed in his office. Allison did not like going to the dentist one bit and even checking her teeth was an ordeal. I had to hold her down, restrain her hands and try to distract her by singing or counting and she usually howled and resisted every step of the way. If she had her chain and suncatcher or a toy she usually threw these, hoping we would let her go get them. When the dentist examined Allison's teeth he had to put a metal thimble-like apparatus over his finger to prevent Allison from biting him and to allow him to open her jaw wide enough so he could see inside her mouth, but he had to be quick. If he found evidence of cavities we had to make arrangements for Allison to have a general anesthetic because of her fear and non-compliance. About every other year we had to make the appropriate

arrangements to have actual dental work done and booked a surgical suite in advance. The dentist used this time when Allison was under anesthesia to thoroughly check her teeth, do x-rays, clean her teeth and fill any cavities he found. Fortunately Allison's teeth were quite strong, but because she ground her teeth when she was younger she often developed cavities in her back molars and the difficulties we had in brushing teeth did not help.

After this check up Alli needed to have some work done and on the day of the procedure Cheryl came with us. I always brought someone with me because Allison was groggy and restless after she came out of the anesthetic and I needed to watch her carefully on the ride home, so I needed a driver. Upon our arrival Cheryl and I took Allison directly into the operating room and stayed with her until she was anesthetized. It bothered me when Allison drifted into unconsciousness, so I didn't stay in the room long and I usually left the building for an hour or so as soon as she was "out." Even staying in the waiting room was just too difficult for me to endure, because Allison was monitored throughout and I could hear her heartbeat and the sounds of the drilling. Cheryl and I went for coffee and returned just as the dentist finished and we went to the recovery room to wait until Allison regained consciousness. Allison came out of the anesthesia fighting; her arms and legs were flying and she was not about to stay on the stretcher, even though she was groggy and her legs were like rubber. We had to lift her into a wheelchair and almost hold her in because she just wanted to get out of there. However, she had to be assessed and we could not leave until she had recovered from the anesthesia. Going to the dentist was always a traumatic experience, but we had to have her teeth looked after.

In April of 1999 Allison's general practitioner in Okotoks moved away, so we had to find a new doctor for Allison. Cheryl requested that we consider sending Allison to their family doctor, a man they had great confidence in and because his office was in High River, this would be more convenient for Cheryl. We had Allison's records transferred and Cheryl and I took Allison to meet this doctor and review her history. It wasn't a week later that Allison had a major seizure. Gord and I were driving to a hockey banquet and I suddenly told Gord I had to call Cheryl. It was unusual for me to use the cell phone, but for some reason I had a strange feeling and knew I had to make this call. Sure enough, Allison had just had the seizure moments before and Cheryl

was just thinking about calling us to inform us of the situation. We were all a little spooked with my intuition, but glad that I had this strange feeling and acted on it because it would have been difficult for Cheryl to get in touch with us otherwise. Cheryl and Bill had things under control, but Gord and I went to their home after spending a short time at the banquet. We took Alli to the doctor the next day and her blood level was a bit low and the dosage of her medication was increased. Allison had frequent blood tests in the next few weeks and we had to increase her medication dosage a couple more times before the end of April. Each time we had to do this, Allison was drowsy and it took her some time to adjust to the new dosage. Achieving the optimal blood levels was problematic because with an increase in dosage, Allison became obsessed with food, causing her to gain weight. Following a significant weight gain she might require another increase in the dosage of her medication and so the cycle went. However, by the end of May it seemed as if we had found the correct dosage for Allison, her blood levels were in the desired range and we all relaxed a little.

In July the epilepsy returned. On the day after Alli's birthday, Cheryl was bringing her home to be with us and she had four eleven-year-old girls in the van with her because she was taking them all out to dinner and the movies to celebrate Jade's eleventh birthday. They planned to drop Allison off on their way to Calgary. Allison was in the front passenger seat beside Cheryl and suddenly she arched back over her right shoulder. Jade saw this and initially thought Allison was reaching back to her, but quickly realized Allison was in trouble and going into a convulsion when she saw Allison's eyes roll back. Jade called out to her mom and once Cheryl realized what was happening, she immediately pulled the car over onto the shoulder to protect and attend to Alli until the seizure was over. Fortunately Allison was wearing a seat belt. Once the seizure was over, because they were not far from our home, Cheryl drove while Jade attended to Allison. She crawled up between the two front seats and was holding Allison's upper torso in her arms, protecting her head, in spite of the fact that she was a whole lot smaller than Alli. A few moments later they arrived at my door and Cheryl and I brought Allison into the house. After Allison was safely in our home, Cheryl took the girls on to Calgary. They were all frightened and needed an explanation as to what had just happened. Cheryl and Jade explained epilepsy to Jade's friends and they sat and talked about

the event over dinner. They had a number of questions and once they had a better understanding of what had happened to Allison, some of the mystery and misconceptions of epilepsy had been cleared up for them. Cheryl and her daughter were able to reduce their fear and had taught them some important lessons. Jade made a point of telling them what should be done if they ever witnessed someone having a seizure and her friends were quite impressed with not only her knowledge, but how she had handled the situation with Allison.

Allison's blood was checked the next morning and her blood levels of Valproic Acid were in the therapeutic range and were, in fact, higher than they had ever been. These results were cause for alarm, because Alison's anticonvulsant was not being effective. The earliest appointment we could get with her neurologist was in December. However, Allison's general practitioner talked to the neurologist and we were assured that she would be well monitored until she went for the appointment with the specialist. Alli's medication regime was altered and we gave the drug in divided doses, three times a day rather than twice, hoping that this would keep her blood levels more even. Allison was obviously not feeling well and began to lose weight, dropping to under ninety-five pounds over the summer. Even the Valproic Acid was not making her hungry.

We were all nervous about Allison and in mid-August she had another seizure. This time it occurred in the car when Gord was taking her back to the Holmes residence one Saturday morning. He managed to get to their home, lifted Allison out of the car and laid her down on the lawn. Bill saw what was happening and he came out to assist Gord. This seizure lasted over five minutes and of course we were alarmed. I feared that she might end up in status epilepticus like she did ten years earlier and I could not accept waiting until December to see a neurologist. In desperation I called my own neurologist and he made arrangements for Allison to be seen by another specialist in epilepsy but we still had to wait a month. In the meantime my neurologist consented to treat Allison although epilepsy was not his area of expertise. He believed there was still room for a higher dose of Valproic Acid before it might become toxic and he increased her medication again and indicated that he would see her if further problems arose.

The saga continued and just three weeks later Allison had another seizure. This time Gord and I had taken her to watch an equestrian

show and we were sitting in the handicapped section. She suddenly arched back and went into convulsions. This seizure lasted more than five minutes, she became quite blue in color and was slow to respond afterwards. I was not willing to wait another day to have Alli seen by a neurologist, so we had one of the bystanders call an ambulance. Paramedics arrived and administered oxygen and once the ambulance arrived we took her to the hospital. Allison was assessed in the emergency department and prescribed a new medication to be given in addition to the Valproic Acid. We were instructed to contact our own doctor on Monday. Allison was discharged and I called the new neurologist the following morning and he made some adjustment in her medications and arranged to see her the following morning in his epilepsy clinic on an emergency basis.

Cheryl and I took Allison for the appointment and this doctor was very thorough and we were both impressed with him. He ordered a battery of tests, including an EEG, CAT Scan and MRI, because he felt she needed a complete neurological workup given her recent problems and he wanted the results for his records. He explained that often Valproic Acid stops working after several years and suggested that we needed to continue with the combination of drugs. The new drug was Lamictal and it too was not without side effects and dangers, so we had to gradually increase the dosage at the same time as reducing the Valproic Acid dosage. Allison's neurological tests were completed over the next few weeks and she was responding favorably to the new combination of medications and was seizure free, much to our relief. I discovered that I was able to handle the return of Allison's seizures somewhat better. I was not happy about them, but I was not as stressed and anxious. I no longer felt the same intensity of fear and loss of control I had previously experienced. Perhaps it was because of the additional support Gord and I had from the Holmes family, but in addition, perhaps I was beginning to conquer some of my fears through my increased faith and trust.

Allison's behavior following seizures continued to concern us. She was still in an altered state of consciousness, her balance was poor, she resisted any assistance or attempts to support or even hold on to her in any way and she insisted on going up and down the stairs and around and around the house, visiting every room. At times we even had to take her outside to walk off this agitation. Cheryl and Bill lived in a split-level house and had a growing concern about the stairs and the risk and

potentially disastrous consequences if Alli fell down them at the onset of a seizure or during the postictal stage. It was difficult if not impossible to keep her away from the stairs. I was aware of Cheryl and Bill's anxiety and I wondered if they might decide that keeping Allison in their home was just too difficult for them. They called and asked to meet with us and we almost felt a sense of impending doom. But we were underestimating their commitment and love for our daughter. Rather than giving up, they came up with a solution that was amazing. They had decided to build a new house, a bungalow, as soon as possible. In fact they had already put their house on the market, contacted a builder and were in the process of designing a house that would be much safer for Allison. Alli's room would be close to Bill and Cheryl's on the main floor and Keara and Jade were to have bedrooms downstairs. They planned to have a gate at the top of the stairs, which could be closed off, providing for Alli's safety. Gord and I were overwhelmed by their plans and how much they were willing to do for the sake of Allison. Regardless of the added expense, they were willing to change their lives in order to provide a safe environment for our daughter. They assured us they had dreams of building a new home some day anyway and had just moved their plans forward a few years. In our hearts we knew that their love and devotion for Allison was the main reason behind their decision to move and this was testimony to their strong

Jade, Allison and Keara, 1999.

commitment to her. Throughout the building process they had taken Allison to see the house several times, but as the moving date was getting closer, she was becoming quieter and seemed anxious about something. Cheryl began packing their belongings well in advance and this might have been of concern to Allison; maybe she thought she was going to be abandoned. It wasn't until February and they were moved in and Allison found all her things in her new room that she relaxed.

Allison settled in to her new surroundings and it appeared that we had control of those chains of epilepsy, which was the dark side of Allison's disability, and we all had a great deal more sunshine in our lives. Other than the seizures, Allison was generally very well, so once her epilepsy was under control she was back to being happy and healthy. She gained back the weight she had lost and enjoyed all the activities and social events living with the Holmes provided her with. In fact, there came a time when it was obvious that Allison couldn't wait to get back to the Holmes' residence after a weekend with us. As soon as Cheryl and Bill arrived to get Allison on Sundays, she was ready to go. She stood up, went to the door and if we weren't quick to get her dressed

Kris, Allison and Gord, 1999.

for the outdoors, she walked out to the car without her coat and in her stocking feet. We liked to have a few minutes to visit, but Allison had no time for that. Cheryl asked me one day if Allison's behavior upset me and I assured her that it did not. Allison could not tell me in words that

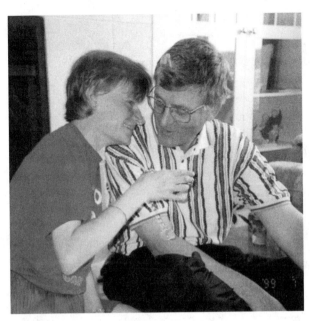

Allison with Gord.

she was happy living with the Holmes, but her actions spoke for her. Besides, Gord and I were getting older, there wasn't as much activity in our house and she got rather bored after a few days. When she was with them she had lots of people around, there was so much stimulation and she loved all the action in their house. Gord and I had the consolation that she was every bit as excited to see us when we picked her up on Friday afternoons. Allison was fortunate to have two homes and two families that loved her.

Bill and Cheryl had had to have their dog Cruise put down just before they moved into their new house because he developed serious health problems. Although they did not have a dog for six weeks, Cheryl weakened and they got a new puppy, named Bentley. This was a border collie-cocker spaniel cross that was full of energy. Bentley loved Allison and crawled all over her, rarely letting her out of his sight. In fact at one point he was too diligent in herding Allison and would not let her leave the family room, so Bill had to intervene and train the dog to give Alli a little more space. This dog often slept in Allison's room and on occasion alerted Cheryl when Alli got up in the night. Allison and Bentley became friends and often shared toys and generally enjoyed each other's company. A year or so later they got another dog, a small black poodle named Jazz, and Allison had two dogs to entertain her and

be her faithful companions.

As well as providing a safe and loving home environment for our daughter, Cheryl kept watch over Allison's day program, communicating with Foothills AIM Society on a regular basis. Of course Gord and I were involved in the decisions regarding Allison's care, but Cheryl looked after the day-to-day issues, which was a considerable relief to me. Each year we had a combined family meeting with the person in charge of overseeing the client's programs at AIM and this was held at the Holmes' residence. Bill and Cheryl's parents, as well as some of their close friends were invited because they were also involved in Alli's life. We discussed issues regarding Allison's care and programs, reflected back on the past year and planned goals for the upcoming year. Everyone was encouraged to have input and Allison's best interests were at the forefront of the discussion. Further to this we received regular written evaluations and summaries of Allison's progress from the AIM Society. Communication was important, allowing all of us to be informed about the things that were going on in Allison's life. Cheryl started a written communication book in which Allison's support partners at work wrote daily messages, reporting on Allison's day. This was useful because Allison herself could not tell us what had transpired and if issues arose, they could be handled immediately.

Gord and I maintained open communications with the Holmes family and they were always so positive when we talked to them about Alli. They usually had some interesting story to tell us about their week with her. During the week Cheryl and I talked on the phone and often after our conversation Cheryl put Allison on so I could talk to her. Alli loved to talk on the phone and at first Cheryl held the phone up to Allison's ear and she just listened. I talked to her, sang to her and eventually she started "talking" back. It was a riot! I asked a question and Alli would respond with her noises. If I sang to her, she often laughed or even hummed along and when I counted, she would join in. Sometimes it seemed she had a great deal to say and would jabber on in her own way, almost like a small child using jargon. Although she was not saying many words, she would blurt out a long rendition, including changes in the inflection of her voice and it sounded like she was telling me something very important. All I had to do was add a few comments and encouragement and Allison would continue on. Eventually Allison held the phone herself and she started to walk around the house when

she talked to me, copying Cheryl's habit. When she had had enough of our conversation, she handed the phone back to Cheryl. If Cheryl didn't follow Allison around, Alli would simply put the phone down on her bed, a counter or on the floor when she had enough and when she did this I knew our discussion was over. One time I was talking to her and Allison pushed a button on the phone cutting me off, so I tried to call Cheryl back but the line was busy. A few minutes later Cheryl called me and she was laughing uproariously. Allison had brought the phone back to her and Cheryl started talking, telling me that Allison was finished with our conversation. Cheryl discovered that she was not talking to me at all, but to her mother-in-law, Dorothy. Allison had pushed the redial button and the last call had been made to her. At first Dorothy couldn't understand what was happening, but she recognized Allison's voice and her sounds and thought Bill or Cheryl had dialed for her, so she and Alli had a conversation. It was a good thing the last call had been a local one and not to one of the Holmes' friends living in another country!

Ever since Allison moved in with the Holmes family, we noticed that not only was she happier than she had been for a long time, but she had an increase in her vocalizations. She had been counting to ten, singing her ABCs and a few words of *Oh Canada* for some time. Bill in particular encouraged Allison to sing along with him and Alli started to sing and say more actual words. Her favorite song was *You are my Sunshine* and she often said the word "sunshine." At Christmas she sang along with the songs *Away in a Manger*, *Silent Night* and *Jingle Bells*, often completing whole lines of the lyrics. Allison loved birthdays, anyone's, and we could count on her singing most of the words of *Happy Birthday*. Cheryl and Bill also encouraged Allison to talk and we noticed that Allison would say, "let's go" or "here we go" when they came to pick Allison up on Sundays. Alli was developing a repertoire of words and most times she was imitating, but sometimes she would come out with appropriate responses, unprompted. Each time she uttered any words we were all thrilled. Some of her favorites were "funderful," "alright," "you are my sunshine," "oh what fun," "hi," "yeah" and "no." When the telephone rang she said "hello." One day Jade and one of her friends were talking in Jade's bedroom as only teenaged girls can. Allison had been downstairs and when she came up, Bill asked her what those girls were talking about down there. Allison replied in a very clear voice, "the boys." Jade couldn't believe it when her dad told her about Alli's

response later and she confirmed that they had indeed been talking about boys. It was obvious that Allison had been listening. One of the most touching things for me was when Allison first said the words "I love you." Those three words were sweet music to my ears and I had waited a long time to hear them from Allison. She had heard those words many times from us and in many songs, but she had not spoken them until she was in her late twenties.

At one point after their move, Cheryl and Bill approached us with concerns about Allison's future, asking that they be added to our wills to ensure that if something did happen to us, they would be able to continue looking after her. They handled this carefully, not wanting to suggest that we might not be around long, but wanted to have things in order to prevent future legal problems and we recognized that this was just good planning. They wanted to ensure that they would continue to be involved in Allison's life. Gord and I consulted a lawyer who specialized in family law and persons with disabilities and she was a tremendous help. We became more informed about the Dependent Adults Act and legal issues. We had assumed that because we were Allison's parents, this would be enough protection for her, but found out that we needed to make a formal application to become her legal guardians now that she was an adult. After we went through the process we were informed that we would have to repeat this every six years, providing proof that we were acceptable guardians for our daughter. I found this hard to believe, but it was explained to us that not all parents have the best interests of their children at heart and this system was in place to protect people with disabilities from abuse and to ensure that the government funding was being used to meet the needs of the disabled person.

Along with applying to become Allison's legal guardians, we revised and updated our wills. We named a nephew, Michael, as executor and guardian for Allison in the event of our death or anything else that would preclude us from being able to provide for her. We had Personal Directives and Enduring Power of Attorney forms drawn up. Originally we wanted to name Bill and Cheryl as Allison's guardians, but we learned that it would create a conflict of interest and they would no longer be able to provide residential support in the case of our deaths; this was not the scenario we wanted. Michael and his wife Claudia consented to become Allison's legal guardians and although they would be responsible for looking after the legal issues and Allison's finances, Bill

and Cheryl would continue to care for her and have a say as to her future and living arrangements. It was all very complicated, but these things needed to be attended to. We did not want Derek to have to be responsible for his sister and wanted to be sure that both of our children would be treated fairly. All parents should have their affairs in order, but there are special considerations when there is a disabled person involved. None of us liked to think about death or such eventualities, but it is prudent to have the appropriate arrangements made.

The year 2000 was one of transitions for us. Gord and I had planned to retire from our full-time teaching positions at the age of fifty-five, although we had no intentions of retiring completely. Gord planned to continue working in his summer hockey camp program and no doubt would find other jobs to do. My goal was to retire from my full time position in 2000 with the intention of continuing teaching nursing on a part time basis. However, this involved teaching in the clinical area, supervising students in the hospital and because of my headaches and residual symptoms this was something I knew I was unable to handle physically. I had to re-examine goals and think seriously about my future. I realized that even working half time had been a strain for me in the past couple of years and decided that it was time for me to retire from teaching nursing. My ultimate goal was to be able to continue to care for Allison and I hoped I would be able to do this for a long time, so my health became my priority. It was hard for me to even think of retiring, so much of my identity had been connected with my role as a nursing instructor. On the other hand, I had been teaching for thirty years and I recognized that the time had come for me to relinquish this, to find other ways to define myself and let it go. I did experience somewhat of an identity crisis in the transition but once again had to trust that things would work out. I retired officially in August of 2000 and Gord joined me the end of September that year. We both felt good about the changes that were about to happen in our lives and we looked forward to shifting gears and taking more time to be together, traveling and moving into the next phase of our lives. We felt very positive and secure in knowing that our children were both doing well and had meaningful lives of their own. Our goal for our first year of retirement was to take time to rest, to travel and just relax into this next stage. We made a commitment not to work for several months, except for Gord when he was planning for and operating hockey school. We

planned four two-to-three week holidays over the next few months utilizing some of our time-shares. We had some concerns about how Alli would react to us being away, because in the past if we were gone for more than a few days she became sad and upset, missing us. Cheryl had to deal with the reactions and Allison often presented some behavioral problems. We found that Allison was able to handle our travels just fine as long as we were not away for more than three weeks at a time and we talked to her on the phone regularly. By calling her we were letting her know we were still in her life and she was better able to cope with our physical absence. Cheryl and I altered our schedule for those months were we coming and going on our trips. After we got home we brought Allison home to be with us for a few days during the week and she was with us on all of the weekends we were home.

By the spring of 2001 our travels were over and we settled into a routine, once again alternating weekends with Allison. We thoroughly enjoyed the time we had taken to travel and recuperate and were ready to once again stay home and build our lives centered around our home in Heritage Point. Our weekends with Allison were special and we made a point of taking her on various outings. Gord and I spent many mornings working out at the gym and Gord, already an avid runner, had dreams of training for a marathon. I was no longer able to run because of my problems with dizziness and balance, but found I could walk on a treadmill and could compensate for my difficulties by hanging on to the handrails. We had the time to do many things we had always wanted to do and we were enjoying our time together.

Over the summer Gord was busy with hockey school and I helped out with registrations. I brought Allison home to be with me on weekends and for ten days while the Holmes family went on their holiday in July. I concentrated on my health and fitness by going swimming, walking and playing golf and I was able to find a balance between my activities and rest and felt so much better when I took care of myself. I had made significant changes in my lifestyle and came to appreciate what life was like without a great deal of stress. I had been taking courses in Healing Touch and was in the process of becoming a certified healing touch practitioner myself, although I knew this would not become a career, but a way in which I could help my friends and family. I realized that in giving to another in this way, I too received healing energy and benefited.

In the fall we started a tradition in our neighborhood at Heritage Point to help us develop a sense of community and meet the new residents in the area. One Friday night each month we got together for what we called Flop Night. Everyone gathered at one house early in the evening, bringing appetizers and beverages and we visited, caught up on the news, wound down after the week and nibbled on all the delicious snacks. Allison was welcome to attend these events and our new friends and neighbors learned to appreciate and accept her. At Christmas time we had an evening of caroling at the home of a talented, musical family. The woman of the house was a piano teacher and her husband was a professional singer and we all gathered around their grand piano, singing carols. Allison was in her glory. She made a point of positioning herself beside the piano at the feet of this marvelous singer and rocked to the music all evening. Furthermore, she discovered they had stained glass tree ornaments that she was allowed to pluck from their Christmas tree and enjoy for the evening.

Cheryl was particularly good at problem solving and whenever an issue came up about Allison she tried to consider all the factors and figure out the meaning. Allison began wetting the bed in the fall of 2001 and this did not make sense to any of us. It had not been happening when she was home with us, but Cheryl had to deal with it a couple of times a week. In the past Allison had problems with bed wetting during stressful times, but she seemed happy, things were going well in her day program and we could not identify any precipitating factors causing this problem. To try to prevent it we reduced Alli's fluid intake after supper and this made a difference, although on occasion that didn't even help. Then Cheryl figured it out. Allison wet her bed on those nights after she had been swimming in her day program at AIM and she had been swimming two afternoons a week. When Alli swam, she drank a great deal of pool water. To compound the problem, the water in the pool was salt water, so even though she had taken on a great deal of fluid when swimming, she was thirsty after because of the additional sodium in her system. Once Cheryl recognized this she let Alli have some juice when she came home in the afternoon after swimming, but severely limited her drinking after supper and made sure she took her to bathroom a few extra times in the evening. It didn't always work, but at least we knew the bedwetting was not due to stress or a reaction to something negative in Allison's life.

Gord decided to return to coaching hockey in the fall of 2001, which curtailed any plans to travel for the next several months. I agreed that he should continue to pursue his passions and I knew I would be able to find enough to do. In many ways I still missed teaching nursing and struggled somewhat with issues around finding a purpose and other ways in which I could contribute to society. For years I had dreamed about writing a book about Allison and autism some day, but had never actualized this dream. I thought I didn't have the time and did not even know how to start such an onerous project. In the past I had enjoyed writing many poems and skits related to work, my friendships, and Allison. After spending a weekend with my sister in October, I realized that I could write my story. My sister provided me with the incentive to launch my project and I also received encouragement from my family and friends. In my writing I could fulfill my own personal dream and in a way, could continue to teach others. I knew I had many stories to tell based on personal experiences and believed that others might be able to learn from my experiences. Writing became my passion, my new profession and I was on a mission.

In January of 2002 we celebrated the five-year anniversary of Allison living with the Holmes family. Cheryl and Bill had Gord and I

Allison and the Holmes family at their five-year anniversary of living together, January, 2002.

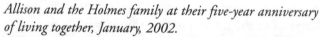

over for dinner and we had a party with their family. We had a great deal to celebrate, not only the fact that the residential program was working well, but Allison had been seizure free for a year and a half and she was healthy. Above all else, she has had a life that was fulfilling, meaningful and brought her pleasure. Allison has had a unique relationship with each member of the Holmes family and they have all been involved in her life, contributing in such positive ways. We have had many happy and interesting stories to reflect on. Keara was now in school and one day she told Cheryl that she wanted to help with Allison more. She told her mom that Cheryl was not going to be able to look after Allison for-ever and it was time she took on more responsibility with Allison so she could take over when Cheryl was too old. As a result, Keara took on the responsibility of helping her mom get Allison ready in the morning and putting Alli's seat belt on in the car. Jade had always helped in caring for Allison as well and if her mom was not home at bedtime, she got Alli undressed and brushed her teeth, so Bill just had to put her to bed. Out of respect for Alli, Bill did not like to be responsible for undressing her or changing her clothes. Allison loved to go to Jade's soccer games and other sports activities and was one of Jade's best fans. There was no question about Allison's love for Bill and his musical talents, strange noises he made for her and how he teased and humored her. Cheryl was the ultimate care-provider and advocated for Allison in so many ways. The Holmes' had taught Allison many things since she began her life with them, including flushing the toilet, thanks to Keara. When she first went there Alli did not sit up to the table very long and in fact, rarely ate a meal sitting down, but they had taught her to sit nicely at mealtimes. They got her to drink milk, something she had not done for us. She could put on her deodorant, take her pill in a pincer grasp when they handed it to her, put her clothes in the laundry along with numer-ous other skills. The mutual love and respect between Alli and this fam-ily was something to treasure.

In reflecting back over the past several years I was able to see and appreciate how much we have been through, how much we have learned and how much we had to celebrate. I had recovered consider-ably and have found a way to accept and live with my ongoing headaches and symptoms. Gord and I were doing what we wanted to do. He was coaching hockey, his passion, and still had his hockey school to concentrate on. I was well underway in writing my book, fulfilling

my dream. Our son Derek and his family were doing well and were planning to build their first home and we had two delightful grandchildren. Our lives were overflowing with blessings and we had so much to be thankful for.

Allison had much to be thankful for as well. She had two families who loved, cared for and supported her, two places to call home and two bedrooms that have been decorated especially for her. In both homes she had her own CD player and tape recorder and several tapes, CDs and her own special videos. Toy boxes overflowing with her treasures and favorite toys and a supply of suncatchers and chains have been available to her, to help her to feel secure. Alli has always had a "toy of the day" and when she misplaced it she was on a hunt, opening cupboards, drawers, and stripping the beds. She was usually able to conscript one of us to help her find what she was looking for. She had copies of her favorite Dr. Suess books and friends and family members willing to read these rhyming stories to her. Her love of and need for children's toys, stories and music has been accepted and respected. Music had been very much part of her life and she had the companionship of two dogs. In spite of her inability to speak, she had compensated and learned effective ways to communicate, making her wishes and needs known. Her life has been full of caring people and she has had many friends who have accepted and valued her. Allison has always lived in the present, with no cares about what time it was or what she should be doing. She has been the ultimate human "being," not human "doing." Allison has had all her needs met and she has not had to worry about mundane things like finances, mortgages or taxes. She has been welcomed into the communities in which she has lived and many people have been interested in her and wanting to help her and understand more about her disabilities. Other people have been willing to reach out to her and have appreciated her specialness. The staff of Foothills Advocacy in Motion Society have supervised her residential and day programs and provided her with meaningful jobs and recreational opportunities, advocating for persons with disabilities. She has been fortunate that she has lived in a country, province and communities that value and provides for those who are disabled.

In writing my book, I have reflected on and revisited the many stories and events of our lives. I realized how meaningful my life with Allison has been and how much I personally have learned from her. Our

extraordinary experiences together have shaped the development of my values, beliefs and philosophies, helping me to grow mentally and spiritually. She has taught me many valuable lessons about unconditional love, patience, persistence, trust, wisdom, faith and the unique value of being human, to name a few. Allison is ageless and in her innocence she has lived in perpetual childhood and this is sometimes enviable. In imagining her perceptions of the world and her heightened sensory experiences, I have been able to appreciate more beauty, more love and more depth in the surroundings and environment around us. Allison has been in my life for many reasons and she has taught me well. In fact, she has been a teacher for many people and will continue to bring light and love to those who are fortunate enough to know her. Our journey is ongoing and no doubt there will be more "chains and suncatchers" along the way, providing us with more opportunities for personal growth. Some of my stories have reflected our heartbreaks and sorrows, but even more have expressed our joys and triumphs.

I have been able to identify many positive aspects and advantages that I have had in having an autistic daughter. I have never had to put up with backtalk from Allison and she is a wonderful confidante. I have told her all my secrets, knowing with certainty that she will not ever divulge my innermost thoughts and feelings. I have always known where she was and with whom, and I have not had to worry about her smoking, drinking, taking drugs or driving too fast. These could be viewed as distinct advantages for a parent. As I have traveled with Allison on her journey with autism, my goals have changed. Initially her father and I wanted to make her well, to rid her of this affliction and help her break free of the bondage of her disability. I have read many books about autism and some stories about miracle cures and at one time had hopes and dreams of finding a cure for Alli. But only a small percentage of children with autism are cured and once I accepted the fact that I could not alleviate her autism, I had to find meaning for it, a way to reframe her disability in a positive way. I have realized that her life did have meaning, meaning because of her autism. My goals and attitudes had changed and I tried to focus on the positive aspects of my life with her, on providing her with as much love and quality in her life as I could. Gord and I were not alone in our ventures, heartbreaks and struggles and have had many special people that have eased our way, supporting us, loving us and helping us along this journey. Through

Allison we have had experiences we never would have had if she were not autistic and she has brought many wonderful and caring people into our lives. Although we have had many difficult times and have had to help Allison deal with the trials, shadows and chains of autism, mental retardation and epilepsy, juxtaposed with those are the joys, those rays of sunshine, those powerfully positive experiences that reflect her gifts and Allison's inner beauty. She has shown us that disabled people can be happy, can have meaningful lives and in a very special way, contribute to our communities. Allison has a way of catching sunbeams with her suncatchers and transforming them into rainbows and a myriad of colors and shapes and if we pay attention, we too can transform our beliefs, values and our lives in fulfilling our destiny.

Although each person has unique needs and some have to live with disabilities, in the final analysis we are all human beings sharing our lives on this planet, learning and living together, trying to give meaning to our lives. If the truth were known, at times aren't we all a little handicapped; a little retarded, a little autistic, a little blind, a little deaf, a little less than "normal"? If we can learn to accept one another, appreciate each person's uniqueness and learn from one another, perhaps we can make this world a better place. Life is a paradox and Allison has experienced both the dark and light sides of autism. This has been her destiny, part of a grand, divine plan. She has lived with her disabilities surrounded by countless people supporting and caring for her throughout her continuing journey with autism. In writing the following poem, I give tribute to my daughter Allison; I honor her and thank her for sharing her journey with me.

My Tribute To Allison

My heart is filled with the wonder of you
You have such a beautiful soul.
There are so many things that I need to say
Things I really want you to know.
We've come to this earth to learn and to love
Our journey has taken us far.
Our paths have crossed and become entwined
So we can know who we are.
Our journey began the day you were born
And I held you to my breast
I wept with joy and offered my thanks

In my heart I felt truly blessed.

Your early years were rocky and rough
And questions did arise,
You were withdrawn from our world and so distant at times
For reasons I could not surmise.

You have endured your life in this world of autism
And your spirit is so strong,
Your world at times has been lonely and strange
But with us you will always belong.

You never scored well on psychology tests
But I've always believed in you so,
You are not able to show all the things that you know
And the real Truth you already know.

Quality your small dog, your friend and companion
Was constantly at your side,
She gave you her love, made you feel secure
And you both liked to go outside.

When you grew up and the time had come
That I knew I must let you go,
I had to step back, let you walk on your path
To carry on with the work of your soul.

Although it took time we found you a place
A place you could call your own,
I know we had help, we were undoubtedly blessed
With a family that opened their home.

And now you have others to love and to teach
Your light will show them the way,
They love you well and take good care of you
And they too are learning each day.

Your specialness is the gift that you bring
To those whose lives you have touched
Your innocence you share and your love shines through
To others you mean so much.

I am so proud of you and the jobs that you do
As you work in the program at AIM.
With friends you recycle and your life is fulfilled
AIM Society is gaining some fame.

Your family will always be there for you
Your brother I know you adore,

He has a family now and there's a thing
about love -
There always is room for some more.

You and your Dad have been able to share
A bond with an amazing style,
You are the light of his life, his so precious
gift
You always could make your Dad smile.

There still are some things I don't under-
stand
The seizures that cause so much fear,
No doubt there's a reason, they're a part of
the plan
Though the lesson as yet is not clear.

I admire you and I'm devoted to you,
I pray that life gives you pleasure,
I love and accept you just the way that you
are
You truly are a treasure.

You do not judge, you make few demands
You have a simple way of living,
When we make mistakes or miss knowing your needs
You have a exceptional way of forgiving.

I know you are wise and your soul is pure
Love is the essence of your heart,
The road we have traveled has brought us rewards
This I understood from the very start.

I have learned a great deal from my life here with you
My lessons have been so dear,
I have come to believe things are meant to be
And trust is replacing my fear.

You have always been a part of me
And I've been a part of you,
As soul mates on this journey in life
Our love is tried, tested and true.

I thank you, my love, our dance will go on
You have given so much to me,
How grateful I am to be walking with you
On this sweet path of our destiny.

Kris Jones graduated from the University of Alberta Hospital School of Nursing in 1966 and in 1973 she received her BSc in Nursing from the University of Alberta. Kris taught at the Foothills Hospital School of Nursing, a three-year diploma course, from 1967 to 1974. Kris joined the faculty at Mount Royal College in Calgary in 1975 as a part time or sessional instructor in the two-year Nursing Diploma Program and became a full time faculty member in 1979. In 1991 she received her Masters Degree in Education from the University of Calgary with a focus on teaching and learning.

She presented workshops on Canine Companions for Independence through Mount Royal College Continuing Education Department and was a guest speaker for Pet Access League Society and at a conference for parents of children with hearing deficits. On many occasions Kris has been a guest lecturer in different courses at Mount Royal College and at the University of Calgary in the Calgary Conjoint Nursing Program. In these classes she presented information about the

challenges facing families with a disabled member, the disability of autism and her lived experiences in raising her daughter, Allison. In 1992 her nursing students nominated her for the Distinguished Faculty Award. She remained at Mount Royal College until she retired in August 2000. She has been a member, Director, Vice President, and President of the Board of Directors for the High River, Alberta, based program, Foothills Advocacy in Motion Society, which provides day and residential programs for adults with disabilities. She has completed several courses in Healing Touch. Kris is married and lives with her husband, Gord, south of Calgary. Her interests include speaking and lecturing about autism, writing, travel, fitness, swimming and golf.

AGMV Marquis

MEMBER OF SCABRINI MEDIA

Quebec, Canada
2002